Jonathan S. Harbour

Sams **Teach Yourself**

Windows®
Phone 7
Game Programming

in **24**
Hours

SAMS 800 East 96th Street, Indianapolis, Indiana

Sams Teach Yourself Windows® Phone 7 Game Programming in 24 Hours

ISBN-13: 978-0-672-33554-9

ISBN-10: 0-672-33554-9

Library of Congress Cataloging-in-Publication Data is on file.

Printed in the United States of America

First Printing November 2011

Trademarks

All terms mentioned in this book that are known to be trademarks or service marks have been appropriately capitalized. Sams Publishing cannot attest to the accuracy of this information. Use of a term in this book should not be regarded as affecting the validity of any trademark or service mark.

Warning and Disclaimer

Every effort has been made to make this book as complete and as accurate as possible, but no warranty or fitness is implied. The information provided is on an "as is" basis. The author and the publisher shall have neither liability nor responsibility to any person or entity with respect to any loss or damages arising from the information contained in this book.

Bulk Sales

Sams Publishing offers excellent discounts on this book when ordered in quantity for bulk purchases or special sales. For more information, please contact

U.S. Corporate and Government Sales
1-800-382-3419
corpsales@pearsontechgroup.com

For sales outside of the U.S., please contact

International Sales
international@pearsoned.com

Editor-in-Chief
Greg Wiegand

Executive Editor
Neil Rowe

Development Editor
Mark Renfrow

Managing Editor
Kristy Hart

Project Editor
Andrew Beaster

Copy Editor
Cheri Clark

Indexer
Ken Johnson

Proofreader
Sarah Kearns

Technical Editor
Jim Perry

Publishing Coordinator
Cindy Teeters

Book Designer
Gary Adair

Composition
Nonie Ratcliff

Contents at a Glance

Sams Teach Yourself Windows Phone 7 Game Programming in 24 Hours

Table of Contents

Contents

About the Author

Jonathan S. Harbour has been programming video games since the 1980s. His first game system was an Atari 2600, which he played with, disassembled, on the floor of his room as a kid. He has written on numerous subjects such as C++, C#, Basic, Java, DirectX, Allegro, Lua, DarkBasic, Pocket PC, and game consoles. He is the author of another recent book titled *XNA Game Studio 4.0 for Xbox 360 Developers*. He holds a Master's degree in Information Systems Management. Visit his web log and game development forum at www.jharbour.com/forum, and his Facebook page at www.facebook.com/jharbourcom.

Dedication

Dedicated to FASA Corporation founders Jordan Weisman and L. Ross Babcock III, whose games continue to inspire.

Acknowledgments

Thank you to the editorial staff at Sams for their hard work in getting this book polished and into print: Neil Rowe, Mark Renfrow, Andy Beaster, Cheri Clark, Ken Johnson, Sarah Kearns, Nonie Ratcliff, and a special thanks to Jim Perry for his technical advice. I enjoyed working with all of you and hope we can do it again soon.

We Want to Hear from You!

As the reader of this book, *you* are our most important critic and commentator. We value your opinion and want to know what we're doing right, what we could do better, what areas you'd like to see us publish in, and any other words of wisdom you're willing to pass our way.

You can email or write me directly to let me know what you did or didn't like about this book—as well as what we can do to make our books stronger.

Please note that I cannot help you with technical problems related to the topic of this book, and that due to the high volume of mail I receive, I might not be able to reply to every message.

When you write, please be sure to include this book's title and author, as well as your name and phone or email address. I will carefully review your comments and share them with the author and editors who worked on the book.

Email: feedback@samspublishing.com

Mail: Neil Rowe
            Executive Editor
            Sams Publishing
            800 East 96th Street
            Indianapolis, IN 46240 USA

Reader Services

Visit our website and register this book at www.samspublishing.com/register for convenient access to any updates, downloads, or errata that might be available for this book.

Introduction

This book was written with the beginner in mind. Each of the 24 hours in this book is short and succinct, usually teaching one basic subject and building on previous hours. The subjects covered in this book are geared primarily toward rendering on the small Windows Phone 7 screen. A *lot* of attention is given to sprite animation, since this seems to be the main focus of games for this platform. This book is not a "geeky" or "gadget" guide to the Windows Phone 7 platform. There are no hours devoted to the Windows Phone 7 hardware capabilities, and there is no overview of available applications in the marketplace.

This book is entirely focused on programming games with XNA Game Studio 4.0, targeting the Windows Phone 7 platform, and gets to the point quickly. This book does not try to cover every aspect of programming with XNA Game Studio 4.0. The goal of this book is to teach a relative beginner how to get graphics on the screen of a phone device, how to get user input via the touchscreen, and how to interact with the user. A lot of attention is given to user input, animation, and interaction. This requires a significant investment of time into graphical user interface (GUI) programming, which features prominently in these pages.

Our development tool of choice is obvious: Visual Studio 2010 Express for Windows Phone (with total emphasis on the C# language). This book does not spend much time covering Silverlight, although one small example of a Silverlight application is presented as a comparison to XNA. Nor is 3D rendering a high priority in this book. XNA's rendering capabilities are similar on all XNA platforms. *Most* of the same 3D rendering code will run on Windows, Xbox 360, and Windows Phone 7 without modification. The real difference is that custom shader effects are not supported on Windows Phone 7. The first hour will help you get up and running with the development environment.

Audience and Organization

This book assumes that the reader is new to the Windows Phone 7 platform, and new to XNA Game Studio 4.0. It assumes that the reader has a basic working knowledge of the C# language, but moves at a reasonable pace. This book does go deep into some advanced concepts, such as animation and collision response, but this is *not* a heavy rendering book. This is far more of a *gameplay* book, with much time spent on building user interfaces and doing animation. There just aren't enough pages to cover everything we want to explore with the Windows Phone 7 platform and also cover rendering, which is a *monumental* subject. Rendering a mesh with BasicShader is easy enough that an hour was not devoted to it.

Following is a list of the hours in this book with a short description of each hour.

1. Introduction to Windows Phone 7

This first hour introduces the platform and explains both the benefits of portability and the limitations in terms of gameplay potential that a designer or producer would find informative.

2. Getting Started with Visual C# 2010 for Windows Phone

This hour explains how to set up the development environment and create a project in both XNA and Silverlight (for comparison).

3. Printing Text

This hour might seem a bit premature, but printing text on the screen using a sprite font is very helpful at the earliest stage of programming a phone device.

4. Getting User Input

The next subject of importance is user input. This hour shows how to use the touch-screen to get user input, with coverage of touch features.

5. Drawing Bitmaps

This hour shows how to add an art file to the project, load it up as a bitmap, and draw it to the screen. This is the first step in making a game.

6. Treating Bitmaps as Sprites

The next step is to bring a static bitmap to life, so to speak, which is the goal of this hour.

7. Transforming Sprites

After a sprite has basic properties and methods in the form of a class, we can use those features to transform a sprite—that is, move it on the screen.

8. More Sprite Transforms: Rotation and Scaling

We add to the basic translation capability of a sprite by giving it the capability to rotate and scale itself.

9. Advanced Linear and Angular Velocity

Delving into user interaction and gameplay, we add important code that makes it possible to move and rotate a sprite more realistically on the screen based on velocity rather than manual transforms.

10. When Objects Collide

Collision detection literally makes a game possible, for without it a game is merely a graphics demo without the capability to interact with the player.

11. Managing Lots of Sprites

At a certain point in a game's development, there tends to be quite a bit of repetitive code. We leverage that code in a way that makes it easy to add and remove sprites from a game and interact with them using a list.

12. Sprite Color Animation

The first hour on animation starts off slowly by just covering color animation, but this sets up a framework for more advanced forms of animation to come.

13. Sprite Transform Animation

Although our sprite class can already transform itself, the code must be manually written to perform specific transforms. Transform animation is a means to perform transforms with an algorithm rather than with manual code.

14. Sprite Frame Animation

The traditional form of "cartoon" animation involves flipping one frame over another to create the impression of movement. We use that technique to add support for frame animation to our sprites.

15. Transforming Frame Animations

This hour shows how to add transform animation support to framed animations, while previously these two were not possible at the same time. The code developed in this hour makes simultaneous multiple animations possible.

16. Drawing with Z-Index Ordering

This hour shows how to give each sprite a priority number so that it will show up under or over other sprites.

17. Using Location Services (GPS)

All Windows Phone 7 devices have a GPS receiver as part of the hardware specification. We can use this for some creative gameplay for multiplayer games.

18. Playing Audio

The audio system of Windows Phone 7 is a bit different from that of other XNA platforms, so we discuss the differences here while learning to write code to load and play audio files.

19. Reading and Writing Files Using Storage

Unlike with a Windows PC, we cannot just read and write to any file in the system with a Windows Phone 7 device. In this hour, we learn to use the storage space to read and write files, for the purpose of reading in game levels and saving game state.

20. Creating a Graphical User Interface

Most of the animation code developed previously contributes to this hour, which shows how to create several types of GUI controls, including a button, a label, and sliders.

21. Finite State Gameplay

This hour explores an important gameplay concept, keeping track of state for an object or the whole game itself. We use this concept to enable multiple "screens" that can be switched to and from by the user.

22. The Physics of Gravity

The first of three hours devoted to a sample game, this hour goes over the algorithm for simulating gravity between two massive objects in space.

23. Rocket Science: Acceleration

Combining simulated gravity with acceleration gives us code that can cause objects to affect each other realistically in space.

24. The Black Hole Game

The final hour presents a complete game for the reader to explore on a fun subject. The code presented for this game can be used for other types of games as well.

Conventions Used in This Book

The following styles are found throughout the book to help the reader with important points of interest.

This is the "Watch Out" style. These boxes present important information about the subject that the reader may find helpful in order to avoid potential problems.

Watch Out!

This is the "Did You Know" style. These boxes provide additional information about a subject that may be of interest to the reader.

Did you Know?

This is the "By the Way" style. These boxes usually refer the reader to an off-topic subject of interest.

By the Way

Resource Files

The resource files that accompany this book are available for download online. This affords us the benefit of being able to update the resource files at any time, whereas a more traditional CD-ROM would be "set in stone." Plus, if you are a serious developer, downloading the files online will be faster than inserting a CD-ROM and copying the files to your system anyway!

The resource files may be downloaded from the Sams/Pearson website or from the author's website at www.jharbour.com/forum. In addition, a link to the resources is posted at the author's Facebook page at www.facebook.com/jharbourcom.

PART I

Introduction

HOUR 1

Making Games for Windows Phone 7

What You'll Learn in This Hour:

▶ **Getting started with Windows Phone 7**
▶ **Windows Phone 7 as a game platform?**
▶ **History of the platform**
▶ **Hardware specifications**

This hour begins our exploration of game programming on Microsoft's new smartphone platform, Windows Phone 7. I can say "new" here because it really is a whole new platform, built from the ground up. As you will learn in this hour, the old Windows Mobile division at Microsoft has undergone some major changes, and the older platform of Windows Phone 6.5 was not used as a basis for the new 7. Instead, 7 was created from the ground up around an all-new version of the core operating system, Windows CE. The exciting thing about this new platform is the exceptional development tool Microsoft has created for it: XNA Game Studio 4.0. One might argue that XNA was updated from 3.1 to 4.0 solely for this new smartphone because the Windows, Xbox 360, and Zune HD support was already exceptional in XNA 3.1. In 4.0, we have out-of-the-box support for Windows Phone 7, so we'll focus, in this hour, on exploring the new smartphone operating system.

Getting Started with Windows Phone 7

There are two ways we can develop games for Windows Phone 7: Silverlight and XNA Game Studio. Although Silverlight does have basic graphics capabilities, those capabilities are provided to support applications and are not ideally suited for games. XNA, on the other hand, was developed *specifically* for game development!

Before learning all about XNA Game Studio 4.0, Visual C# 2010, projects, configurations, Xbox Live, App Hub, and other great things that will interest a game developer, we need to first understand this new platform. Windows Phone 7, which we might call WP7 for short, is an operating system for smartphone devices.

In "the old days," if you knew how to turn on a computer, you were called a "computer geek." It didn't really matter if you knew how to do anything with a computer; it was just assumed by many (especially in the older generations) that turning it on required knowledge of the black arts in electronics wizardry. That seems to be the case with most new technology, which people will tend to resist and perhaps even fear to a certain degree. When cars were first invented at the dawn of the automobile industry, people who drove around in a "horseless carriage" were considered snobbish, among the wealthy class—that is, until Henry Ford built a car that just about anyone could afford to buy. Not only did *most* people *not* have a computer in the early days, but most people at the time did not even begin to know how to go about buying one.

I'm speaking in terms of the time period around the mid- to late-1970s, at the dawn of the personal computer (PC) age. At that time, PCs were few and far between, and a kid who owned a Commodore PET, a Tandy TRS-80, or an Apple was a rare and lucky kid indeed! Most big businesses used big mainframe computers to do the most time-consuming tasks of any business—accounting, payroll, and taxes. But even at this time period, most white-collar employees who worked in an office did not have a PC. Imagine that! It's unheard-of today! Today, the first thing a new employee must have is a cubicle or an office with a PC. And, not just that, but a *networked* PC with Internet access.

Windows Phone 7 as a Game Platform?

There was a time not too many years ago when just having a PC was enough to do your work—programming, software engineering, computer-aided design (CAD), word processing, accounting. Even in the 1980s, it was rare for every employee to have a PC at his or her desk, and even more rare for families to have a PC in their homes. A lot of kids might have had a Nintendo Entertainment System (NES) or Sega Master System (SMS) or the older Atari 2600, all of which used cartridge-based games. A step up from these video game systems were the true PCs of the time, such as the Apple II, Commodore 64, Amiga, Atari 400/800, and Atari ST. No computer enthusiasts at the time used an IBM PC at home! MS-DOS was a *terrible* operating system compared to the other, more user-friendly ones. If you wanted to do programming, you would naturally gravitate to the consumer PCs, not the business-oriented IBM PC. Now, at the time, the Apple Macintosh was pretty expensive and the ordinary kid would prefer an Apple II, but that was the start of the Mac, back in the 1980s (although it has been completely redesigned several times before reaching the modern OS X).

Well, today the world sure is a different place. If we just ignore how powerful computers are today, just look at all the hand-held systems—they're everywhere! The Nintendo DS family and the Sony PlayStation Portable (PSP) family are the two leading competitors of hand-held video game systems, and they can do almost anything that their big brothers (Nintendo Wii and Sony PS3) can do, including online play. These things are everywhere! You can't walk through a store or a mall without seeing kids carrying some sort of mobile video game system with them, not to mention phones. And it's not just kids, but adults have their toys too, like Apple iPhone, iPod, and iPad, for which some really great games are available! One of my favorites is Plants vs Zombies by PopCap Games. You can also get the game for Xbox 360, Mac, Windows, and Nintendo DS. And you know what? Some popular games are starting to come out for Windows Phone 7 because it's fairly easy to port an Xbox 360 game to Windows Phone 7.

So what is Windows Phone 7 all about? Obviously, since you're reading this book, you are interested in programming games for the device. That goes without saying, but what is development for this platform really like? What's it all about? We have to ask ourselves these questions because developing a game that you want to be taken seriously requires a pretty big investment of time, if not money. Most likely, anyone looking at Windows Phone 7 for game development is already experienced with XNA Game Studio. If you have never used this development tool, the next hour will be helpful because we'll be creating projects and working with Visual C# quite a bit. I'll assume that you might not have any experience with Visual Studio, but I do not want to annoy experienced developers, so bear with me a bit while we cover the basics such as these!

History of the Platform

Windows Phone 7 follows a long history of mobile devices from Microsoft, dating clear back to the Pocket PC in 2000. Pocket PC competed directly with the market leader of the time, Palm. The Palm Pilot was arguably the progenitor of all hand-sized mobile computers today, including cellphones.

Interestingly enough, I would not consider Apple's iPhone as an evolutionary leap beyond Palm Pilot—ignoring the many devices that have entered the market in the intervening years of the past decade. The iPhone does not follow in the lineage of "mobile computer" dating back to the Palm Pilot and Pocket PC because it was derived from Apple's wildly successful iPod. The iPod should have been invented by

Sony, the company responsible for the "Walkman" generation of portable music players. Everyone in the 1980s and early 1990s owned a "Walkman," regardless of the brand, in the same vein that everyone has played with a "Frisbee," despite these being brand names with competing companies making similar products. We Americans, due to targeted advertising, come to associate whole industries with a single product name, merely out of habit.

At any rate, you might have heard the term "podcast." The term is rather generalized today to mean audio streamed or recorded in digital form for playback on a digital media player. But the concept was invented by Apple for the iPod and iTunes (including iTunes University), which now work with video files as well as audio files. While everyone was caught up in the Napster lawsuits, Apple was busy developing iTunes and began selling music in a revolutionary new way: *per track* instead of *per album*. Have you ever heard a catchy new song on the radio and wanted to buy it for your iPod, Microsoft Zune, Creative Zen, or similar media player? Well, in the past decade, you would buy the whole CD and then rip the tracks into MP3 with software such as Windows Media Player or Winamp. This point is debatable, but I would argue that Apple iTunes proved that digital music sales can be a commercial success, highly profitable both for the recording artists and for the service provider (iTunes). Amazon is probably the second case example that proves this is now a commercially successful way to sell music.

The point is, iPod was so successful that it evolved into the iPhone and iPad, and competing companies have been trying to keep up with Apple in both of these markets now for *years*! The iPod and its relatives are *insanely great*, which is why everyone wants one. More than a fashion statement, Apple understood what the consumer wanted and made it for them. What did customers want? Not a do-everything *badly* device, but a do-the-most-important-thing *great* device. In contrast, many companies hire "experts" to conduct consumer studies, and then spend millions trying to convince customers that they really want and need that product. This might be one good way to break into a relatively unknown market or to adjust the feature set of a product according to consumer interest. But the situation Apple finds itself in today is enviable, and with that comes emulation.

The previous iteration of Windows Mobile was called Windows Phone 6.5, and over a dozen hardware manufacturers and networks supported it, from Acer to HP to Samsung. Prior to that, Windows Phone 5 revolutionized the platform with a GPU (graphics processing unit) for 3D rendering.

The current Windows Phone 7's operating system traces its roots directly back to the original Pocket PC operating system released in 2000. Pocket PCs came with a *stylus*, much like the one used on a Nintendo DS. This allows for precise input coordinates, necessary for apps like a spreadsheet (a portable version of Excel called Pocket Excel was available). However, stylus input can be tedious in today's hustle-and-bustle environment, where it is more convenient to use a thumb to do things on the device's touchscreen. Who wants to fish out a stylus just to tap a silly pop-up button (which Microsoft developers are notoriously fond of) when a thumb or another finger will do the trick?

> The online capabilities of the Sega Dreamcast video game console were made possible thanks to Windows CE. If you look at the front of the Dreamcast case, you will find a Windows CE logo.

To get technical, Windows Phone 7 is based on the Windows Mobile operating system, a new name for the classic Windows CE operating system. Windows CE goes back quite a few years. "Pocket PC" was a marketing name for Windows CE 3.1. Developers at the time used Microsoft eMbedded Visual Tools 3.0 (see Figure 1.1) to develop for Windows CE 3.1. This was a modified version of Visual Studio 6 for Windows CE that was actually a *remarkable* development environment! It was stable, fully featured, and *free*! This might be considered an early predecessor of the Express Editions now made available free by Microsoft. At the time, there were many Pocket PC models available, but the most notable ones were from Casio, HP, Dell, and Compaq.

FIGURE 1.1
Microsoft
eMbedded
Visual C++ 3.0.

Microsoft supported game development on the Pocket PC (Windows CE 3.1) by providing a low-level library called the Game API. It was nowhere near as powerful as DirectX for rendering; but neither was the Game API at the slower level of the Windows GDI (graphics device interface). No, the Game API did give access to the actual bits of the video memory, making it possible to write a low-level blitter (a term derived from the "bit-block transfer" form of memory copying). Many developers worked on sprite renderers and game libraries using the Game API, and a book was published on the subject—*Pocket PC Game Programming: Using the Windows CE Game API*, by Prima-Tech—in 2001. Some copies are still floating around if you're curious about "the early days" and the predecessor of WP7. At the time, developers had their choice of eMbedded Visual Basic or eMbedded Visual C++, but today we're developing games for WP7 using XNA and C#. In that 2001 book is a rudimentary game library surrounding `WinMain()` and the other Windows core code necessary when working in C++, as well as integrated Game API built into a series of classes.

I created one published game using the library from that early book, an indie game called Perfect Match, shown in Figure 1.2. It was sold on mobile sites such as www. Handango.com. Since I lost contact with the artist who did all the renderings, the game could not be updated or ported to any newer systems. By the way, the screen resolution was 240×320 in portrait orientation, and most games were designed to be played this way; but you'll note that many WP7 games require the player to tilt the device sideways (landscape orientation). This is something that was not common back in the Pocket PC days, but it makes sense now.

FIGURE 1.2
Perfect Match,
a Pocket PC
2000 game.

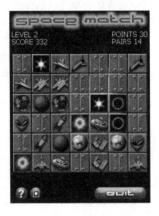

Another example from the time period is the final sample game in the book, a multiplayer game called Pocket Air Hockey, shown in Figure 1.3. This was a quick game, but even now, looking back on it, I think the chat keypad and networking code were quite good for a book example. I used the Windows Sockets (winsock) library with threading. To develop the game, I had two Pocket PCs (a Casio Cassiopeia and an HP Jornada) each equipped with a Hawking CF LAN card plugged into the top expansion port with blue CAT5 network cables going into each one. Can you imagine that? (There were also 802.11b Wi-Fi cards available for the Compact-Flash adapter port.) I just don't think anyone was really into developing multiplayer games for this platform at the time.

FIGURE 1.3
Pocket Air
Hockey, a net-
worked multi-
player game.

There was no single processor standard for the original Pocket PC 2000 devices, but three came to be used: Hitachi SH-3, NEC VR MIPS, and StrongARM. The ARM processor would become the single standard for Pocket PC 2002. The reason there have been so many releases in recent years, compared to the past, without significant updates to the core operating system (Windows CE) is that there's a need to keep up with the aggressive cellphone market's demand for *change*, even when change is not entirely necessary. When a company releases some trivial new feature in one of its phones, all competitors must come up with a compelling reason for customers to choose *their* phone instead. The carrier networks (T-Mobile, AT&T, and Verizon, primarily) also push hard for new devices and plans to maintain their customers and attract new customers. So, Windows Mobile 6 might not even be recognizable between 2007 and 2009, but the changes are primarily cosmetic, but also have to do with user input and application support. This market has been chaotic, to say the least! Table 1.1 is a historical list of releases for the platform.

TABLE 1.1 History of Windows Mobile

Year	Core	Product Name
1994	CE 1.0	Windows CE 1.0
1997	CE 2.0	Windows CE 2.0
2000	CE 3.1	Pocket PC 2000
2002	CE 3.2	Pocket PC 2002
2003	CE 4.2	Windows Mobile 2003
2004	CE 4.2	Windows Mobile 2003 SE
2005	CE 5.0	Windows Mobile 5
2007	CE 5.2	Windows Mobile 6

TABLE 1.1   History of Windows Mobile

Year	Core	Product Name
2008	CE 5.2	Windows Mobile 6.1
2009	CE 5.2	Windows Mobile 6.5
2010	CE 6.0	Windows Phone 7

Windows Phone 7 was planned for release in 2009 with a core based on Windows CE 5.0—a core dating back to 2005. The core was just too old, so development failed. At that point, a stopgap product was released (Windows Phone 6.5) while Windows Phone 7 went back to the drawing board. The Windows Mobile team ended up rebuilding the new platform from scratch around the new Windows CE 6.0 core for release the following year (2010).

Hardware Specifications

What we have today in the WP7, a completely new operating system built from the ground up around the Windows CE 6.0 core, is a modern touch-enabled architecture with no resemblance to the Windows desktop computer operating system. It took many years, but Microsoft finally perfected the platform! No longer must mobile users tap with a stylus. A sample phone built by Samsung and connected to the AT&T network is shown in Figure 1.4. WP7 competes directly with two other smartphones in the industry today: Apple iPhone and Google Android. Apple is a closed architecture, meaning only Apple builds iPhone devices. WP7 and Android, on the other hand, are not so much *mobile devices* as they are *operating systems*. That is why there are many devices available in the Android and WP7 format—but there is only one iPhone. From a developer's point of view, this openness makes life more difficult. Android, for instance, may be *too open*, with many different screen sizes and hardware specs. Developing a game for iPhone? That's a piece of cake, as far as specifications go, because there is only one (although, admittedly, adjustments to the settings are required for iPad due to its larger screen resolution).

Table 1.2 shows the common hardware specifications among most of the models available at the time of this writing. The most notable thing about the specifications is that they now follow a basic standard across all manufacturers. Apple has proven that extreme openness and flexibility are not always desirable traits in mobile hardware. One of the difficulties facing Android developers today is the need to support many different hardware devices in a single code base. Windows Mobile developers had to deal with a similar problem in Windows Phone 6.4 and earlier versions, but as you can see, WP7 has a much simpler subset of hardware specifications. This is a *good thing* for developers, greatly simplifying the code, allowing developers to focus on game design and gameplay rather than hardware idiosyncrasies among the different makes and models.

FIGURE 1.4
A Windows
Phone 7 device
built by Samsung.

TABLE 1.2   Windows Phone 7 Hardware Specifications

Component	Specification
CPU	1GHz Qualcomm
Screen Size	3.50–4.50
Resolution	480×800
Memory	8–16GB
Wi-Fi	802.11g
Network	3G
Accelerometer	Yes
GPS	Yes
FM Radio	Yes
Camera	5+ MP 720p

Summary

WP7 is an awesome integration of many technologies that have evolved over the years, beginning with the early Windows CE and Pocket PC devices, to the modern, powerful smartphone of today with advanced 3D rendering capabilities that truly bring cutting-edge gaming into the palm of your hand. We will get started writing some code for this platform in the very next hour.

Q&A

Q. *Given the history of Windows Mobile, what is a likely future for Windows Phone and other smartphone devices?*

A. This answer is subjective, but one can extrapolate a trend by observing the history of Windows Mobile, XNA Game Studio, and services such as Xbox Live and iTunes, to draw a reasonable conclusion about the future. Smartphones and touch tablets like iPad already do what we need them to do, replacing desktop PCs for the most part. Pocket PC users 10 years ago might have been pleasantly surprised by the progress but not in awe, because this technology is evolving at a predictable pace. They will become cheaper and more capable, but should still be recognizable 10 years down the road.

Q. *What improvements might be made to the development tools for smartphones beyond the current batch of tools for Windows Phone, iPhone, and Android?*

A. Developers have only one choice for iPhone, and that's Xcode/Objective-C. For Android, it's primarily a Java-based environment, but a C++ SDK is also available. For Windows Phone, we have the equally fully featured and *free* Visual C# for Windows Phone environment, which can build projects based on Silverlight and XNA using C#.

Workshop

Quiz

1. What is the standard screen resolution of Windows Phone 7 devices?

2. What is the core operating system of Windows Phone 7?

3. What are the two development tools we can use to build apps and games for Windows Phone 7?

Answers

1. 480×800

2. Windows CE

3. Silverlight and XNA

Exercises

Visit the App Hub website to see the apps and games that are available for the Windows Phone 7 platform, which will give you a feel for the type of game you would like to see published in the App Hub store. The website is http://www.microsoft.com/windowsphone/en-us/apps/default.aspx.

Getting Started with Visual C# 2010 for Windows Phone

What You'll Learn in This Hour:

- ▶ Using Visual C# 2010 Express
- ▶ Creating Silverlight projects and using Expression Blend
- ▶ Creating XNA Game Studio projects

In this hour, we will explore the development environment used to write code for the Windows Phone 7 *platform* (a word that encompasses *all* devices running the mobile operating system). If you are an experienced developer, some of the information in this hour might seem redundant or too basic. The goal is to provide information specific to Windows Phone development for a developer who might already know another language but who is new to Visual C# 2010 and/or XNA Game Studio. We'll take a leisurely pace early on so that we can cover all the basics and won't need to repeat key steps in later hours, such as how to create a new project. Each hour will still stand on its own, in terms of the information presented, and won't require one to have gone through the hours one at a time in order. This hour will be all about creating projects and using Visual C#. We will explore all the project types that are available for Windows Phone.

Visual C# 2010 Express

At the time of this writing, the current version of the development tool for Windows Phone 7 is Visual Studio 2010. To make development simple for newcomers to the Windows Mobile platform, Microsoft has set up a package that will install everything you need to develop, compile, and run code in the emulator or on a physical Windows Phone device—*for free*. The download URL at this time is http://www.microsoft.com/express/Phone. If you are using a licensed copy of Visual Studio 2010, such as the Professional, Premium, or Ultimate edition, then you will find XNA Game Studio 4.0 and related tools at http://create.msdn.com (the App Hub website). The App Hub website, shown in Figure 2.1, also contains links to the development tools.

FIGURE 2.1
The App Hub website has download links to the development tools.

The most common Windows Phone developer will be using the free version of Visual C# 2010, called the Express edition. This continues the wonderful gift Microsoft first began giving developers with the release of Visual Studio 2005. At that time, the usual "professional" versions of Visual Studio were still available, of course, and I would be remiss if I failed to point out that a *licensed* copy of Visual Studio is required by any person or organization building software for business activities (including both for-profit and nonprofit). The usual freelance developer will also need one of the professional editions of Visual Studio, if it is used for profit. But any single person who is just learning, or any organization that just wants to evaluate Visual Studio for a short time, prior to buying a full license, can take advantage of the free *Express editions*. I speak of "editions" because each language is treated as a separate product. The professional editions include all the languages, but the free Express editions, listed here, are each installed separately:

▶ Visual C# 2010 Express

▶ Visual Basic 2010 Express

▶ Visual C++ 2010 Express

The version of Visual Studio we will be using is called Visual Studio 2010 Express for Windows Phone. This is a "package" with the Windows Phone SDK already prepackaged with Visual C# 2010 Express. (Despite the name, "Visual Studio" here supports only the C# language.) It's a nice package that makes it very easy to get started doing Windows Phone development. But if you are using Visual Studio 2010 Professional (or one of the other editions) along with the Windows Phone SDK, you will see a *lot* more project templates in the New Project dialog, shown in Figure 2.2.

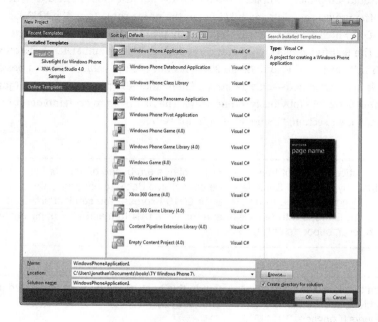

FIGURE 2.2
The New Project dialog in Visual C# 2010 Express.

▶ Windows Phone Application (Visual C#)

▶ Windows Phone Databound Application (Visual C#)

▶ Windows Phone Class Library (Visual C#)

▶ Windows Phone Panorama Application (Visual C#)

▶ Windows Phone Pivot Application (Visual C#)

▶ Windows Phone Game (4.0) (Visual C#)

▶ Windows Phone Game Library (4.0) (Visual C#)

▶ Windows Game (4.0) (Visual C#)

▶ Windows Game Library (4.0) (Visual C#)

▶ Xbox 360 Game (4.0) (Visual C#)

▶ Xbox 360 Game Library (4.0) (Visual C#)

▶ Content Pipeline Extension Library (4.0)

▶ Empty Content Project (4.0) (Visual C#)

As you can see, even in this limited version of Visual Studio 2010, all the XNA
Game Studio 4.0 project templates are included—not just those limited to Windows
Phone. The project templates with "(4.0)" in the name come from the XNA Game
Studio SDK, which is what we will be primarily using to build Windows Phone
games. The first five project templates come with the Silverlight SDK. That's all we
get with this version of Visual Studio 2010. It's not even possible to build a basic
Windows *application* here—only Windows Phone (games or apps), Windows (game
only), and Xbox 360 (obviously, game only). The first five project templates are covered in the next section, "Using Silverlight for WP7."

Did you notice that all of these project templates are based on the C# language?
Unfortunately for Visual Basic fans, we cannot use Basic to program games or
apps for Windows Phone using Visual C# 2010 Express. You can install Visual
Basic 2010 Express with Silverlight and then use that to make WP7 applications.
XNA, however, supports only C#.

We don't look at Xbox 360 development in this book at all. If you're interested in
the subject, see my complementary book *XNA Game Studio 4.0 for Xbox 360
Developers* [Cengage, 2011].

Using Silverlight for WP7

Microsoft Silverlight is a web browser plug-in "runtime." Silverlight is not, strictly
speaking, a development tool. It might be compared to DirectX, in that it is like a
library, but for rich-content web apps. It's similar to ASP.NET in that Silverlight applications run in a web browser, but it is more capable for building consumer applications (while ASP.NET is primarily for business apps). But the *way* Silverlight
applications are built is quite different from ASP.NET—it's more of a *design* tool with
an editing environment called Expression Blend. The design goal of Silverlight is to
produce web applications that are rich in media support, and it supports all standard web browsers (not just Internet Explorer, which is a pleasant surprise!), including Firefox and Safari on Mac.

Using Expression Blend to Build Silverlight Projects

Microsoft Expression Blend 4 is a free tool installed with the Windows Phone package that makes it easier to design Silverlight-powered web pages with rich media content support. Blend can be used to design and create engaging user experiences for Silverlight pages. Windows application support is possible with the WPF (Windows Presentation Foundation) library. A key feature of Blend is that it separates design from programming. As you can see in Figure 2.3, the New Project dialog in Blend lists the same project types found in Visual C# 2010 Express.

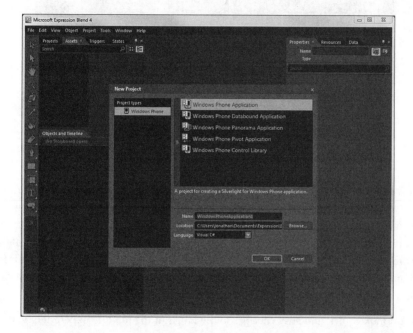

FIGURE 2.3
Expression Blend is a Silverlight development tool for web designers.

Let's create a quick Expression Blend project to see how it works. While working on this quick first project, keep in mind that we're not building a "Blend" project, but a "Silverlight" project—*using* Blend. Blend is a whole new Silverlight design and development tool, not affiliated with Visual Studio (but probably based on it). The Silverlight library is already installed on the Windows Phone emulator and actual phones.

Here's how to create the project:

1. Create a Windows Phone Application project using the New Project dialog. Click File, New Project.

2. Blend creates a standard project for Windows Phone, complete with an application title and opening page for the app.

3. Run the project with Project, Run Project, or by pressing F5. The running program is shown in Figure 2.4.

FIGURE 2.4
Our first project with Expression Blend.

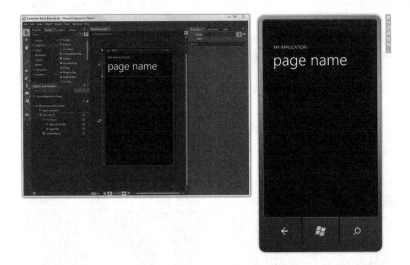

This is a useless app, but it shows the steps needed to create a new project and run it in the Windows Phone emulator. Did you notice how large the emulator window appears? That's full size with respect to the screen resolution of WP7. As you'll recall from the first hour, the resolution is 480×800. That is enough pixels to support 480p DVD movies, but not the 740p or 1080p HD standards. Still, DVD quality is great for a phone! And when rotated to landscape mode, 800×480 is a lot of screen real estate for a game too.

You can make quick and easy changes to the labels at the top and experiment with the design controls in the toolbox on the left. Here you can see that the application title and page title have been renamed, and some images and shapes have been added to the page. Pressing F5 again brings it up in the emulator, shown in Figure 2.5.

Now that you've seen what's possible with Expression Blend's more designer-friendly editor, let's take a look at the same Silverlight project in Visual Studio 2010.

Silverlight Projects

The Silverlight runtime for WP7 supports some impressive media types with many different audio and video codecs, vector graphics, bitmap graphics, and animation. That should trigger the perimeter alert of any game developer worth their salt! Silverlight brings some highly interactive input mechanisms to the Web, including accelerometer motion detection, multitouch input (for devices that support it), camera, microphone input, and various phone-type features (like accessing an address book and dialing).

FIGURE 2.5
Making quick changes to the page is easy with Expression Blend.

To find out whether your preferred web browser supports Silverlight, visit the installer web page at http://www.microsoft.com/getsilverlight/get-started/install.

By the Way

The Visual Studio 2010 project templates specific to Silverlight are highlighted in bold in the list below. These are the same project templates shown in Expression Blend!

- ▶ **Windows Phone Application (Visual C#)**
- ▶ **Windows Phone Databound Application (Visual C#)**
- ▶ **Windows Phone Class Library (Visual C#)**
- ▶ **Windows Phone Panorama Application (Visual C#)**
- ▶ **Windows Phone Pivot Application (Visual C#)**
- ▶ Windows Phone Game (4.0) (Visual C#)
- ▶ Windows Phone Game Library (4.0) (Visual C#)
- ▶ Windows Game (4.0) (Visual C#)
- ▶ Windows Game Library (4.0) (Visual C#)
- ▶ Xbox 360 Game (4.0) (Visual C#)
- ▶ Xbox 360 Game Library (4.0) (Visual C#)
- ▶ Content Pipeline Extension Library (4.0)
- ▶ Empty Content Project (4.0) (Visual C#)

Let's create a quick project in Visual Studio in order to compare it with Expression Blend. You'll note right away that it is not the same rich design environment, but is more programmer oriented.

▼ **Try It Yourself**

Comparing Visual Studio with Expression Blend

Let's create a new project in Visual C# 2010 in order to compare it with Expression Blend. Follow these steps:

1. Open the New Project dialog with File, New Project.

2. Next, in the New Project dialog, choose the target folder for the project and type in a project name, as shown in Figure 2.6.

FIGURE 2.6
Creating a new Silverlight project in Visual C# 2010 Express.

3. Click the OK button to generate the new project shown in the figure. Not very user-friendly, is it? First of all, double-clicking a label does not make it editable, among other limitations (compared to Expression Blend). Where are the control properties? Oh, yes, in the Properties window in Visual Studio. See Figure 2.7. This is also very data-centric, which programmers love and designers loathe. The view on the left is how the page appears on the device (or emulator); the view on the right is the HTML-like source code behind the page, which can be edited.

4. Bring up the Properties window (if not already visible) by using the View menu. Select a control on the page, such as the application title. Scroll down in the Properties to the Text property, where you can change the label's text, as shown in Figure 2.8. Play around with the various properties to change the horizontal alignment, the color of the text, and so on. Open the Toolbox (located on the left side of Visual Studio) to gain access to new controls such as the Ellipse control shown here.

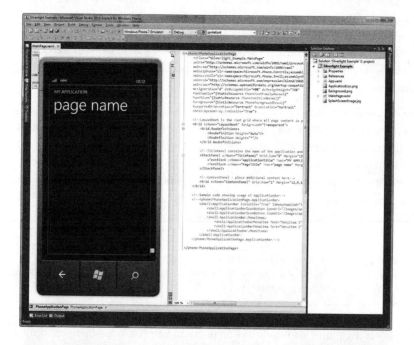

FIGURE 2.7
The new Silverlight project has been created.

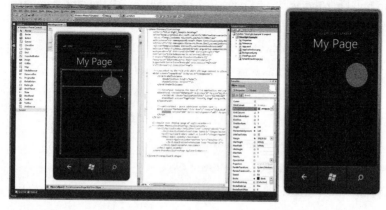

FIGURE 2.8
Adding content to the Silverlight page.

XNA Game Studio

XNA Game Studio 4.0 was released in the fall of 2010. (From now on, let's just shorten this to "XNA" or "XNA 4.0", even though "Game Studio" is the name of the SDK, and "XNA" is the overall product name.) XNA 4.0 saw several new improvements to the graphics system, but due to the hardware of the Xbox 360, XNA is still based on Direct3D 9 (not the newer versions, Direct3D 10 or 11). This is actually very good news for a beginner, since Direct3D 9 is much easier to learn than 10 or 11. Although XNA abstracts the C++-based DirectX libraries into the C#-based XNA Framework, there is still much DirectX-ish code that you have to know in order to build a capable graphics engine in XNA. While XNA 4.0 added WP7 support, it simultaneously *dropped* support for Zune (the portable multimedia and music player).

I have a Zune HD, and it's a nice device! It can play 720p HD movies and even export them to an HDTV via an adapter and HDMI cable. It plays music well too. But, like many consumers, I just did not have much incentive to go online and download *games* for the Zune. This is, of course, purely a subjective matter of opinion, but it's disappointing for game developers who put effort into making games for Zune. Fortunately, the code base is largely the same (thanks to XNA and C#), so those Zune games can be easily ported to WP7 now.

Did you Know?

> Rendering states, enumerations, return values, and so forth are the same in XNA as they are in Direct3D, so it could be helpful to study a Direct3D book to improve your skills as an XNA programmer!

The project templates for Windows Phone might surprise you—there are only *two*! We can build a Windows Phone *game* or a *game library*. All the other templates are related to the other platforms supported by XNA.

- ▶ Windows Phone Application (Visual C#)
- ▶ Windows Phone Databound Application (Visual C#)
- ▶ Windows Phone Class Library (Visual C#)
- ▶ Windows Phone Panorama Application (Visual C#)
- ▶ Windows Phone Pivot Application (Visual C#)
- ▶ **Windows Phone Game (4.0) (Visual C#)**
- ▶ **Windows Phone Game Library (4.0) (Visual C#)**
- ▶ Windows Game (4.0) (Visual C#)

▶ Windows Game Library (4.0) (Visual C#)

▶ Xbox 360 Game (4.0) (Visual C#)

▶ Xbox 360 Game Library (4.0) (Visual C#)

▶ Content Pipeline Extension Library (4.0)

▶ Empty Content Project (4.0) (Visual C#)

Let's build a quick XNA project for Windows Phone to see what it looks like. We'll definitely be doing a lot of this in upcoming chapters since XNA is our primary focus (the coverage of Silverlight was only for the curious—grab a full-blown Silverlight or Expression Blend book for more complete and in-depth coverage.

Try It Yourself ▼

Creating Your First XNA 4.0 Project

Let's create a new XNA 4.0 project in Visual C# 2010, so we can use this as a comparison with the previous project created with Expression Blend. Follow these steps:

1. Create a new project. We'll be basing these tutorials around Visual Studio 2010 Express for Windows Phone. The processes will be similar to using the Professional version, but you will see many more project templates in the New Project dialog. Open the File menu and choose New Project. The New Project dialog is shown in Figure 2.9.

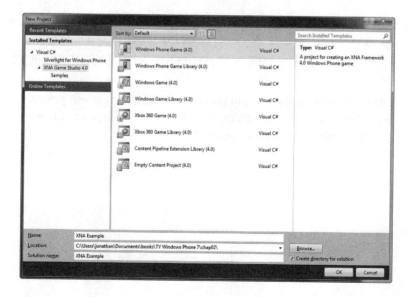

FIGURE 2.9
Creating a new XNA 4.0 project.

2. The new project has been created. Note, from Figure 2.10, the code that has been automatically generated for the XNA project. If you have ever worked with XNA before, this will be no surprise—the code looks exactly like the generated code for Windows and Xbox 360 projects!

FIGURE 2.10
The new XNA 4.0 project has been created.

3. Run the project with Build, Run, or by pressing F5. The emulator will come up, as shown in Figure 2.11. Doesn't look like much—just a blue screen! That's exactly what we want to see, because we haven't written any game code yet.

4. Add a SpriteFont to the Content project. Right-click the content project, called XNA ExampleContent(Content) in the Solution Explorer. Choose Add, New Item, as shown in Figure 2.12.

FIGURE 2.11
Running the
XNA project in
the Windows
Phone emulator.

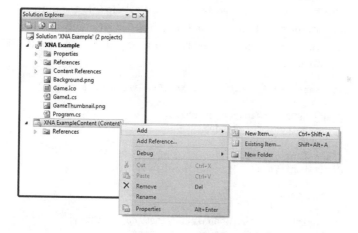

FIGURE 2.12
Adding a new
item to the con-
tent project.

5. In the Add Item dialog, choose the Sprite Font item from the list, as shown
in Figure 2.13, and leave the filename as `SpriteFont1.spritefont`.

FIGURE 2.13
Adding a new
SpriteFont con-
tent item to the
project.

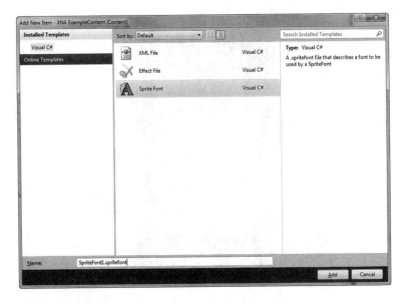

6. Create the font variable. The comments in the code listing have been removed to make the code easier to read. We'll dig into the purpose of all this code in the next hour, so don't be concerned with understanding all the code yet. Type in the two new bold lines of code shown here to add the font variable.

```
public class Game1 : Microsoft.Xna.Framework.Game
{
    GraphicsDeviceManager graphics;
    SpriteBatch spriteBatch;

    //new font variable
    SpriteFont font;

    public Game1()
    {
        graphics = new GraphicsDeviceManager(this);
        Content.RootDirectory = "Content";
        TargetElapsedTime = TimeSpan.FromTicks(333333);
    }
```

7. Load the font. Enter the two new lines shown in bold in the LoadContent method.

```
protected override void Initialize()
{
    base.Initialize();
}
```

```
protected override void LoadContent()
{
    spriteBatch = new SpriteBatch(GraphicsDevice);

    //load the font
    font = Content.Load<SpriteFont>("SpriteFont1");
}

protected override void UnloadContent()
{
}
```

8. Print a message on the screen. Using the `SpriteBatch` and `SpriteFont`
    objects, we can print any text message. This is done from the `Draw`
    method—add the code highlighted in bold.

```
protected override void Update(GameTime gameTime)
{
    if (GamePad.GetState(PlayerIndex.One).Buttons.Back ==
        ButtonState.Pressed)
        this.Exit();

    base.Update(gameTime);
}

protected override void Draw(GameTime gameTime)
{
    GraphicsDevice.Clear(Color.CornflowerBlue);

    //print a message
    spriteBatch.Begin();
    string text = "HELLO FROM XNA!";
    Vector2 pos = font.MeasureString(text);
    spriteBatch.DrawString(font, text, pos, Color.White);
    spriteBatch.End();

    base.Draw(gameTime);
}
}
```

9. Run the program using Debug, Start Debugging, or by pressing F5. The pro-
    gram will come up in the emulator, shown in Figure 2.14. Now there's just
    one big problem: The font is too small, and the screen needs to be rotated
    to landscape mode so we can read it!

10. Click the emulator window to cause the little control menu to appear at the
    upper right. There are two icons that will rotate the window left or right,
    allowing us to switch from portrait to landscape mode. All XNA projects
    will default to portrait mode by default. Landscape mode is shown in
    Figure 2.15.

FIGURE 2.14
The text message is displayed in the emulator—
sideways!

FIGURE 2.15
Rotating the emulator window to landscape mode for XNA projects.

11. Enlarge the font. We're almost done; there's just one final thing I want to show you how to do here. Open the font file you created, `SpriteFont1.spritefont`. Change the size value from 14 to 36. Now rerun the project by pressing F5. The new, large font is shown in Figure 2.16.

FIGURE 2.16
Enlarging the
font to make it
more readable.

XNA or Silverlight: What's the Verdict?

We have now seen two projects developed with the two different, and somewhat competing tools: XNA and Silverlight. Which should we choose? This is really a matter of preference when it comes to developing a game. Although XNA is far more capable due to its rendering capabilities, Silverlight *can* be used to make a game as well, with form-based control programming. For portable, touchscreen *applications*, it's a given: Silverlight. But for serious game development, XNA is the only serious option.

Summary

We covered quite a bit of information regarding Visual Studio 2010, the project templates available for Windows Phone, and the value-added tool Expression Blend. A sample project was presented using Expression Blend with a corresponding Silverlight project in Visual Studio, as well as an XNA project. We're off to a good start and already writing quite a bit of code! In the next hour, you will create your first Windows Phone game.

Q&A

Q. *Given the obvious appeal of Expression Blend for designing rich media web pages, why would anyone choose to build a Silverlight website using Visual Studio rather than Expression Blend?*

A. Expression Blend is a designer's tool. Although it is very easy to use and is more useful to a designer, there are some limitations in its capabilities beyond what is built into Blend, whereas a Visual Studio project has add-on libraries and .NET available for more professional needs, such as a business site that connects to a database.

Q. *Given that XNA games running on Windows Phone can run in either landscape or portrait mode, what are some advantages and disadvantages of each of these two screen orientations?*

A. Answers will vary.

Workshop

Quiz

1. What is the name of Microsoft's rich web content runtime library?

2. What is the default resolution of an XNA game running on Windows Phone?

3. What is the default screen orientation of an XNA game running on Windows Phone?

Answers

1. Silverlight

2. 800×480

3. Landscape mode

Exercises

Design your own Silverlight-powered web page using Expression Blend, made to look like a blog-style site using the various text and image controls available.

HOUR 3

Printing Text

This hour takes the next logical step in programming the WP7 with XNA 4.0. You have learned how to create a new Windows Phone project in Visual C# 2010. We will touch on that subject again in this hour while learning about fonts and text drawing code. There are actually quite a lot of interesting features available to us for working with text and fonts in an XNA program. There are several royalty-free fonts included with XNA, which can each be used to draw text in any font point size with special effects such as italic and bold. We will explore the runtime capabilities of the font system to render text in different colors (including alpha blending), color animation, and even scaling.

What You'll Learn in This Hour:

- ▶ **Creating the Font Demo project**
- ▶ **Adding a new font to the Content project**
- ▶ **Learning to use the** `SpriteFont` **class**
- ▶ **Printing text**

Creating the Font Demo Project

At first glance, the text output capabilities of XNA seem to be pretty straightforward, but with a little know-how and experimentation, we find that XNA offers us some really great features for printing text on the little Windows Phone screen. The code here, as elsewhere in this book, will be the standard "XNA" fare, meaning the code would look the same on other platforms supported by XNA (namely, Windows and Xbox 360). Let's first get started by creating the project.

A *font* in XNA is nothing more than a text file—at least, from the programmer's point of view. When the project is compiled, XNA uses the text file to create a bitmap font on a memory texture and use that for printing text on the screen.

This is a time-consuming process, which is why the font is created at program startup rather than while it's running. Let's create a new project and add a font to it.

▼ **Try It Yourself**

Creating a New XNA Project

Follow these steps to create a new XNA project in Visual C# 2010:

1. Start up Visual Studio 2010 Express for Windows Phone (or whichever edition of Visual Studio 2010 you are using).

2. Bring up the New Project dialog, shown in Figure 3.1, from either the Start Page or the File menu.

FIGURE 3.1
Creating the Font Demo project.

3. Choose Windows Phone Game (4.0) from the list of project templates.

4. Type in a name for the new project (the example is called Font Demo).

5. Choose the location for the project by clicking the Browse button, or by typing the folder name directly.

6. Click OK to create the new project.

The new project is generated by Visual Studio and should look similar to the project shown in Figure 3.2.

FIGURE 3.2
The newly generated Font Demo project.

Adding a New Font to the Content Project

At this point, you can go ahead and run the project by pressing F5, but all you will see in the Windows Phone emulator is a blue screen. That is because we haven't written any code yet to draw anything. Before we can print text on the screen, we have to create a font, which is added to the Content project.

In XNA 4.0, most game assets are added to the Content project within the Solution, where they are compiled or converted into a format that XNA uses. We might use the general term "project" when referring to a Windows Phone game developed with XNA, but there might be more than one project in the Solution. The "main project" will be the one containing source code for a game. Some assets, however, might be located just within the source code project, depending on how the code accesses those assets. Think of the Content project as a container for "managed" assets.

A Visual Studio "Solution" is the overall wrapper or container for a game project, and should not be confused with "projects" that it contains, including the Content project containing game assets (bitmap files, audio files, 3D mesh files, and so on).

Did you Know?

In this example, both the Solution and the main project are called "Font Demo," because Visual Studio uses the same name for both when a new Solution is generated. Now, let's add a new font to the Content project. Remember that the Content project is where all game assets are located.

1. Select the Content project in Solution Explorer to highlight it, as shown in Figure 3.3.

FIGURE 3.3
Highlighting the
Content project.

2. Open the Project menu and choose Add New Item. Optionally, you can right-click the Content project in Solution Explorer (Font DemoContent (Content)) to bring up the context menu, and choose Add, New Item.

3. The Add New Item dialog, shown in Figure 3.4, appears. Choose Sprite Font from the list. Leave the name as is (SpriteFont1.spritefont).

FIGURE 3.4
Adding a new
Sprite Font.

A new .spritefont file has been added to the Content project, as shown in Figure 3.5. Visual Studio opens the new file right away so that you can make any changes you want to the font details. The default font name is Segoe UI Mono, which is a monospaced font. This means each character of the font has the same width (takes up the same amount of horizontal space). Some fonts are *proportional*, which means each character has a different width (in which case, "W" and "I" are spaced quite differently, for instance).

FIGURE 3.5
A new Sprite Font has been added to the Content project.

The SpriteFont1.spritefont file is just a text file, like a .CS source code file, but it is formatted in the XML (Extensible Markup Language) format. You can experiment with the font options in the .spritefont descriptor file, but usually the only fields you will need to change are FontName and Size. Here is what the font file looks like with all comments removed:

```
<?xml version="1.0" encoding="utf-8"?>
<XnaContent xmlns:Graphics =
"Microsoft.Xna.Framework.Content.Pipeline.Graphics">
  <Asset Type="Graphics:FontDescription">
    <FontName>Segoe UI Mono</FontName>
    <Size>14</Size>
    <Spacing>0</Spacing>
    <UseKerning>true</UseKerning>
```

```
<Style>Regular</Style>
<CharacterRegions>
  <CharacterRegion>
    <Start>&#32;</Start>
    <End>&#126;</End>
  </CharacterRegion>
</CharacterRegions>
</Asset>
</XnaContent>
```

> Visual Studio Solution (.sln) and project (.csproj) files also contain XML-format-ted information!

Table 3.1 shows the royalty-free fonts included with XNA 4.0. Note that some fonts come with italic and bold versions even though the SpriteFont description also allows for these modifiers.

TABLE 3.1   XNA Fonts

Font Name	Font Name	Font Name
Andy Bold	Jing Jing	Kootenay
Lindsey	Miramonte	Miramonte Bold
Moire Bold	Moire ExtraBold	Moire Light
Moire Regular	Motorwerk	News Gothic
News Gothic Bold	OCR A Extended	Pericles
Pericles Light	Pescadero	Pescadero Bold
Quartz MS	Segoe Keycaps	Segoe Print
Segoe Print Bold	Segoe UI Mono	Segoe UI Mono Bold
Wasco Sans	Wasco Sans Bold	Wasco Sans Bold Italic
Wasco Sans Italic		

> For practical purposes, "Solution" and "project" are interchangeable terms, refer-ring to the same thing. We will not try to differentiate between them in this book.

Learning to Use the `SpriteFont` Class

We can create as many fonts as we want in an XNA project and use them at any time to print text with different styles. For each font you want to use in a project, create a new `.spritefont` file. The name of the file is used to load the font, as you'll see next. Even if you want to use the same font style with a different point size, you must create a separate `.spritefont` file (although we will learn how to scale a font as a rendering option).

Try It Yourself ▼

Loading the SpriteFont Asset

To use a `SpriteFont` asset, first add a variable at the top of the program. Let's go over the steps:

1. Add a new variable called `SpriteFont1`. You can give this variable a different name if you want. It is given the same name as the asset here only for illustration, to associate one thing with another.

```
public class Game1 : Microsoft.Xna.Framework.Game
{
    GraphicsDeviceManager graphics;
    SpriteBatch spriteBatch;

    //create new font variable
    SpriteFont SpriteFont1;
```

2. Create (instantiate) a new object using the `SpriteFont1` variable, and simultaneously load the font with the `Content.Load()` method. Note the class name in brackets, `<SpriteFont>`. If you aren't familiar with template programming, this can look a bit strange. This type of coding makes the code cleaner, because the `Content.Load()` method has the same call no matter what type of object you tell it to load.

```
protected override void LoadContent()
{
    // Create a new SpriteBatch, which can be used to draw textures.
    spriteBatch = new SpriteBatch(GraphicsDevice);

    // TODO: use this.Content to load your game content here

    SpriteFont1 = Content.Load<SpriteFont>("SpriteFont1");
}
```

▲

If the `Content` class did not use a templated `Load()` method, we would need to call a different method for every type of game asset, such as `Content.LoadSpriteFont()`, `Content.LoadTexture2D()`, or `Content.LoadSoundEffect()`.

There is another important reason for using a template form of `Load()` here: We can create our own *custom* content loader to load our own asset files! XNA is very extendable with this capability. Suppose you want to load a data file saved by your own custom level editor tool. Instead of manually converting the level file into text or XML, which XNA can already read, you could instead just write your own custom content loader, and then load it with code such as this:

```
Content.Load<Level>("level1")
```

The ability to write code like this is powerful, and reflects a concept similar to "late binding." This means the C# compiler might not know exactly what type of object a particular line of code is referring to at compile time, but the issue is sorted out later while the program is running. That's not *exactly* what's happening here, but it is a similar concept, and the easiest illustration of template programming I can think of.

These are just possibilities. Let's get back to the `SpriteFont` code at hand!

Printing Text

Now that we have loaded the `.spritefont` asset file, and XNA has created a bitmap font in memory after running the code in `LoadContent()`, the font is available for use. We can use the `SpriteFont1` object to print text on the screen using `SpriteBatch.DrawString()`. Just be sure to always have a matching pair of `SpriteBatch.Begin()` and `SpriteBatch.End()` statements around any drawing code. That directive applies to both text and sprites, which we will learn about in Hour 5, "Drawing Bitmaps."

▼ **Try It Yourself**

Printing the Text

Here are the steps you may follow to print some text onto the screen using the new font we have created:

1. Scroll down to the `Draw()` method in the code listing.

2. Add the code shown in bold.

```
protected override void Draw(GameTime gameTime)
{
    GraphicsDevice.Clear(Color.CornflowerBlue);
```

```
    // TODO: Add your drawing code here

    string text = "This is the Segoe UI Mono font";
    Vector2 position = new Vector2(20, 20);

    spriteBatch.Begin();
    spriteBatch.DrawString(SpriteFont1, text, position, Color.White);
    spriteBatch.End();

    base.Draw(gameTime);
}
```

Run the program by pressing F5. The WP7 emulator comes up, as shown in Figure 3.6.

FIGURE 3.6
Printing text in the Font Demo program.

The version of `SpriteBatch.DrawString()` used here is the simplest version of the method, but other *overloaded* versions of the method are available. An *overloaded method* is a method such as `DrawString()` that has two or more different sets of parameters to make it more useful to the programmer. There are actually *six* versions of `DrawString()`. Here is an example using the sixth and most complex version. When run, the changes to the text output are dramatic, as shown in Figure 3.7!

```
float rotation = MathHelper.ToRadians(15.0f);
Vector2 origin = Vector2.Zero;
Vector2 scale = new Vector2(1.3f, 5.0f);
spriteBatch.DrawString(SpriteFont1, text, position, Color.White,
    rotation, origin, scale, SpriteEffects.None, 0.0f);
```

FIGURE 3.7
Experimenting
with different
DrawString()
options.

Summary

As you have learned in this hour, the font support in XNA takes a little time to set up, but after a font has been added, some very useful and versatile text printing capabilities are available. We can print text via the SpriteFont.DrawString() method, with many options available such as font scaling and different colors.

Q&A

Q. *What if I want to use a custom TrueType font (.ttf) file that I really like in my game?*

A. You can include the font file in the project directory and XNA will look for it when you try to load it with Content.Load(). Just be careful not to distribute any nonlicensed font files with your game. The fonts included with XNA are free, but not all font files are public domain. Many of the Windows fonts (such as Times New Roman) are licensed and cannot be distributed with a game.

Q. *How can I print a message that's centered on the screen?*

A. Take a look at the SpriteFont.MeasureString() method, which returns a Vector2 containing the dimensions of the string that you can use to center the text based on the width and height of the screen and the text.

Workshop

Quiz

1. What version of `Content.Load<>()` should be used to load a font?

2. What class contains the `DrawString()` method used to print text based on a font?

3. How many royalty-free fonts does XNA 4.0 come with?

Answers

1. `Content.Load<SpriteFont>()`

2. `SpriteBatch`

3. 28

Exercises

For further study, try adding several more fonts to the project created in this hour, and then experiment with the different options in the `.spritefont` files, such as name and size, and print each font in a different color. Also, try out the different overloads of `DrawString()` to find the one that you like the best.

HOUR 4

Getting User Input

What You'll Learn in This Hour:

- ▶ Exploring touch screen input
- ▶ Simulating touch input
- ▶ Using gestures on the touchscreen

This hour delves into the user input system of XNA Game Studio 4.0, with an emphasis only on those features relevant to the Windows Phone. We actually have a somewhat easier time of it regarding input on the phones, because there's just one practical form of input—the touchscreen. With just one form of input, our games will have to treat the screen as an array of discrete squares, more like a *grid* of squares. It will really be next to impossible to get a precise pixel location when using one's finger! A general position can be determined by taking the center of a small rectangle or circular area representing a "touch" event, but it is quite different from mouse input. But for all practical purposes, a single point on the screen does ultimately represent the touch or tap position. We will explore these issues and more this hour.

Exploring Windows Phone Touchscreen Input

Programming a game's input system really does require a lot of design consideration ahead of time because all we really can use is the touchscreen! Oh, there is an accelerometer that can be used for input, but it is a rare and often niche game that uses the accelerometer to read the phone's orientation (the angle and position at which it is being held). The touchscreen, for all practical purposes, is treated like mouse input without a visible mouse cursor. Windows programmers will have a slightly harder time adjusting than someone who has been working with the Xbox 360 or another console, which already requires an adjustment in one's assumptions about user input. Windows games are a cakewalk, with 100-plus keyboard keys, the mouse, *and* an optional controller! That's a lot of input! On the Windows Phone, though, all we have is the touchscreen. So we need to make the most of it, being mindful that a user's finger is rather large compared to the precise input of a mouse cursor.

For the purpose of detecting input for a game, the most obvious method might be to just detect the touch location and convert that to an average coordinate—like mouse input. But the Windows Phone touchscreen is capable of *multitouch*, not just single-touch input. Although the screen is very small compared to a tablet or PC screen, it is still capable of detecting input from up to *four* fingers at once. To develop a multitouch game, you will need the actual Windows Phone hardware—either a real phone or an unlocked development model (with no phone service).

Multitouch is a significant feature for the new phone! For our purposes here, however, we will just be concerned with single "tap" input from one finger, simulated with mouse motion in the emulator. We can do a single tap with a mouse click, or a *drag* operation by touching the screen and moving the finger across the screen. Again, this will have to be done with your mouse for development on the emulator (unless your Windows system uses a touchscreen!).

> You will not be able to test multitouch in the emulator without a multitouch screen on your Windows development system or an actual Windows Phone device.

Simulating Touch Input

The key to touch input with a WP7 device with XNA is a class called TouchPanel. The XNA services for mouse, keyboard, and Xbox 360 controller input are not available in a WP7 project. So, for most XNA programmers, TouchPanel will be a new experience. Not to worry; it's similar to the mouse code if we don't tap into the multitouch capabilities.

The TouchPanel class includes one very interesting property that we can parse— MaximumTouchCount represents the number of touch inputs that the device can handle at a time.

The second class that we need to use for touch input is called TouchCollection. As the name implies, this is a collection that will be filled when we parse the TouchPanel while the game is running. TouchCollection has a State property that is similar to MouseState, with the enumerated values Pressed, Moved, and Released.

Try It Yourself ▼

The Touch Demo Project, Step by Step

Let's create a sample project to try out some of this code. I'll skip the usual new project instructions at this point since the steps should be familiar by now. Just create a new project and add a font so that we can print something on the screen. I've used Moire Bold 24 as the font in this example.

1. Add some needed variables for working with text output. (The code for the touchscreen input system will be added shortly.)

```
public class Game1 : Microsoft.Xna.Framework.Game
{
    GraphicsDeviceManager graphics;
    SpriteBatch spriteBatch;

    SpriteFont MoireBold24;
    Vector2 position;
    Vector2 size;
    string text = "Touch Screen Demo";
```

2. Initialize the font and variables used in the program.

```
protected override void LoadContent()
{
    spriteBatch = new SpriteBatch(GraphicsDevice);

    MoireBold24 = Content.Load<SpriteFont>("MoireBold24");

    size = MoireBold24.MeasureString(text);
    Viewport screen = GraphicsDevice.Viewport;
    position = new Vector2((screen.Width - size.X) / 2,
        (screen.Height - size.Y) / 2);
}
```

3. Write the update code to get touch input.

```
protected override void Update(GameTime gameTime)
{
    if (GamePad.GetState(PlayerIndex.One).Buttons.Back ==
ButtonState.Pressed)
        this.Exit();

    //get state of touch inputs
    TouchCollection touchInput = TouchPanel.GetState();

    //look at all touch points (usually 1)
    foreach(TouchLocation touch in touchInput)
    {
        position = new Vector2(touch.Position.X - size.X / 2,
```

```
                            touch.Position.Y - size.Y / 2);
            }

        base.Update(gameTime);
    }
```

4. Print the message on the screen at the touch coordinates.

```
protected override void Draw(GameTime gameTime)
{
    GraphicsDevice.Clear(Color.CornflowerBlue);

    spriteBatch.Begin();
    spriteBatch.DrawString(MoireBold24, text, position, Color.White);
    spriteBatch.End();

    base.Draw(gameTime);
}
```

Figure 4.1 shows the output of the program running in the WP7 emulator. Although the static figure doesn't show movement, the message "Touch Screen Demo" moves on the screen with touch input! On a real Windows Phone device, this would work with finger input on the screen.

Did you Know?

The Windows Phone hardware specification calls for *at least* four simultaneous touchscreen inputs!

FIGURE 4.1
The text message moves based on touch input.

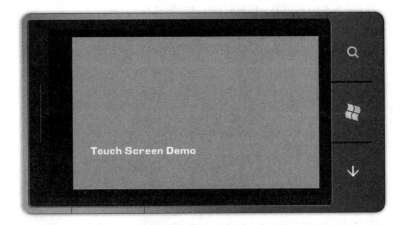

How to Simulate More Inputs

What if you really do have a great design for a multitouch game but have no way to test it (that is, you do not have a WP7 device or a touchscreen for your Windows

PC)? One alternative is to develop and test your game with *simulated inputs* for each finger, and then test each input separately in the emulator. This actually works quite well! Suppose your game requires one input to move a ship left or right on the screen, and another input to fire a weapon. The easy approach is to just leave the ship's movement alone (presumably at the center of the screen without movement) to test the firing input. When that is working satisfactorily, then you might test left-to-right movement input with random or regular shooting intervals. This is how most developers will approach the problem.

Using Gestures on the Touchscreen

A related capability of the TouchPanel class is a *gesture* interface. This is potentially a really *great* feature for WP7 games, so don't pass it up! A gesture is essentially nonverbal communication with your hands. A gesture on a touchscreen might be to flick an object across the screen rather than dragging to the exact location where you want it to go. Instead of manually moving something one direction or another, one might just *flick it* in the general direction. So, it's up to the game to interpret the gestures based on the game's user interface design.

Since gesture input can be used in place of touch input, you might want to just use gesture input instead. If all you need for your game is single-touch input, a tap gesture would work in place of the mouselike touch code seen previously. The main difference between the two methods is that gesture input does *not* support multitouch.

XNA supports gestures with the same TouchPanel class used for touch input. Here are the contents of the GestureType enumeration:

- ▶ None
- ▶ Tap
- ▶ DoubleTap
- ▶ Hold
- ▶ HorizontalDrag
- ▶ VerticalDrag
- ▶ FreeDrag
- ▶ Pinch
- ▶ Flick
- ▶ DragComplete
- ▶ PinchComplete

Gesture-based input does *not* support multitouch. Only a single gesture (with one finger) can be used at a time.

By the Way

To use gesture input, we have to enable it, because gesture input is not automatic. There are obvious problems with input if all gestures are enabled by default, because the game will behave erratically with flick gestures in a game using a lot of "drag"-style input to move and interact with the game. Even the simplest of arcade-style or puzzle games will involve some dragging of the finger across the screen for input, and this could be misinterpreted as a flick if the intended movement is too fast. To enable both tap and flick gestures, add this line to the constructor, Game1(), or LoadContent():

```
TouchPanel.EnabledGestures = GestureType.Tap | GestureType.Flick;
```

A simple example can be added to the Update() method of the Touch Demo to see how it works. Note that the first if condition is *required*. Trying to read a gesture when none is available will cause an exception!

```
if (TouchPanel.IsGestureAvailable)
{
    GestureSample gesture = TouchPanel.ReadGesture();
    if (gesture.GestureType == GestureType.Tap)
    {
        position = new Vector2(gesture.Position.X - size.X / 2,
            gesture.Position.Y - size.Y / 2);
    }
}
```

Running this code, you might be surprised to find that the tap gesture is more like a mouse click-and-release event. Click-dragging does not produce the gesture! You can see for yourself by commenting out the touch input code in the Touch Demo program, and running just the gesture code instead. If you're really interested in gesture input, a real WP7 device is a must-have! The emulator just doesn't satisfy. If you are doing WP7 development for profit, a dev device or an actual Windows Phone device (with carrier subscription) is a good investment.

Summary

Touch input can be quite satisfying to a game designer after working with the traditional keyboard and mouse, because it offers the potential for very creative forms of input in a game. Although regular multitouch input will be the norm for most Windows Phone games, the ability to use gestures also might prove to be fun.

Q&A

Q. *What options are there for developing a multitouch game for Windows Phone?*

A. A hardware touchscreen is required, on either a Windows development PC (via the emulator and a touch-sensitive screen) or an actual Windows Phone device. Multitouch cannot be tested on a nontouchscreen with the emulator.

Q. *What is perhaps the biggest issue that a developer should consider when planning to port a game from Windows or Xbox 360 to the small Windows Phone platform?*

A. Aside from the most obvious issue of down-scaling the graphics and the smaller screen size, the most challenging issue is converting keyboard and mouse, or controller, input to touchscreen input.

Workshop

Quiz

1. What is the name of the XNA class that provides multitouch input?
2. What is the name of the collection that stores the position of each touch location?
3. Which gesture is equivalent to a mouse click or touch position?

Answers

1. `TouchPanel`
2. `TouchLocation`
3. `GestureType.Tap`

Exercises

The sample program in this hour caused a text message to follow the touch input on the screen. Modify the example so that the text message appears to be "selected" instead when the user touches it. The selection might be to draw the text with a larger scale or to change the font color, or both.

HOUR 5

Drawing Bitmaps

What You'll Learn in This Hour:

- ▶ **Adding a bitmap file to the project**
- ▶ **Loading a bitmap**
- ▶ **Drawing a bitmap**
- ▶ **Transparency**

This hour will dig into one of the most vital subjects of game programming: bitmaps. A bitmap is a 2D image, also known as a texture in the realm of 3D programming. Bitmap images can be created in memory, but they are more often loaded from an existing bitmap *file*. The most common file types are BMP, PNG, and JPG. For games, we want high-quality bitmaps without lossy compression (in which pixels are changed to shrink the file size). The BMP format does work well but it has fallen out of favor in recent years due to format incompatibilities (such as some BMP files supporting an alpha channel, and some not). A good compromise is the PNG format, which offers decent file size and 32-bit ARGB color. For the sake of discussion, images will just be referred to as "bitmaps" regardless of the file format. In this hour, we'll learn to add bitmap files to the Content project, and then load and draw them. This is the basis for most games!

Adding a Bitmap File to an XNA Project

Bitmap programming is the precursor to sprite programming, which is where we really want to go in order to draw game characters, ships, or whatever the game calls for. We can't draw a 3D shape with just a bitmap, although bitmaps are used as *textures* when rendering in 3D. A texture is an image wrapped around the 3D shape, such as a tree, a car, or a human figure. Texturing can get pretty complex! Fortunately, we'll start with the basics of 3D in a later hour and learn how to draw with lights and special effects. But first we need to learn 2D or *bitmap* programming.

There's so much we can do with bitmaps in XNA! I'm eager to jump right into the advanced rendering stuff, but we'll start off at a steady pace and first learn the basics. In the *next hour*, we'll do some really fascinating things with bitmaps, like scaling and rotation.

We need to create a new project for our explorations of bitmap programming. Let's begin with a new project.

Try It Yourself

Adding a Bitmap Asset to an XNA Project

Follow these steps to create the Bitmap Demo project that we will use as an example while learning how to load and draw bitmaps in this hour:

1. Create a new Windows Phone (4.0) project called Bitmap Demo.

2. Create or find a bitmap file containing an image you want to draw. The example uses an image of a spaceship that you can borrow. The bitmap file is a 32-bit PNG with a transparent region (via alpha channel). We will go over transparency in more detail in upcoming chapters.

> The spaceship bitmap was created by Ron Conley for a free game called *Starflight— The Lost Colony*, which can be downloaded from www.starflightgame.com.

3. Right-click the Content project in Solution Explorer (it is called Bitmap Demo-Content (Content)), as shown in Figure 5.1. From the context menu that comes up, choose Add, Existing Item.

FIGURE 5.1
Adding an existing bitmap file to the project.

An optional (and easier) way to add a file to the Content project is by just dragging it from Windows Explorer onto the Content project in Solution Explorer.

Did you Know?

4. The Add Existing Item dialog should come up. Select the bitmap file you want to add to the project. The file is added to the project as shown in Figure 5.2.

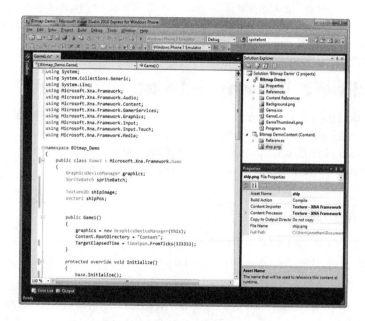

FIGURE 5.2
The ship.png file has been added.

5. If the Properties window is not visible, open it with View, Properties Window. When you select an asset file in the Content project, the file's properties will be shown. Note the properties in the case of ship.png. Both the Content Importer and the Content Processor properties are automatically set to Texture - XNA Framework. This means that XNA recognized the file type and will process it as a texture. If you look at the other items in the drop-down list, you should find the following:

- ▶ Effect - XNA Framework

- ▶ Autodesk FBX - XNA Framework

- ▶ Sprite Font Description - XNA Framework

- ▶ WAV Audio File - XNA Framework

- ▶ WMA Audio File - XNA Framework

- ▶ WMV Video File - XNA Framework

- ▶ XACT Project - XNA Framework
- ▶ X File - XNA Framework
- ▶ XML Content - XNA Framework

These are the types of asset files XNA recognizes automatically. You can also create your own custom content importer to convert data files of any type to work with XNA—although you still have to write the code to read the file. We will be using asset files from most of the items on this list in upcoming chapters.

Loading a Bitmap File as an Asset

The name of the bitmap file added to the project is important, but the extension is not. The ship.png file added in the preceding Try It Yourself tutorial will be converted into a file called ship.xnb when compiled, and will be recognized by the name "ship" in the content manager. Let's see how to load the bitmap.

Try It Yourself

Writing Code to Load a Bitmap File

Follow these steps to write the code to load a bitmap file:

1. Add two new variables near the top of the Game1 class definition (where other global variables are found) as shown. The first variable is of type Texture2D, which is a class for bitmaps. The second is a Vector2 to keep track of the position of the bitmap on the screen.

```
public class Game1 : Microsoft.Xna.Framework.Game
{
    GraphicsDeviceManager graphics;
    SpriteBatch spriteBatch;

    //texture variable
    Texture2D shipImage;

    //position variable
    Vector2 shipPos;
```

2. Load the "ship" bitmap in the LoadContent() method and set the position to (0,0).

```
protected override void LoadContent()
{
    spriteBatch = new SpriteBatch(GraphicsDevice);
```

```
    //load the ship bitmap
    shipImage = Content.Load<Texture2D>("ship");
    shipPos = Vector2.Zero;
}
```

If XNA cannot find an asset file that your code tries to load with `Content.Load()` in the program's main `LoadContent()` method, an exception error will be generated!

Drawing a Bitmap with SpriteBatch

After adding the bitmap file as an asset item to the Content project, adding the variables, and loading the bitmap as a Texture2D, we can now draw the bitmap onto the screen. For that, we need to jump down to the Draw() method. Here is the easiest way to draw a bitmap:

```
protected override void Draw(GameTime gameTime)
{
    GraphicsDevice.Clear(Color.CornflowerBlue);

    //begin drawing
    spriteBatch.Begin();

    //draw the bitmap
    spriteBatch.Draw(shipImage, shipPos, Color.White);

    //finish drawing
    spriteBatch.End();

    base.Draw(gameTime);
}
```

The output from this program is shown in Figure 5.3.

SpriteBatch is an XNA core class that can draw both bitmaps and text, with many variations of the Draw() and DrawString() methods. In the next hour, we will work with SpriteBatch.Draw() extensively, exploring all of its capabilities. Let's look at all the overloaded variations of Draw() here to get a feel for these capabilities. We will study these in more detail in the next hour.

The *first* parameter is always a Texture2D. The *second* parameter is always the destination—either a Rectangle or a Vector2. Beyond those two are a variety of parameters that make it possible to perform the following actions:

▶ Rotate

▶ Scale

▶ Animate

▶ Flip horizontally

▶ Flip vertically

FIGURE 5.3
The Bitmap
Demo program.

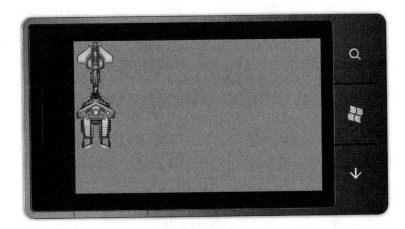

We will learn to use these special effects in upcoming chapters, as well as take a peek under the hood of the `SpriteBatch.Begin()` and `SpriteBatch.End()` methods that have been so mysterious up to this point. We have used only the second version, although the first one is easy enough to follow as well. Overloads 3 to 7 will be examined in the next hour and others following *in depth*, so think of this as just a sneak peek! Some of this code might be hard to read, because these are the definitions of the methods. I'm only going into this much detail now for `Draw()` because we will use it a *lot*!

```
public void Draw(Texture2D texture, Rectangle destinationRectangle,
    Color color);

public void Draw(Texture2D texture, Vector2 position, Color color);

public void Draw(Texture2D texture, Rectangle destinationRectangle,
    Rectangle? sourceRectangle, Color color);

public void Draw(Texture2D texture, Vector2 position,
    Rectangle? sourceRectangle, Color color);

public void Draw(Texture2D texture, Rectangle destinationRectangle,
    Rectangle? sourceRectangle, Color color, float rotation,
    Vector2 origin, SpriteEffects effects, float layerDepth);

public void Draw(Texture2D texture, Vector2 position,
    Rectangle? sourceRectangle, Color color, float rotation,
    Vector2 origin, float scale, SpriteEffects effects, float layerDepth);
```

```
public void Draw(Texture2D texture, Vector2 position,
    Rectangle? sourceRectangle, Color color, float rotation,
    Vector2 origin, Vector2 scale, SpriteEffects effects,
    float layerDepth);
```

Drawing Bitmaps with Transparency

The ship.png file used in the example in this hour has an alpha channel and draws without showing the background pixels around the shape of the actual ship inside the bitmap. Let's learn how to create an alpha channel. I'll use Gimp because it's a free graphics editor and it has many features similar to the uber-powerful Adobe Photoshop (download Gimp from www.gimp.org).

XNA will draw an image transparently if it has an alpha channel, and we don't need to do anything extra for this to happen. This really makes life easier for an XNA game programmer. If you supply XNA with a bitmap file containing transparent pixels, it will draw that image with transparency.

I have used many graphics editors, including Photoshop, PaintShop Pro, Corel-DRAW, and Gimp. Although each behaves somewhat differently, they all share a similar toolset, including the ability to work with alpha channels. The instructions here for Gimp will be basically similar for other graphics editors.

Did you Know?

Try it Yourself ▼

Creating an Alpha Channel

Let's take a look at how to create an alpha channel. To add a transparency layer to an image, you need to locate the Magic Wand tool available in most graphics editors.

1. After selecting the Magic Wand tool, click somewhere in the background (which should be a solid color). The Magic Wand locates the edges of the game object and highlights everything around it, as shown in Figure 5.4. Another, more precise way to select a background is with the Color Picker or the Select by Color tool.

2. Now that you have a selection available, you can create a layer mask. In Gimp, open the Layer menu and choose Mask, Add Layer Mask, as shown in Figure 5.5.

3. The Add Layer Mask dialog shown in Figure 5.6 comes up. Choose the Selection option and check the Invert Mask option; then click the Add button.

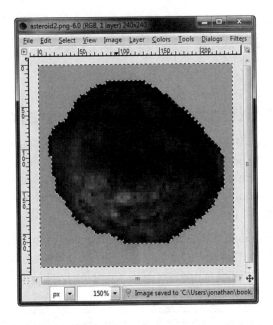

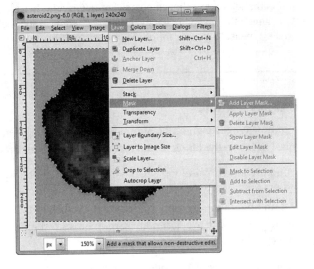

If you have a complex image and would like to exclude many portions of it in order to select the boundary of the real image, you can hold down the Shift key while clicking with the Fuzzy Select (or Magic Wand) tool inside portions of the image to add new selections.

FIGURE 5.6
The Add Layer
Mask dialog is
used to choose
options for a
layer mask.

4. The next step is to apply the layer mask. You can tell Gimp to apply the
mask using the Layer menu, then Mask, Apply Layer Mask, as shown in
Figure 5.7.

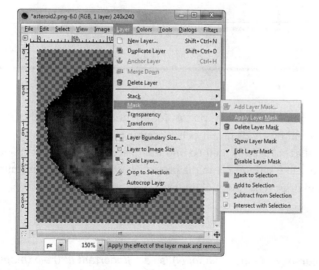

FIGURE 5.7
Applying the
new layer mask
makes it per-
manent.

5. In the final figure, shown in Figure 5.8, the alpha channel has been created based on the masked selection. The checkerboard background behind
the asteroid image shows the transparent region. The result looks very nice!
You can load this image into your XNA project, and it will draw with transparency so that the outer edges of the image (where the solid background is

located) will not overwrite the background of the screen. Just be sure to save the file using a bitmap file format that supports transparency *and* works with XNA. The most common formats are PNG and TGA.

FIGURE 5.8
The asteroid image now has a masked transparency layer.

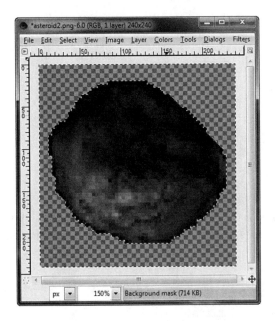

Summary

This hour began a journey that will last for essentially the rest of the book. Most of our attention will be on 2D graphics in upcoming chapters, with all the variations of the SpriteBatch.Draw() method and the special effects that are possible with it. Being able to add a bitmap file to the project (with transparency information), and then load and draw it, is essential for every XNA programmer.

Q&A

Q. *Transparency (via alpha channel) is very important in the bitmaps used in a game. What happens if a game character is not saved with transparency in the bitmap file?*

A. The background pixels around the character will draw, erasing the background, and the bitmap will look like a square image on the screen.

Q. *What service does the* `SpriteBatch` *class provide to an XNA game?*

A. The ability to draw bitmaps and text.

Workshop

Quiz

1. What are the three *significant* bitmap file formats supported by XNA?

2. What is the name of the XNA class used to load a bitmap file?

3. What is the name of the XNA class that contains the bitmap data in memory?

Answers

1. BMP, PNG, and JPG

2. `ContentManager`

3. `Texture2D`

Exercises

The Bitmap Demo project simply demonstrates how to load and draw a bitmap, and because of the need for simplicity, it doesn't do much! What if we were to adjust the `shipPos` variable (a `Vector2`, as you'll recall) so that it moves with touch input? We studied touch input in the preceding hour, so it should be fairly easy to adapt this program by adding the touch input code to it. Cause the ship bitmap to follow the user's touch inputs on the screen.

PART II

Sprite Programming

HOUR 6

Treating Bitmaps as Sprites

What You'll Learn in This Hour:

- ▶ Bringing bitmaps to life
- ▶ Drawing lots of bitmaps
- ▶ Limitations of global variables
- ▶ A simple `Sprite` class
- ▶ Drawing a lot of sprites

This hour continues to explore the capabilities of XNA's bitmap drawing features via the SpriteBatch class. As we learned in the preceding hour, bitmaps are the building blocks of most 2D and 3D games. Although a game could be designed using just 2D vectors or 3D wireframes—perhaps in a retro style as a homage to such games of the 1970s when graphics hardware was not yet able to rasterize bitmaps—there is little reason to use lines today in a properly designed game. Bitmaps are the name of the game today, for both 2D and 3D games. A bitmap-based 2D game will have small "flat" game characters, vehicles, or avatars to represent the gameplay, whereas a mesh- and matrix-based 3D game will have rendered objects in the game with such effects as real-time lighting and realistic surfaces with reflection and textured bumpiness.

Bringing Bitmaps to Life

A sprite is a bitmap with benefits. XNA provides the SpriteBatch class to draw bitmaps with the SpriteBatch.Draw() method, of which there are several overloaded variants. But despite the name, SpriteBatch does not give us "sprite" capabilities from the gameplay perspective. SpriteBatch is a rendering class, used solely for drawing, not "managing" game entities traditionally known as "sprites." The difference might seem a subtle one, but it's actually quite a distinction. SpriteBatch might have been a somewhat incorrect name for the class. The "Batch" part of the name refers to the way in which "bitmaps" (not sprites) are drawn—in a *batch*. That is, all *bitmap drawing* via SpriteBatch.Draw() is put into a queue and then *all* the drawing is done quickly when SpriteBatch.End() is called. It's faster to perform many draw calls at once in this manner, since the video card is going to be switching state only once. Every time SpriteBatch.Begin() and SpriteBatch.End() are called, that involves a state change (which is very slow in terms of rendering). The fewer state changes that happen, the better!

SpriteBatch.Draw() can handle animation, rotation, scaling, and translation (movement). But, without *properties*, we have to write custom code to do all of these things with just global variables. It can get tedious! We will see how tedious by writing an example using all global variables. Then, for comparison, we'll write a simple Sprite class and convert the program. This is not just an illustration of how useful object-oriented programming can be (which is true) but to show *why* we need a Sprite class for gameplay.

SpriteBatch.Draw() works fine. We don't need an alternative replacement because it can do anything we need. But the code to draw sprites is very specific. If we don't want to manually draw every character, or vehicle, or avatar in the game, we have to automate the process in some manner. The key to making this work is via *properties*. A property is a trait or an attribute that partially describes something. In the case of a person, one property would be gender (male or female); other properties include race, height, weight, and age. No single property fully describes a person, but when all (or most) of the properties are considered, it gives you a pretty good idea of what that person looks like.

The simplest and most common property for a sprite is its position on the screen. In the previous hour, we used a variable called Vector2 shipPos to represent the position of the bitmap, and a variable called Texture2D shipImage to represent the image. These two variables were properties for a game object—a spaceship to be used in a sci-fi game. Wouldn't it be easier to manage both of these properties inside a Sprite class? Before we do that, let's see whether it's really that big of a deal to keep track of properties with global variables.

Drawing Lots of Bitmaps

Let's create a short example. Now, working with just one bitmap is a piece of cake, because there's only one call to SpriteBatch.Draw(), only one position variable, and only one image variable. When things get messy is when about five or more bitmaps need to be manipulated and drawn. Up to that point, managing variables for four or so images isn't so bad, but as the number climbs, the amount of manual code grows and becomes unwieldy (like a giant two-handed sword).

```
Vector2 position1, position2, position3, position4, position5;
Texture2D image1, image2, image3, image4, image5;
```

It's not just declaring and using the variables that can be a problem. It's the ability to *use* any more than this practically in a game's sources. But let's give it a try anyway for the sake of the argument. Figure 6.1 shows the output for this short program, which is a prototype for a solar system simulation we'll be creating in this hour. The source code is found in Listing 6.1.

LISTING 6.1 Source code for the Many Bitmaps Demo program, a precursor to a larger project.

```
public class Game1 : Microsoft.Xna.Framework.Game
{
    GraphicsDeviceManager graphics;
    SpriteBatch spriteBatch;

    Vector2 position1, position2, position3, position4, position5;
    Texture2D image1, image2, image3, image4, image5;

    public Game1()
    {
        graphics = new GraphicsDeviceManager(this);
        Content.RootDirectory = "Content";
        TargetElapsedTime = TimeSpan.FromTicks(333333);
    }

    protected override void Initialize()
    {
        base.Initialize();
    }

    protected override void LoadContent()
    {
        spriteBatch = new SpriteBatch(GraphicsDevice);
```

```
        image1 = Content.Load<Texture2D>("sun");
        image2 = Content.Load<Texture2D>("planet1");
        image3 = Content.Load<Texture2D>("planet3");
        image4 = Content.Load<Texture2D>("planet2");
        image5 = Content.Load<Texture2D>("planet4");

        position1 = new Vector2(100, 240-64);
        position2 = new Vector2(300, 240-32);
        position3 = new Vector2(400, 240-32);
        position4 = new Vector2(500, 240-16);
        position5 = new Vector2(600, 240-16);
    }

    protected override void Update(GameTime gameTime)
    {
        if (GamePad.GetState(PlayerIndex.One).Buttons.Back ==
            ButtonState.Pressed)
            this.Exit();

        base.Update(gameTime);
    }

    protected override void Draw(GameTime gameTime)
    {
        GraphicsDevice.Clear(Color.Black);

        spriteBatch.Begin();
        spriteBatch.Draw(image1, position1, Color.White);
        spriteBatch.Draw(image2, position2, Color.White);
        spriteBatch.Draw(image3, position3, Color.White);
        spriteBatch.Draw(image4, position4, Color.White);
        spriteBatch.Draw(image5, position5, Color.White);
        spriteBatch.End();

        base.Draw(gameTime);
    }
}
```

Running into Limits with Global Variables

The Many Bitmaps Demo program wasn't too difficult to deal with, was it? I mean, there were only five bitmaps to draw, so we needed five position variables. But what if there were 20, or 50, or 100? With so many game objects, it would be impossible to manage them all with global variables. Furthermore, that's bad programming style when there are better ways to do it. Obviously, I'm talking about arrays and collections. But not only is it a quantity issue with regard to the global variables, but if we want to add another property to each object, we're talking about adding another 20, 50, or 100 variables for that new property!

Let's rewrite the program using an array. Later in the hour, we'll work with a list, which is a container class, but for this next step, an array is a little easier to follow. Here is a new version using arrays. The new source code is found in Listing 6.2.

LISTING 6.2   New source code for the program rewritten to more efficiently store the planet bitmaps and vectors in arrays.

```
public class Game1 : Microsoft.Xna.Framework.Game
{
    GraphicsDeviceManager graphics;
    SpriteBatch spriteBatch;

    Texture2D[] images;
    Vector2[] positions;

    public Game1()
    {
        graphics = new GraphicsDeviceManager(this);
        Content.RootDirectory = "Content";
        TargetElapsedTime = TimeSpan.FromTicks(333333);
    }

    protected override void Initialize()
    {
        base.Initialize();
    }

    protected override void LoadContent()
    {
        spriteBatch = new SpriteBatch(GraphicsDevice);

        images = new Texture2D[5];
        images[0] = Content.Load<Texture2D>("sun");
        images[1] = Content.Load<Texture2D>("planet1");
        images[2] = Content.Load<Texture2D>("planet3");
        images[3] = Content.Load<Texture2D>("planet2");
        images[4] = Content.Load<Texture2D>("planet4");

        positions = new Vector2[5];
        positions[0] = new Vector2(100, 240-64);
        positions[1] = new Vector2(300, 240-32);
        positions[2] = new Vector2(400, 240-32);
        positions[3] = new Vector2(500, 240-16);
        positions[4] = new Vector2(600, 240-16);
    }

    protected override void Update(GameTime gameTime)
    {
        if (GamePad.GetState(PlayerIndex.One).Buttons.Back ==
            ButtonState.Pressed)
            this.Exit();

        base.Update(gameTime);
    }

    protected override void Draw(GameTime gameTime)
    {
        GraphicsDevice.Clear(Color.Black);

        spriteBatch.Begin();
        for (int n = 0; n < 5; n++)
        {
            spriteBatch.Draw(images[n], positions[n], Color.White);
```

```
        }
        spriteBatch.End();

        base.Draw(gameTime);
    }
}
```

As you examine the code in this version of the program, what stands out? I notice that in ContentLoad(), the initialization code is actually a bit more complicated than it was previously, but the code in Draw() is shorter. We're not counting lines of code, but in Draw(), the for loop could accommodate 100 or 1,000 objects with the same amount of code. This is the most significant difference between this and the previous program—we now can handle any arbitrary number of objects.

We could shorten the code in LoadContent() even further by building the filename for each planet. The key is to make the asset names consistent. So, if we rename "sun" to "planet0", then loading the assets becomes a simple for loop. Here is an improvement:

```
protected override void LoadContent()
{
    spriteBatch = new SpriteBatch(GraphicsDevice);

    images = new Texture2D[5];
    positions = new Vector2[5];
    for (int n = 0; n < 5; n++)
    {
        string filename = "planet" + n.ToString();
        images[n] = Content.Load<Texture2D>(filename);
    }

    positions[0] = new Vector2(100, 240 - 64);
    positions[1] = new Vector2(300, 240 - 32);
    positions[2] = new Vector2(400, 240 - 32);
    positions[3] = new Vector2(500, 240 - 16);
    positions[4] = new Vector2(600, 240 - 16);
}
```

The positions array must still be set manually due to the differences in the sizes of the planet images. But I think we could automate that as well by looking at the width and height of each image. The point is not just to make the code shorter, but to find ways to improve the code, make it more versatile, more reusable, and easier to modify. Using a consistent naming convention for asset files will go a long way toward that end.

Creating a Simple `Sprite` Class

Now let's experiment with some code that actually does something interesting besides drawing fixed images. We'll start by creating a simple class to encapsulate a sprite, and then add some features to make the `Sprite` class useful. This will be a hands-on section where we build the `Sprite` class in stages. If you are an experienced programmer, you may skip this section.

Creating the `Sprite` Class

Let's begin with a new project. The project type will be, as usual, Windows Phone (4.0), and the name is Sprite Demo. In the `Game1.cs` file, which is the main source code file for the game, we're going to add the new `Sprite` class to the top of the file, above the `Game1` class. After a while, the `Sprite` class can be moved into its own file called `Sprite.cs`. I find this more convenient while working on a new class. See Listing 6.3 for the complete source code.

> Classes do not *need* to be stored in unique source code files; that's a practice to keep a large project tidy and easier to maintain. But it is acceptable (and often practical) to define a new class inside an existing file. This is especially true when several classes are closely related and you want to better organize the project. The best practice, though, for large classes, is to define each class in its own file.

Watch
Out!

LISTING 6.3   Source code for the new project with included `Sprite` class.

```
public class Sprite
{
    public Texture2D image;
    public Vector2 position;
    public Color color;
}
public class Game1 : Microsoft.Xna.Framework.Game
{
    GraphicsDeviceManager graphics;
    SpriteBatch spriteBatch;
    Viewport viewport;
    Sprite sun;

    public Game1()
    {
        graphics = new GraphicsDeviceManager(this);
        Content.RootDirectory = "Content";
        TargetElapsedTime = TimeSpan.FromTicks(333333);
    }
```

```
protected override void Initialize()
{
    base.Initialize();
}

protected override void LoadContent()
{
    spriteBatch = new SpriteBatch(GraphicsDevice);

    //get screen dimensions
    viewport = GraphicsDevice.Viewport;

    //create sun sprite
    sun = new Sprite();
    sun.image = Content.Load<Texture2D>("sun");
    //center sun sprite on screen
    float x = (viewport.Width - sun.image.Width) / 2;
    float y = (viewport.Height - sun.image.Height) / 2;
    sun.position = new Vector2(x,y);
    //set color
    sun.color = Color.White;
}

protected override void Update(GameTime gameTime)
{
    if (GamePad.GetState(PlayerIndex.One).Buttons.Back ==
        ButtonState.Pressed)
        this.Exit();

    base.Update(gameTime);
}

protected override void Draw(GameTime gameTime)
{
    GraphicsDevice.Clear(Color.Black);

    spriteBatch.Begin();
    //draw the sun
    spriteBatch.Draw(sun.image, sun.position, sun.color);
    spriteBatch.End();

    base.Draw(gameTime);
}
}
```

By the Way

The code listings in this book omit the using statements at the beginning of every XNA project, as well as the namespace line and surrounding brackets, to focus on just the functional part of a program, only when that code is generated by Visual Studio. You should assume that those lines *are required* to compile every example listed herein.

Scope and Clarity

This is how most classes begin life, with just some public properties that could have been equally well defined in a `struct`. In fact, if you just want to create a quick container for a few variables and don't want to deal with a class, go ahead and do it. Structures (defined as `struct`) can even have constructor methods to initialize their properties, as well as normal methods. But in a `struct`, there is no scope; everything is public. In contrast, everything in a class is private by default. This would work, for example:

```
struct Sprite
{
    Texture2D image;
    Vector2 position;
    Color color;
}
```

But one limitation with a `struct` is room for growth; with a class, we can make changes to scope (which means changing whether individual properties and methods are visible outside of the class). At this simplistic level, there's very little difference between a `class` and a `struct`. Some programmers differentiate between them by using `struct`s *only* as property containers, with no methods, reserving methods only for defined classes. It's ultimately up to you!

An OOP (object-oriented programming) "purist" would demand that our image, position, and color properties be defined with *private* scope, and accessed via property methods. The difference between property *variables* and property *methods* is fuzzy in C#, whereas they are very clear-cut in a more highly precise language such as C++. Let's see what the class will look like when the three variables (image, position, and color) are converted into private properties with public accessor methods.

```
public class Sprite2 //"good" OOP version
{
    Texture2D p_image;
    Vector2 p_position;
    Color p_color;

    public Texture2D image
    {
        get { return p_image; }
        set { p_image = value; }
    }
    public Vector2 position
    {
        get { return p_position; }
        set { p_position = value; }
    }
    public Color color
    {
```

```
        get { return p_color; }
        set { p_color = value; }
    }
}
```

> In general, I prefer to not hide property variables (such as `public Texture2D image` in the `Sprite` class), because it just requires extra code to access the property later. This is, again, a matter of preference, and might be dependent on the coding standards of your team or employer. If it's up to you, just focus on writing clean, tight code, and don't worry about making your code "OOP safe" for others.

Initializing the `Sprite` Class with a Constructor

Compared to the original `Sprite` class defined in `Game1.cs`, what do you think of the "safe" version (renamed to `Sprite2` to avoid confusion)? The three variable names have had "p_" added (to reflect that they are now *private* in scope), and now in their place are three "properly defined" properties. Each property now has an accessor method (`get`) and a mutator method (`set`). If you prefer this more highly structured form of object-oriented C#, I encourage you to continue doing what works best for you. But for the sake of clarity, I will use the original version of `Sprite` with the simpler *public* access property variables.

Let's give the `Sprite` class more capabilities. Currently, it's just a container for three variables. A constructor is a method that runs automatically when an object is created at runtime with the new operator, for example:

```
Sprite sun = new Sprite();
```

The term `Sprite()`, with the parentheses, denotes a method—the *default* method since it requires no parameters. Here is ours:

```
public class Sprite
{
    public Texture2D image;
    public Vector2 position;
    public Color color;

    public Sprite()
    {
        image = null;
        position = Vector2.Zero;
        color = Color.White;
    }
}
```

Here, we have a new constructor that initializes the class's properties to some initial values. This is meant to avoid problems later if one forgets to initialize them manually. In our program now, since color is automatically set to Color.White, we no longer need to manually set it, which cleans up the code in LoadContent() a bit.

```
protected override void LoadContent()
{
    spriteBatch = new SpriteBatch(GraphicsDevice);

    //get screen dimensions
    viewport = GraphicsDevice.Viewport;

    //create sun sprite
    sun = new Sprite();
    sun.image = Content.Load<Texture2D>("sun");

    //center sun sprite on screen
    float x = (viewport.Width - sun.image.Width) / 2;
    float y = (viewport.Height - sun.image.Height) / 2;
    sun.position = new Vector2(x,y);
}
```

Writing Reusable Code with Abstraction

A usual goal for an important base game class like Sprite is to abstract the XNA code, at least somewhat, to make the class stand on its own as much as possible. This becomes a priority when you find yourself writing games on several platforms. Within the XNA family, we have Windows, Xbox 360, and Windows Phone. But on a larger scale, it's fairly common to port games to other systems. After you have rewritten your Sprite class a few times for different platforms (and even *languages*, believe it or not!), you begin to see similarities among the different systems, and begin to take those similarities into account when writing game classes.

There are two aspects that I want to abstract in the Sprite class. First, there's loading the image. This occurs in LoadContent() when we simply expose the image property to Content.Load(). Second, there's drawing the sprite. This occurs in Draw(), also when we expose the image property. To properly abstract the class away from XNA, we need our own Load() and Draw() methods within Sprite itself. To do this, the Sprite class must have access to both ContentManager and SpriteBatch. We can do this by passing those necessary runtime objects to the Sprite class constructor. Listing 6.4 contains the new source code for the Sprite class.

LISTING 6.4   Source code for the expanded Sprite class.

```
public class Sprite
{
    private ContentManager p_content;
    private SpriteBatch p_spriteBatch;
    public Texture2D image;
    public Vector2 position;
    public Color color;

    public Sprite(ContentManager content, SpriteBatch spriteBatch)
    {
        p_content = content;
        p_spriteBatch = spriteBatch;
        image = null;
        position = Vector2.Zero;
        color = Color.White;
    }

    public bool Load(string assetName)
    {
        try
        {
            image = p_content.Load<Texture2D>(assetName);
        }
        catch (Exception) { return false; }
        return true;
    }

    public void Draw()
    {
        p_spriteBatch.Draw(image, position, color);
    }
}
```

Putting our new changes into action (in Listing 6.5) reveals some very clean-looking code in LoadContent() and Draw(), with the output shown in Figure 6.2.

LISTING 6.5   Modifications to the project to support the new Sprite features.

```
protected override void LoadContent()
{
    spriteBatch = new SpriteBatch(GraphicsDevice);
    viewport = GraphicsDevice.Viewport;

    //create sun sprite
    sun = new Sprite(Content, spriteBatch);
    sun.Load("sun");

    //center sun sprite on screen
    float x = (viewport.Width - sun.image.Width) / 2;
    float y = (viewport.Height - sun.image.Height) / 2;
    sun.position = new Vector2(x, y);
}

protected override void Draw(GameTime gameTime)
{
```

```
GraphicsDevice.Clear(Color.Black);
spriteBatch.Begin();
sun.Draw();
spriteBatch.End();
base.Draw(gameTime);
}
```

FIGURE 6.2
Demonstrating the Sprite class.

Error Handling

The Sprite.Load() method has error handling built in via a try...catch block. Inside the try block is a call to Content.Load(). If the passed asset name is not found, XNA generates an exception error, as shown in Figure 6.3. We don't want the end user to ever see an exception error, and in a very large game project, it is fairly common for asset files to be renamed and generate errors like this—it's all part of the development process to track down and fix such common bugs.

To assist, the code in Sprite.Load() returns false if an asset is not found—rather than *crashing* with an exception error. The problem is, we can't exit on an error condition from within LoadContent(); XNA is just not in a state that will allow the program to terminate at that point. What we need to do is set a flag and look for it after LoadContent() is finished running.

I have an idea. What if we add a feature to display an optional error message in a pre-shutdown process in the game loop? All it needs to do is check for this error state and then print whatever is in the global errorMessage variable. The user would then read the message and manually shut down the program by closing the window. Let's just try it out; this won't be a permanent fixture in future chapters, but you may continue to use it if you want to. First, we need some new variables.

FIGURE 6.3
An exception
error occurs
when an asset
cannot be
found.

```
//experimental error handling variables
bool errorState;
string errorMessage;
SpriteFont ErrorFont;
```

Next, we initialize them.

```
public Game1()
{
    graphics = new GraphicsDeviceManager(this);
    Content.RootDirectory = "Content";
    TargetElapsedTime = TimeSpan.FromTicks(333333);
    errorMessage = "";
    errorState = false;
}
```

And in LoadContent(), we need to trap the exception error (note that "sun" was
temporarily renamed to "sun1" to demonstrate the exception error).

```
//create sun sprite
sun = new Sprite(Content, spriteBatch);
if (!sun.Load("sun1"))
{
    errorState = true;
    errorMessage = "Asset file 'sun' not found.";
    return;
}
```

Draw() is where the error handling process comes into play.

```
protected override void Draw(GameTime gameTime)
{
    GraphicsDevice.Clear(Color.Black);
    spriteBatch.Begin();

    //experimental error handler
    if (errorState)
    {
        spriteBatch.DrawString(ErrorFont, "CRITICAL ERROR",
            Vector2.Zero, Color.Red);
        spriteBatch.DrawString(ErrorFont, errorMessage,
            new Vector2(0,100), Color.Red);
    }
    else
    {
        sun.Draw();
    }

    spriteBatch.End();
    base.Draw(gameTime);
}
```

When run again with the new error handling code in place, the previous exception error now becomes a nice in-game notification, as shown in Figure 6.4.

FIGURE 6.4
The exception error has been handled nicely.

Summary

We've just scratched the surface of what will be possible with the new Sprite class in this hour. Over the next several chapters, the class will be enhanced significantly, making it possible—with properties and methods—to perform transformations (translation, rotation, scaling) on a sprite, as well as animation. This hour got the subject off to a great start already!

Q&A

Q. *Are there any other aspects of XNA's core game features that you might abstract into the* Sprite *class, or some other class for that matter?*

A. Answers will vary; user input is a good answer.

Q. *What would be the benefit of a custom class to "contain" a number of sprites at an even higher level?*

A. One benefit might be a sprite *manager* class.

Workshop

Quiz

1. What two XNA core classes do we pass to the Sprite constructor to make it more independent and self-contained?

2. What XNA class is used for the image property of our Sprite class?

3. How are errors trapped in C#?

Answers

1. ContentManager and SpriteBatch

2. Texture2D

3. With a try...catch block

Exercises

Our new Sprite class is already quite functional and could be used to make a small game already with artwork of a fixed nature (that is, no animation or transforms other than movement). Using the Sprite class, write a small demo that causes a ball to "bounce" inside the screen boundary of the Windows Phone display.

HOUR 7

Transforming Sprites

What You'll Learn in This Hour:

▶ **Translating (moving) a sprite**
▶ **Using velocity as movement over time**
▶ **Moving sprites in a circle**

In this hour, we continue to study sprite programming, going beyond the basics into *transforms*. Transform simply means *to change*. Therefore, *transforming* a sprite means to *change* it—more specifically, to change its *properties*. At present, we have only three sprite properties (image, position, and color), which are already more than enough to effect changes right on the screen with the help of `SpriteBatch`. `Draw()`. In the graphics programming realm, "transform" usually refers to three things that can be done to a sprite or 3D mesh: *translation, rotation*, and *scaling*. The same three affect both 2D and 3D game objects. Translation means *movement*, the transform we will study first. The other two—rotation and scaling—will be covered in the next hour.

Translating (Moving) a Sprite

Sprite translation, or movement, can be done directly or indirectly. The direct approach involves writing code to move a sprite specifically to one location or another. The indirect approach involves setting up properties and variables that cause the sprite to move on its own based on those properties—we only write code that updates and draws the sprite, but the properties determine the movement. Although it is possible to cause a sprite to move in an arc or to follow a curve, that is not the type of movement we will be discussing in this hour. Instead, we'll see how to move a sprite a short distance per frame (and remember, although an XNA game normally draws at 60 fps, a WP7 game runs at only 30). The "curves" our sprites will follow are actually complete circles, as you'll see in the Solar System Demo coming up.

The math calculations we will perform in this hour to translate (move) a sprite are based on the 2D Cartesian coordinate system, represented in Figure 7.1. There are two axes, X and Y, which is why we refer to it as a "2D" system. Both the X and the Y axes start at the center, which is called the *origin*, residing at position (0,0). The X axis goes left (-) and right (+) from the origin. The Y axis goes down (-) and up (+) from the origin.

FIGURE 7.1
2D Cartesian coordinates are composed of two axes, X and Y.

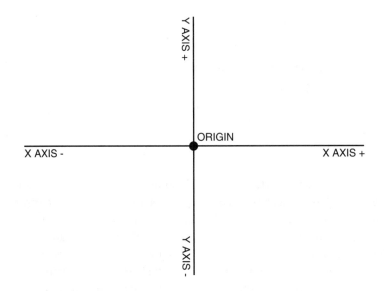

When making trigonometric calculations to transform a sprite's position, the Y value must be *reversed*. If you look at the figure, you can see why! On a computer screen, as well as the WP7 screen, the origin (0,0) is located at the upper left, with X increasing right and Y increasing down. Since the Cartesian system represents Y positive going *up*, any Y coordinates we calculate must be reversed, or *negated*. This can be done by multiplying every Y result by -1.

Moving the position of a sprite needn't be overly complicated. This is the easiest of the three transforms that we can calculate, because the calculation can just be skipped and the point can be moved to the desired target position (at this early stage). See Figure 7.2.

By the Way

We learn how to actually translate a point along a path in Hour 9, "Advanced Linear and Angular Velocity." This is used for such things as firing a rocket or missile from a jet airplane or rocketship pointed in any direction.

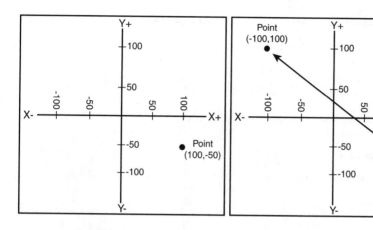

FIGURE 7.2
Translation
(movement)
from one point
to another.

Using Velocity as Movement Over Time

Velocity can be calculated as distance over time. Mathematically, the formula is V = D / T. This calculation is more useful *after* a certain distance has been traveled in a certain amount of time, to figure out the average speed. But it is not as useful when it comes to moving sprites across the screen. For that purpose, we need to set a certain velocity *ahead of time*, while the distance and time variables are not as important. Let's add a new velocity property to our ever-evolving Sprite class. Since velocity is a public property, we can use it outside of the class. Just for fun, let's add a new method to the class to move the sprite based on velocity, as shown in Listing 7.1.

LISTING 7.1   Adding a new property to our Sprite class.

```
public class Sprite
{
    private ContentManager p_content;
    private SpriteBatch p_spriteBatch;
    public Texture2D image;
    public Vector2 position;
    public Vector2 velocity;
    public Color color;

    public Sprite(ContentManager content, SpriteBatch spriteBatch)
    {
        p_content = content;
        p_spriteBatch = spriteBatch;
        image = null;
        position = Vector2.Zero;
        color = Color.White;
    }

    public bool Load(string assetName)
    {
        try
        {
```

```
        image = p_content.Load<Texture2D>(assetName);
    }
    catch (Exception) { return false; }
    return true;
}

public void Draw()
{
    p_spriteBatch.Draw(image, position, color);
}

public void Move()
{
    position += velocity;
}
}
```

The Move() method does something very simple—adds the velocity to the sprite's position. The position will be rounded to the nearest X,Y pixel coordinate on the screen, but the velocity *definitely* will not be represented with whole numbers. Considering a game running at 60 fps, the velocity will be a fraction of a pixel, such as 0.01 (1/100th or 1% of a pixel). At this rate, assuming that the game is running at 60 fps, the sprite will move one pixel in 6/10ths of a second. This is equal to roughly two pixels per second, because 0.01 times 60 is 0.60. See Figure 7.3.

FIGURE 7.3
Sprite velocity in relation to frame rate.

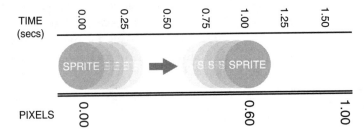

An XNA WP7 program runs at only 30 fps, so expect a difference in performance compared to Windows and Xbox 360 projects (which usually run at 60 fps).

We can put this simple addition to the Sprite class to the test. Included with this hour is an example called Sprite Movement. Open the project and take it for a spin. You'll see that a funny-looking spaceship is moving over a background image, as shown in Figure 7.4, wrapping from right to left as it reaches the edge of the screen. Two asset files are required to run this project: craters800x480.tga and fatship256.tga, also included with the project. The source code is found in Listing 7.2.

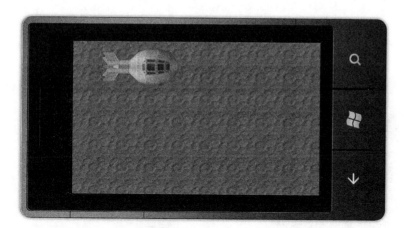

FIGURE 7.4
Testing velocity
with sprite
motion.

LISTING 7.2 Test project for the new and improved `Sprite` class with movement capability.

```
public class Game1 : Microsoft.Xna.Framework.Game
{
    GraphicsDeviceManager graphics;
    SpriteBatch spriteBatch;

    Sprite background;
    Sprite ship;

    public Game1()
    {
        graphics = new GraphicsDeviceManager(this);
        Content.RootDirectory = "Content";
        TargetElapsedTime = TimeSpan.FromTicks(333333);
    }

    protected override void Initialize()
    {
        base.Initialize();
    }

    protected override void LoadContent()
    {
        spriteBatch = new SpriteBatch(GraphicsDevice);

        background = new Sprite(Content, spriteBatch);
        background.Load("craters800x480");

        ship = new Sprite(Content, spriteBatch);
        ship.Load("fatship256");
        ship.position = new Vector2(0, 240 - ship.image.Height / 2);
        ship.velocity = new Vector2(8.0f, 4.0f);
    }

    protected override void Update(GameTime gameTime)
    {
```

```
        if (GamePad.GetState(PlayerIndex.One).Buttons.Back ==
            ButtonState.Pressed)
            this.Exit();

        //move the sprite
        ship.Move();

        //rebound from top and bottom
        if (ship.position.Y < -70 ¦ ship.position.Y > 480 - 185)
        {
            ship.velocity.Y *= -1;
        }

        //wrap around right to left
        if (ship.position.X > 800)
            ship.position.X = -256;

        base.Update(gameTime);
    }

    protected override void Draw(GameTime gameTime)
    {
        GraphicsDevice.Clear(Color.Black);
        spriteBatch.Begin();

        //draw the background
        background.Draw();

        //draw the sprite
        ship.Draw();

        spriteBatch.End();
        base.Draw(gameTime);
    }
}
```

Moving Sprites in a Circle

We're going to use the sun and planet artwork introduced in the preceding hour to make a simple solar system simulation. The calculations will not be meaningful to an astronomy fan; we just want the planet sprites to rotate around the sun, with no relation to our actual solar system. For this project, we need several planet bitmaps with alpha channel transparency, but because the background will just be black, if the planets have a black background that will suffice.

The sun needs to be positioned at the center of the screen, with the planets moving around it in concentric circular orbits. To make a sprite move in a circle, we need to use basic trigonometry—sine and cosine functions.

To make the code in our Solar System Demo a little cleaner, I've created a quick subclass of Sprite called Planet that adds three properties: radius, angle, and velocity. Notice that the Planet constructor, `Planet()`, calls the `Sprite` constructor using the `base()` call, passing `ContentManager` and `SpriteBatch` as the two required parameters to `Sprite`. The syntax for *inheritance* from a base class is shown in the class definition that follows. This is very helpful as we can count on `Sprite` to initialize itself.

```
public class Planet : Sprite
{
    public float radius;
    public float angle;
    public float velocity;

    public Planet(ContentManager content, SpriteBatch spriteBatch)
        : base(content, spriteBatch)
    {
        radius = 0.0f;
        angle = 0.0f;
        velocity = 0.0f;
    }
}
```

The rest of the source code for the Solar System Demo is up next. There are just four planets, but it is still efficient to use a `List` container to store them rather than using global variables. We're slowly seeing a little more code added to our WP7 "programmer's toolbox" with each new hour and each new example, which is a good thing. There's a lot more code in the initialization part of `ContentLoad()` than in either `Update()` or `Draw()`, but that is to be expected in a program with so few sprites on the screen. Figure 7.5 shows the program running, and the source code is found in Listing 7.3.

FIGURE 7.5
Solar System demo.

LISTING 7.3   The Solar System Demo project code.

```
public class Game1 : Microsoft.Xna.Framework.Game
{
    GraphicsDeviceManager graphics;
    SpriteBatch spriteBatch;
    Viewport screen;
    Sprite sun;
    List<Planet> planets;

    public Game1()
    {
        graphics = new GraphicsDeviceManager(this);
        Content.RootDirectory = "Content";
        TargetElapsedTime = TimeSpan.FromTicks(333333);
    }

    protected override void Initialize()
    {
        base.Initialize();
    }

    protected override void LoadContent()
    {
        spriteBatch = new SpriteBatch(GraphicsDevice);
        screen = GraphicsDevice.Viewport;

        //create sun sprite
        sun = new Sprite(Content, spriteBatch);
        sun.Load("sun");
        sun.position = new Vector2((screen.Width - sun.image.Width)/2,
            (screen.Height - sun.image.Height)/2);

        //create planet sprites
        planets = new List<Planet>();

        //add 1st planet
        Planet planet = new Planet(Content, spriteBatch);
        planet.Load("planet1");
        planet.velocity = 0.2f;
        planet.radius = 100;
        planet.angle = MathHelper.ToRadians(30);
        planets.Add(planet);

        //add 2nd planet
        planet = new Planet(Content, spriteBatch);
        planet.Load("planet2");
        planet.velocity = 0.16f;
        planet.radius = 140;
        planet.angle = MathHelper.ToRadians(60);
        planets.Add(planet);

        //add 3rd planet
        planet = new Planet(Content, spriteBatch);
        planet.Load("planet3");
        planet.velocity = 0.06f;
        planet.radius = 195;
        planet.angle = MathHelper.ToRadians(90);
        planets.Add(planet);
```

```
        //add 4th planet
        planet = new Planet(Content, spriteBatch);
        planet.Load("planet4");
        planet.velocity = 0.01f;
        planet.radius = 260;
        planet.angle = MathHelper.ToRadians(120);
        planets.Add(planet);
    }

    protected override void Update(GameTime gameTime)
    {
        if (GamePad.GetState(PlayerIndex.One).Buttons.Back ==
            ButtonState.Pressed)
            this.Exit();

        //update planet orbits
        foreach (Planet planet in planets)
        {
            //update planet's orbit position
            planet.angle += planet.velocity;

            //calculate position around sun with sine and cosine
            float orbitx = (float)(Math.Cos(planet.angle) * planet.radius);
            float orbity = (float)(Math.Sin(planet.angle) * planet.radius);

            //center the planet so it orbits around the sun
            float x = (screen.Width - planet.image.Width) / 2 + orbitx;
            float y = (screen.Height - planet.image.Height) / 2 + orbity;

            //save new position
            planet.position = new Vector2(x, y);
        }

        base.Update(gameTime);
    }

    protected override void Draw(GameTime gameTime)
    {
        GraphicsDevice.Clear(Color.Black);
        spriteBatch.Begin();

        //draw the sun
        sun.Draw();

        //draw the planets
        foreach (Planet planet in planets)
        {
            planet.Draw();
        }

        spriteBatch.End();
        base.Draw(gameTime);
    }
}
```

Did you find the code in LoadContent() a bit disconcerting, given that the same planet variable was used over and over again for each planet sprite? The important thing is that each one was added to the `planets` list, which became a "group" of sprites. You should do this whenever possible with related sprites, because it greatly simplifies everything about your code!

> We can also use these `sine()` and `cosine()` functions to fire projectiles (such as a missile) from a launcher toward any target at any position on the screen.

Summary

This hour was a quick jaunt through sprite translation (or movement) based on velocity. The Sprite Movement Demo showed how a sprite can be moved automatically based on its `velocity` property, although we still have to step in and manage the event when the sprite reaches a screen edge. Although rotation is a subject of the next hour, we did explore *moving* a sprite around in a circle. This is different from *sprite rotation*, which involves actually changing the image. In our Solar System Demo, the sprite images were not rotated; they remained in a fixed rotation but followed a circular path around the sun using trigonometry.

Q&A

Q. *The trigonometry calculations used to cause the planets to revolve around the sun. Which math function affects the* `position.X` *and which function affects the* `position.Y` *properties?*

A. Sine affects X; cosine affects Y.

Q. *Since the Windows Phone screen is rather small, what is one easy way to fit more game objects on the screen?*

A. Using smaller bitmaps or scaling the sprites.

Workshop

Quiz

1. Why is it necessary to multiply a radius factor by the results of sine or cosine?

2. If a game is running at 30 fps, and a sprite has a velocity of 1.0, how many pixels will the sprite cover in one second?

3. What property causes a sprite to move at a certain rate?

Answers

1. Because without a radius factor, the sprite will rotate very near the center of the star. Radius moves the planet out, away from the center. Remember, sine and cosine return very small values—for example, 0.8314.

2. 30 pixels

3. Velocity

Exercises

Five planet bitmaps are included with this hour, but the Solar System Demo draws only four of the planets. Modify the program so that it can draw all five unique planets by adding the fifth planet at an outer orbit beyond the others.

More Sprite Transforms: Rotation and Scaling

What You'll Learn in This Hour:

▶ **Rotating a sprite**
▶ **Scaling a sprite**

This hour continues the discussion of sprite transforms started in the preceding hour. We learned that a transform involves changing the properties of a game object so that it is altered in some way. In the context of graphics programming, a transform can be translation (movement), rotation, scaling, or any combination of the three. We also learned the difference between *image* rotation and *position* rotation, to prepare for *this* hour. Now we go beyond basic translation into the more complex transforms of rotation and scaling. The basic tenets of this hour (rotation and scaling) lead to very interesting, useful concepts, such as pointing toward a certain direction, and firing bullets, missiles, or other projectiles with the same angle as the ship or airplane that fired them. These are real, actual, applied techniques that you can use right away in your own games!

Rotating a Sprite

XNA performs sprite rotation for us. That, in a nutshell, is the gist of this section on the subject. Digging into the trigonometry reveals that rotation calculations are in relation to the origin of the coordinate system at (0,0). It is possible to rotate a sprite the "hard way" by rotating each pixel of the sprite using the trigonometry functions sine() and cosine() the way they were used in the previous hour to rotate planets around the sun in the Solar System Demo. The same basic principle is used to rotate a sprite, but it is done very quickly in XNA thanks to a very fast SpriteBatch. Draw() method that can handle rotation like a cinch.

By the Way

> Since we have full control over how fast a sprite can rotate or revolve in a scene (such as the planets in the Solar System Demo), it is possible to use rotation with just partial circles to give a sprite complex movements by linking arclike movements together in interesting ways.

Rotation Angles

Not too many years ago, artists on a game project would prerotate all sprites in order to preserve quality. Back in the early days of game development, graphics hardware was very limited—which is why game programming in the "early years" was such a black art, because it required extensive knowledge of the hardware in order to eke out every possible CPU cycle to the fullest. Most games for Nintendo's original NES fit on a 512Kb ROM cartridge. Compare that with games today, in which a single sprite animation stored as a texture might take up a few megabytes.

Figure 8.1 shows an example of the rotation frames often used in early games. The first direction is usually 0 degrees (north), and each successive frame is 45 degrees clockwise, as listed in Table 8.1.

FIGURE 8.1
A sprite pointing in the most common eight directions.

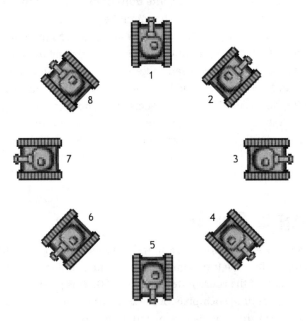

TABLE 8.1 Sprite Rotation Frame Directions and Angles

Direction	Angle/Degrees
North	0
Northeast	45
East	90
Southeast	135
South	180
Southwest	225
West	270
Northwest	315

As the number of frames increases, so does the quality of the rotated animation, at which point we might end up with the 32 frames of rotation shown in Figure 8.2. Despite the large number of animation frames here in the form of a sprite sheet, this is not truly animation; it is just a prerendered rotation sequence. Each angle in the 32 frames of rotation represents 11 degrees of rotation. In this situation, compared to the 8-frame rotation, with 45 degrees per angle, you can see that there are four times as many frames for much higher quality.

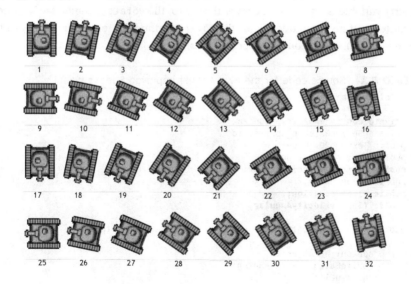

FIGURE 8.2
A 32-frame pre-rotated sprite sheet.

Rotation actually takes place around the origin, and in trigonometric terms, we're still working with the Cartesian coordinate system. Figure 8.3 shows an illustration of a point being rotated around the origin a certain interval.

FIGURE 8.3
Rotation takes place around the origin (0,0) in Cartesian coordinates.

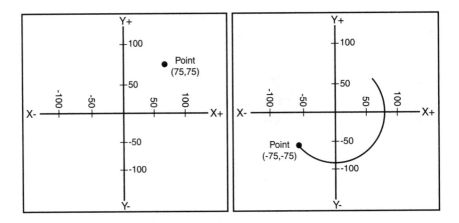

Sprite **Class Changes**

We have been slowly adding new features to the Sprite class over the past two hours, and now the class will receive some much-needed rotation know-how. First, to differentiate between the old velocity and what we will need for *rotational* velocity, I have renamed the old *velocity* variable to velocityLinear, which is still a Vector2. A new variable has been added to the Sprite class called velocityAngular. A support method has been added, called Rotate(). Assuming that the velocityAngular property variable is set to a value other than zero, the Rotate() method will cause the sprite to rotate automatically (as the Move() method did for linear velocity in the preceding hour). Here is our new Sprite class:

LISTING 8.1   Source code for the even further improved Sprite class!

```
public class Sprite
{
    private ContentManager p_content;
    private SpriteBatch p_spriteBatch;
    public Texture2D image;
    public Vector2 position;
    public Vector2 velocityLinear;
    public Color color;
    public float rotation;
    public float velocityAngular;

    public Sprite(ContentManager content, SpriteBatch spriteBatch)
    {
        p_content = content;
        p_spriteBatch = spriteBatch;
        image = null;
        position = Vector2.Zero;
        velocityLinear = Vector2.Zero;
        color = Color.White;
        rotation = 0.0f;
        velocityAngular = 0.0f;
    }
```

```
public bool Load(string assetName)
{
    try
    {
        image = p_content.Load<Texture2D>(assetName);
    }
    catch (Exception) { return false; }
    return true;
}

public void Draw()
{
    p_spriteBatch.Draw(image, position, color);
}

public void Move()
{
    position += velocityLinear;
}

public void Rotate()
{
    rotation += velocityAngular;
    if (rotation > Math.PI * 2)
        rotation = 0.0f;
    else if (rotation < 0.0f)
        rotation = (float)Math.PI * 2;
}
}
```

Drawing with Rotation

Besides the rotation code, some huge changes have had to be made to the Draw()
method to accommodate rotation. We're using the seventh and final overload of the
SpriteBatch.Draw() method, which looks like this:

```
public void Draw( Texture2D texture,
                  Vector2 position,
                  Rectangle? sourceRectangle,
                  Color color,
                  float rotation,
                  Vector2 origin,
                  float scale,
                  SpriteEffects effects,
                  float layerDepth );
```

There are nine parameters in this version of Draw(), which is capable of servicing all
of our sprite needs for the next few chapters. But first things first: the rotation factor.
The fifth parameter requires the rotation value as a float, so this is where we will
pass the new rotation property (added to the preceding class).

For rotation to work correctly, we need to pass the right value for the `origin` parameter. The `origin` defines the point at which rotation will occur. If we pass Vector2.Zero, as in the sample call

```
Vector2 origin = new Vector2(0, 0);
float scale = 1.0f;
p_spriteBatch.Draw(image, position, null, color, rotation, origin,
    scale, SpriteEffects.None, 0.0f);
```

then the origin is set to the upper-left corner of the sprite (0,0), causing the result to look as shown in Figure 8.4, with the image rotation around the upper left.

FIGURE 8.4
The origin parameter defines the point at which rotation takes place.

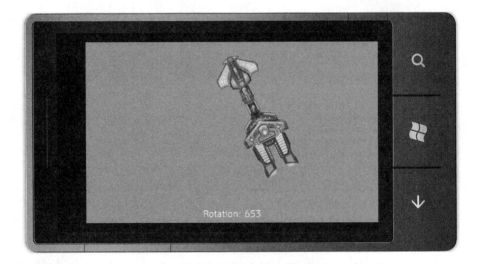

We need to calculate the *center* of the image so that it will rotate correctly from the center of the image rather than the upper-left corner. This can be calculated easily enough using the width and height of the image:

```
Vector2 origin = new Vector2(image.Width/2,image.Height/2);
float scale = 1.0f;
p_spriteBatch.Draw(image, position, null, color, rotation,
    origin, scale, SpriteEffects.None, 0.0f);
```

This is the new and final code for `Draw()` at this point. We will also make minor changes to it again in the next section on scaling. The new version is shown in Figure 8.5.

Changing the origin to the center of the sprite's image affects its *position* as well as rotation center—the origin becomes the focus for the position, even if the sprite is not rotated (with rotation set to 0.0f).

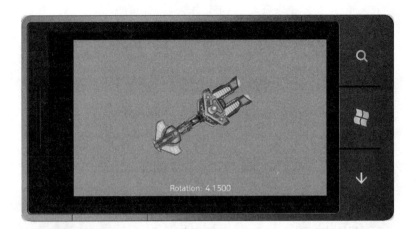

FIGURE 8.5
The sprite now rotates correctly, with the origin set to the center of the image.

Sprite Rotation Demo

For this rotation demo, we will use user input to rotate the sprite either right or left, depending on where the screen is touched, on the right side or left side of the screen. The second screenshot of this demo is shown in Figure 8.5, referenced earlier. Now the sprite is centered on the screen and rotating from the center. Listing 8.2 contains the source code for the test program.

LISTING 8.2   Test program for the new rotation capability of our `Sprite` class.

```
public class Game1 : Microsoft.Xna.Framework.Game
{
    GraphicsDeviceManager graphics;
    SpriteBatch spriteBatch;
    Viewport screen;
    SpriteFont font;
    Sprite ship;

    public Game1()
    {
        graphics = new GraphicsDeviceManager(this);
        Content.RootDirectory = "Content";
        TargetElapsedTime = TimeSpan.FromTicks(333333);
    }

    protected override void Initialize()
    {
        base.Initialize();
    }

    protected override void LoadContent()
    {
        spriteBatch = new SpriteBatch(GraphicsDevice);
        screen = GraphicsDevice.Viewport;

        //create the font
        font = Content.Load<SpriteFont>("WascoSans");
```

```
    //create the ship sprite
    ship = new Sprite(Content, spriteBatch);
    ship.Load("ship");
    ship.position = new Vector2(screen.Width/2, screen.Height/2);
}

protected override void Update(GameTime gameTime)
{
    if (GamePad.GetState(PlayerIndex.One).Buttons.Back ==
        ButtonState.Pressed)
        this.Exit();

    //get state of touch inputs
    TouchCollection touchInput = TouchPanel.GetState();

    //look at all touch points (usually 1)
    foreach (TouchLocation touch in touchInput)
    {
        if (touch.Position.X > screen.Width / 2)
            ship.velocityAngular = 0.05f;
        else if (touch.Position.X < screen.Width / 2)
            ship.velocityAngular = -0.05f;
    }

    base.Update(gameTime);
}

protected override void Draw(GameTime gameTime)
{
    GraphicsDevice.Clear(Color.CornflowerBlue);
    spriteBatch.Begin();

    ship.Rotate();
    ship.Draw();

    string text = "Rotation: " + ship.rotation.ToString("N4");
    Vector2 size = font.MeasureString(text);
    float x = (screen.Width - size.X) / 2;
    spriteBatch.DrawString(font, text, new Vector2(x, 440), Color.White);

    spriteBatch.End();
    base.Draw(gameTime);
}
}
```

Scaling a Sprite

Sprite scaling is also handled by SpriteBatch.Draw(), but it doesn't hurt to learn a little bit about *how* scaling happens. Like rotation, scaling occurs in relation to the origin of the Cartesian coordinate system, used for many trigonometry functions, although the most common we use in game programming are sine() and `cosine()`. Figure 8.6 shows a before-and-after result of an object (represented with just two points, which might be a line). The points are scaled by a factor of 0.5 (50%), resulting in the new positions shown.

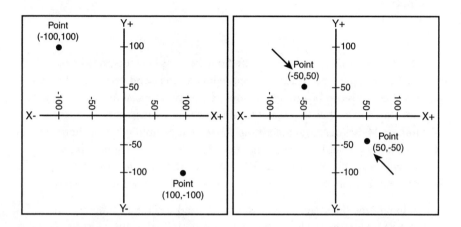

FIGURE 8.6
Scaling also occurs in relation to the origin (0,0).

In our previous example on rotation, the scale factor was hard-coded in the `Sprite.Draw()` method like so:

```
public void Draw()
{
    Vector2 origin = new Vector2(image.Width / 2, image.Height / 2);
    float scale = 1.0f;
    p_spriteBatch.Draw(image, position, null, color, rotation,
        origin, scale, SpriteEffects.None, 0.0f);
}
```

We need to delete this out of `Draw()` and add a new variable to the class's public declaration, with a new initializer in the constructor.

```
private ContentManager p_content;
private SpriteBatch p_spriteBatch;
public Texture2D image;
public Vector2 position;
public Vector2 velocityLinear;
public Color color;
public float rotation;
public float velocityAngular;
public Vector2 scale;

public Sprite(ContentManager content, SpriteBatch spriteBatch)
{
    p_content = content;
    p_spriteBatch = spriteBatch;
    image = null;
```

```
    position = Vector2.Zero;
    velocityLinear = Vector2.Zero;
    color = Color.White;
    rotation = 0.0f;
    velocityAngular = 0.0f;
    scale = new Vector2(1.0f);
}
```

The scale variable is no longer just a mere float, but has been upgraded to a Vector2. This will allow us to scale the sprite horizontally and vertically at different rates, if desired. This can be annoying, however. Every time you need to change the scale value, a Vector2 has to be set. I would much rather just set the scale as a float by default, and have the option of setting the scale individually for the horizontal or vertical axes. This is not because setting a Vector2 is time-consuming, but because the scale will most often be uniform on both axes. We want the most often-used properties and methods to reflect the most common need, not unusual needs.

We need to rename the scale variable to scaleV, and add a new property called scale. After making the modification, scaleV is initialized in the constructor, which sets both the X and the Y values. Anytime Sprite.scale is changed, both the X and the Y properties are changed.

```
scaleV = new Vector2(1.0f);
```

The new scale property looks like this:

```
public float scale
{
    get { return scaleV.X; }
    set {
        scaleV.X = value;
        scaleV.Y = value;
    }
}
```

In the Sprite Scaling Demo coming up shortly, we can scale the sprite very large or very small by simply modifying the Sprite.Draw() method to use Sprite.scaleV (which is a Vector2). It is also now possible to scale the width and height of a sprite. See Figure 8.7.

We're not going to add a scale velocity because that is so rarely needed that if the need does arise, it can be done with a global variable outside of the Sprite class. Or you can go ahead and add that capability to *your* version of the Sprite class if you want! In fact, let's see the complete new version of the Sprite class (in Listing 8.3), just to be thorough, since that was a lot of new information to sort out.

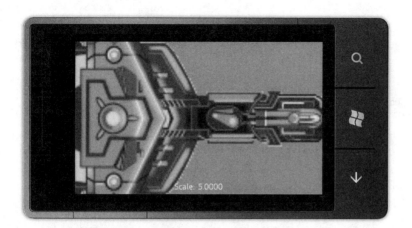

FIGURE 8.7
Scaling a sprite
up to 5× the
normal size.

LISTING 8.3 Source code for the updated Sprite class with new scaling abilities.

```
public class Sprite
{
    private ContentManager p_content;
    private SpriteBatch p_spriteBatch;
    public Texture2D image;
    public Vector2 position;
    public Vector2 velocityLinear;
    public Color color;
    public float rotation;
    public float velocityAngular;
    public Vector2 scaleV;

    public Sprite(ContentManager content, SpriteBatch spriteBatch)
    {
        p_content = content;
        p_spriteBatch = spriteBatch;
        image = null;
        position = Vector2.Zero;
        velocityLinear = Vector2.Zero;
        color = Color.White;
        rotation = 0.0f;
        velocityAngular = 0.0f;
        scaleV = new Vector2(1.0f);
    }

    public float scale
    {
        get { return scaleV.X; }
        set {
            scaleV.X = value;
            scaleV.Y = value;
        }
    }

    public bool Load(string assetName)
    {
        try
```

```
        {
            image = p_content.Load<Texture2D>(assetName);
        }
        catch (Exception) { return false; }
        return true;
    }

    public void Draw()
    {
        Vector2 origin = new Vector2(image.Width / 2, image.Height / 2);
        p_spriteBatch.Draw(image, position, null, color, rotation,
            origin, scaleV, SpriteEffects.None, 0.0f);
    }

    public void Move()
    {
        position += velocityLinear;
    }

    public void Rotate()
    {
        rotation += velocityAngular;
        if (rotation > Math.PI * 2)
            rotation = 0.0f;
        else if (rotation < 0.0f)
            rotation = (float)Math.PI * 2;
    }
}
```

The complete Sprite Scaling Demo is found in Listing 8.4. A view of the program with the scale set very small is shown in Figure 8.8.

FIGURE 8.8
Scaling a sprite
down to 10% of
normal size.

LISTING 8.4 Source code for the updated `Sprite` class with new scaling abilities.

```
public class Game1 : Microsoft.Xna.Framework.Game
{
    GraphicsDeviceManager graphics;
    SpriteBatch spriteBatch;
    Viewport screen;
    SpriteFont font;
    Sprite ship;

    public Game1()
    {
        graphics = new GraphicsDeviceManager(this);
        Content.RootDirectory = "Content";
        TargetElapsedTime = TimeSpan.FromTicks(333333);
    }

    protected override void Initialize()
    {
        base.Initialize();
    }

    protected override void LoadContent()
    {
        spriteBatch = new SpriteBatch(GraphicsDevice);
        screen = GraphicsDevice.Viewport;

        //create the font
        font = Content.Load<SpriteFont>("WascoSans");

        //create the ship sprite
        ship = new Sprite(Content, spriteBatch);
        ship.Load("ship");
        ship.position = new Vector2(screen.Width / 2, screen.Height / 2);

        //rotate the sprite to the right
        ship.rotation = MathHelper.ToRadians(90.0f);
    }

    protected override void Update(GameTime gameTime)
    {
        if (GamePad.GetState(PlayerIndex.One).Buttons.Back ==
            ButtonState.Pressed)
            this.Exit();

        //get state of touch inputs
        TouchCollection touchInput = TouchPanel.GetState();
        foreach (TouchLocation touch in touchInput)
        {
            if (touch.Position.X > screen.Width / 2)
                ship.scale += 0.05f;
            else if (touch.Position.X < screen.Width / 2)
                ship.scale -= 0.05f;
        }

        //keep the scaling within limits
```

```
        if (ship.scale < 0.10f)
            ship.scale = 0.10f;
        else if (ship.scale > 5.0f)
            ship.scale = 5.0f;

        base.Update(gameTime);
    }

    protected override void Draw(GameTime gameTime)
    {
        GraphicsDevice.Clear(Color.CornflowerBlue);
        spriteBatch.Begin();

        ship.Rotate();
        ship.Draw();

        string text = "Scale: " + ship.scale.ToString("N4");
        Vector2 size = font.MeasureString(text);
        float x = (screen.Width - size.X) / 2;
        spriteBatch.DrawString(font, text, new Vector2(x, 440),
            Color.White);

        spriteBatch.End();
        base.Draw(gameTime);
    }
}
```

Summary

That concludes our study of the three basic transforms: translation, rotation, and scaling. These techniques, along with SpriteBatch and some good math formulas, can produce any type of special effect or animated movement that we need for a game, on small game sprites, or even whole backgrounds (give that a try!).

Q&A

Q. *The new transform capabilities added to the* Sprite *class seem to work really well, but wouldn't the code become kind of hard to manage in a real game?*

A. That's true; at a certain point, managing the settings for game object behavior does become a challenge. When that happens, most developers switch to using a scripting language like Lua or Python, which is tied in to the C# game project.

Q. *How would you cause a sprite to perform actions like doing a sliding rotation for a game cut-scene?*

A. We'll get to that topic in a future hour! If you are eager to learn more about it now, see Hour 13, "Sprite Transform Animation."

Workshop

Quiz

1. How do you rotate a sprite at runtime?

2. How do you scale a sprite at runtime?

3. How would you transform a sprite that is animated?

Answers

1. By using the rotation parameter in `SpriteBatch.Draw()`.

2. Again, by using a parameter, `scale`, in `SpriteBatch.Draw()`.

3. This is a complex question that is addressed in Hour 14, "Sprite Frame Animation."

Exercises

Using either the rotation demo or the scaling demo from this hour, modify it so that a *background image* can be rotated and scaled while the spaceship in the foreground remains idle over the background, which will rotate and scale based on various locations on the screen that the user can "touch."

HOUR 9

Advanced Linear and Angular Velocity

What You'll Learn in This Hour:

▶ **Calculating angular velocity**
▶ **"Pointing" a sprite in the direction of movement**

This hour continues along the same path as the preceding hour, regarding sprite transforms, taking it a step further and applying velocity calculations to transform a sprite in useful ways. We will derive the math calculations needed to move a sprite in any desired direction based on its rotation angle (in the top-down view perspective, treating the screen somewhat like a Cartesian coordinate system). Moving a sprite at a desired angle is a very important need in most games, so you will put this technique to use extensively in your own projects. The next related calculations involve "looking" at a desired target point from a source point, and moving toward that target location. This might be perhaps considered the opposite of calculating velocity from a direction angle. In this case, we know *where* we want the sprite to go, but just don't yet know how to point the sprite in the direction of the target. What we're studying in this hour is Newtonian rocket science, just the sort of stuff used to launch space vehicles into orbit! Again, trigonometry comes into use here to solve these problems.

Calculating Angular Velocity

We have done a lot of work already with sprite transforms, so now it's time to put some of these new features to the test in a real-world situation that often comes up in game projects. We'll have a sprite move on the screen based on user input, and move in the direction it is facing. This requires some familiar trigonometry functions used in a creative way.

To begin, we need to understand the starting point for trigonometric calculations. The artwork in a game is often oriented with the "front" or "nose" pointing upward. But in our math calculations, that starting point will always be to the right, or 90 degrees clockwise from the up direction, as shown in Figure 9.1.

FIGURE 9.1
Trigonometry functions assume that angle 0 is right, not up.

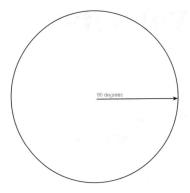

90 degrees

> Math functions dealing with rotation angles and velocities *always* work with radians, not degrees. Using degrees in code is fine, but angles must be converted to radians during calculations. This can be done with `MathHelper.ToDegrees()` and `MathHelper.ToRadians()`.

Watch Out!

We use `cosine()` to calculate the X component, and `sine()` to calculate the Y component for the velocity of an object. In XNA, we can use the `Math.Cos()` and `Math.Sin()` methods to perform these calculations. The sole parameter passed to both of these methods is the `angle` that an object is facing or moving toward.

The angle will be any value from 0 to 360 degrees, including decimal values for partial degrees. When the calculations are made, the angle must be converted to radians. Suppose that the angle is 10 degrees. We convert this to radians with the following:

```
float radians = MathHelper.ToRadians( 10 );
// answer: radians = 0.174532925
```

The angular velocity is calculated using this radian value, rounded to 0.1745 for our purposes (although the complete floating-point value is used with all decimal places in memory):

Velocity X = Cos(0.1745)

Velocity Y = Sin(0.1745)

Figure 9.2 shows a circle with the angle and calculated values.

FIGURE 9.2
Calculating
angular velocity.

The results are X = 0.9848 and Y = 0.1736, as shown in the illustration. Consider the direction the arrow is facing in the illustration (10 degrees). The X and Y velocity values make sense, given that angle. Considering pixel movement on the screen, at this angle a sprite will move in the X axis much more than in the Y axis, a ratio of about five-and-a-half to one (5.5:1). So, when a sprite is moving across the screen at an angle of 10 degrees, it will move 5.5 pixels to the right (+X) for every 1 pixel down (+Y). If the angle were 180, for instance, the arrow would be pointing to the left, which would result in a negative X velocity.

Updating the `Sprite` Class

Some changes are needed for the `Sprite` class to work with the upcoming sample program. There are some new variables and some improvements to the `Draw()` and `Rotate()` methods. To make rotation more versatile, the origin variable (a float) has been moved out of `Draw()` and into the class's public declarations so that it can be modified as a public variable. The `Rotate()` method has some improvements to make its boundary checking more accurate. The changes are included in Listing 9.1.

LISTING 9.1   Yet even more changes to the `Sprite` class!

```
public class Sprite
{
    private ContentManager p_content;
    private SpriteBatch p_spriteBatch;
    public Texture2D image;
    public Vector2 position;
    public Vector2 velocityLinear;
    public Color color;
    public float rotation;
    public float velocityAngular;
    public Vector2 scaleV;
    public Vector2 origin; //new
    public bool alive; //new
    public bool visible; //new
```

```
public Sprite(ContentManager content, SpriteBatch spriteBatch)
{
    p_content = content;
    p_spriteBatch = spriteBatch;
    image = null;
    position = Vector2.Zero;
    velocityLinear = Vector2.Zero;
    color = Color.White;
    rotation = 0.0f;
    velocityAngular = 0.0f;
    scaleV = new Vector2(1.0f);
    origin = Vector2.Zero; //new
    alive = true; //new
    visible = true; //new
}

public float scale
{
    get { return scaleV.X; }
    set
    {
        scaleV.X = value;
        scaleV.Y = value;
    }
}

public bool Load(string assetName)
{
    try
    {
        image = p_content.Load<Texture2D>(assetName);
        origin = new Vector2(image.Width / 2, image.Height / 2); //new
    }
    catch (Exception) { return false; }
    return true;
}

public void Draw()
{
    //Vector2 origin = new Vector2(image.Width / 2, image.Height / 2);
    p_spriteBatch.Draw(image, position, null, color, rotation,
        origin, scaleV, SpriteEffects.None, 0.0f);
}

public void Move()
{
    position += velocityLinear;
}

public void Rotate()
{
    rotation += velocityAngular;
    if (rotation > Math.PI * 2)
        rotation -= (float)Math.PI * 2; //change
    else if (rotation < 0.0f)
        rotation = (float)Math.PI * 2 - rotation; //change
}
}
```

There's a *great* tutorial lesson on all the functions of trigonometry on Wikipedia here: http://en.wikipedia.org/wiki/Trigonometric_functions.

Apache Helicopter Demo

The example for this section is included in the hour resource files, so you may open the project while studying the code in Listing 9.2. This demo draws a small sprite of an Apache helicopter firing bullets at whatever angle it is facing. Touching the top of the screen will cause the chopper's nose to rotate upward. Likewise, touching the bottom of the screen will rotate the chopper's nose downward. Touching the center of the screen will cause the chopper to fire its bullets in its current facing angle. Figure 9.3 shows the program running, and it looks almost like the start of a game! It could be, with a little work! As we continue to improve the Sprite class, the source code for our example programs continue to shrink!

FIGURE 9.3
The Apache helicopter demo.

LISTING 9.2 Source code to the Apache helicopter demo utilizing the improved Sprite class.

```
public class Game1 : Microsoft.Xna.Framework.Game
{
    GraphicsDeviceManager graphics;
    SpriteBatch spriteBatch;
    Viewport screen;
    SpriteFont font;
    Sprite chopper;
    Texture2D bullet;
    Sprite[] bullets;
    float rotation;

    public Game1()
    {
        graphics = new GraphicsDeviceManager(this);
        Content.RootDirectory = "Content";
```

```
        TargetElapsedTime = TimeSpan.FromTicks(333333);
    }

    protected override void Initialize()
    {
        base.Initialize();
    }

    protected override void LoadContent()
    {
        spriteBatch = new SpriteBatch(GraphicsDevice);
        screen = GraphicsDevice.Viewport;

        //create the font
        font = Content.Load<SpriteFont>("WascoSans");

        //create the helicopter sprite
        chopper = new Sprite(Content, spriteBatch);
        chopper.Load("apache");
        chopper.position = new Vector2(120, 240);
        chopper.origin = new Vector2(100, 22);

        //load bullet image
        bullet = Content.Load<Texture2D>("bullet");

        //create bullet sprites
        bullets = new Sprite[10];
        for (int n = 0; n < 10; n++)
        {
            bullets[n] = new Sprite(Content, spriteBatch);
            bullets[n].image = bullet;
            bullets[n].alive = false;
        }
    }

    protected override void Update(GameTime gameTime)
    {
        if (GamePad.GetState(PlayerIndex.One).Buttons.Back ==
            ButtonState.Pressed)
            this.Exit();

        //get state of touch inputs
        TouchCollection touchInput = TouchPanel.GetState();

        //get rotation
        rotation = MathHelper.ToDegrees(chopper.rotation);

        //look at all touch points
        foreach (TouchLocation touch in touchInput)
        {
            if (touch.Position.Y < 180) //top of screen
                rotation -= 1.0f;
            else if (touch.Position.Y > 300) //bottom
                rotation += 1.0f;
            else
                Fire(); //middle
        }
```

```
        //keep rotation in bounds
        if (rotation < 0.0f)
            rotation = 360.0f - rotation;
        else if (rotation > 360.0f)
            rotation = 360.0f - rotation;

        //save rotation
        chopper.rotation = MathHelper.ToRadians(rotation);

        //move the bullets
        for (int n = 0; n < 10; n++)
        {
            if (bullets[n].alive)
            {
                bullets[n].Move();
                if (bullets[n].position.X > 800)
                    bullets[n].alive = false;
            }
        }

        base.Update(gameTime);
    }

    protected override void Draw(GameTime gameTime)
    {
        GraphicsDevice.Clear(Color.CornflowerBlue);
        spriteBatch.Begin();

        //draw the chopper
        chopper.Draw();

        //draw the bullets
        for (int n = 0; n < 10; n++)
        {
            if (bullets[n].alive)
                bullets[n].Draw();
        }

        string text = "Angle: " + rotation.ToString("N4");
        spriteBatch.DrawString(font, text, new Vector2(200, 440),
            Color.White);

        spriteBatch.End();
        base.Draw(gameTime);
    }

    void Fire()
    {
        //look for an unused bullet
        for (int n = 0; n < 10; n++)
        {
            if (!bullets[n].alive)
            {
                bullets[n].alive = true;
                bullets[n].position = chopper.position;
                bullets[n].rotation = chopper.rotation;
                //calculate angular velocity
                float x = (float)Math.Cos(bullets[n].rotation) * 10.0f;
```

```
                float y = (float)Math.Sin(bullets[n].rotation) * 10.0f;
                bullets[n].velocityLinear = new Vector2(x,y);
                break;
        }
    }
  }
}
```

"Pointing" a Sprite in the Direction of Movement

You might be thinking, *Didn't we just do this?* That's an astute question! In fact, in the preceding example, the bullet sprites were pointed in a certain direction, and we just added the angular velocity code to make them move in that direction. Now we're going to do the reverse: Given the direction a sprite is already *moving*, we want it to "point" in that direction so that it looks right. To demonstrate, we'll cause the spaceship sprite to "orbit" around a planet and rotate while moving. To more accurately describe this situation, we want a sprite to *move and point* toward a target.

By the Way

> The trigonometry ("circular") functions we've been using can be considered elementary physics. In a sense, then, we're working on our own simple physics engine here, which is a bit of a stretch but still compelling!

Have you ever played an RTS (real-time strategy) game in which you can select units, then right-click somewhere on the map, and they would move toward that location? That is the basic way most RTS games work. Along the path, if your units encounter enemy units, they will usually fight or shoot at the enemy, unless you tell them to target a specific enemy unit with a similar right-click on it.

Well, we can do something like that with the concept covered here. Oh, there's a lot more involved in an RTS game than just moving toward a destination, but at the core of the game is code similar to what we're going to learn about here.

Calculating the Angle to Target

In the preceding section, we used `Math.Cos()` and `Math.Sin()` to calculate the respective X and Y components of velocity (a `Vector2`). These values could then be used to move a sprite in any desired direction. There's a related calculation we can perform to do the opposite: Given a sprite's current location, and a target location, we can calculate *the angle* needed to get there.

We won't be using sine and cosine to calculate the angle. Those trig functions are useful only if you *know* the angle already. The reverse is, knowing where we are already headed, what is that angle?

This concept is *powerful* in terms of gameplay! Let's say you do know the angle and use it to calculate velocity, then send a bullet on its way, as we did in the preceding example. Okay, that's great. But what if you wanted to slow down that sprite, make it stop, and even begin moving in reverse? Not in terms of a *bullet*, but any sprite, like a spaceship or a car? We can do these things.

> This code could be used to cause one sprite to continually point at another sprite. Instead of using a target screen coordinate, use the location of a moving target sprite instead!

By the Way

The secret behind all this advanced velocity code is another trig function called *arctangent*. Arctangent is an inverse trigonometric function—specifically, the inverse of tangent, which itself is *opposite* over *adjacent* (side a divided by side b), as shown in Figure 9.4. Since I don't want to get into deriving these trig functions, let's just jump to the function name in XNA. There are two versions: Math.Atan(), which takes one parameter, and Math.Atan2(), which takes two parameters (double y, double x). This math function returns the angle whose tangent is the quotient of two specified numbers.

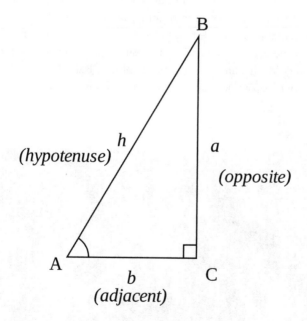

FIGURE 9.4
A right triangle is the basis for trigonometry. Illustration courtesy of Wikipedia.

We can't just pass the position (X and Y) of a target screen coordinate to this function, because the two parameters are actually *delta* values (the difference between the X and Y values of two points). That's not as bad as it sounds, as any math major will tell you. Delta is just the difference between the two points: X2 - X1 and Y2 - Y1.

```
double deltaX = x2 - x1;
double deltaY = y2 - y1;
```

Having these variables ready, we can calculate the angle toward a target with arctangent in XNA like so:

```
double angle = Math.Atan2(deltaY,deltaX);
```

Shuttle Orbit Demo

So now we know how to calculate the angle to a target location. What now? Let's put this new knowledge to use in another sample program. This one will simulate a spaceship orbiting a planet. While it's rotating around the planet, the nose of the ship will rotate so it is oriented in the direction of movement. This isn't exactly moving toward a target on the screen, but given the ship's previous position and the current position, we can figure out what in direction the nose should be pointing *in reverse*. Figure 9.5 shows the program running, showing the space shuttle not just rotating around a planet, but rotating to keep the nose pointing forward. This isn't exactly realistic, because while in orbit, it doesn't matter which direction a ship or satellite is facing—it will continue to orbit the planet. But it looks cool this way in a game, especially to a younger audience. Listing 9.3 contains the source code for the program.

FIGURE 9.5
The spaceship points toward its path while rotating around the planet.

Angle: 0.8465   Radius: 200

LISTING 9.3 Source code for the orbiting spaceship program.

```
public class Game1 : Microsoft.Xna.Framework.Game
{
    GraphicsDeviceManager graphics;
    SpriteBatch spriteBatch;
    Viewport screen;
    SpriteFont font;
    Sprite shuttle, planet;
    float orbitRadius, orbitAngle;
    Vector2 oldPos;

    public Game1()
    {
        graphics = new GraphicsDeviceManager(this);
        Content.RootDirectory = "Content";
        TargetElapsedTime = TimeSpan.FromTicks(333333);
    }

    protected override void Initialize()
    {
        base.Initialize();
    }

    protected override void LoadContent()
    {
        spriteBatch = new SpriteBatch(GraphicsDevice);
        screen = GraphicsDevice.Viewport;

        //create the font
        font = Content.Load<SpriteFont>("WascoSans");

        //create the planet sprite
        planet = new Sprite(Content, spriteBatch);
        planet.Load("planet1");
        planet.scale = 0.5f;
        planet.position = new Vector2(400, 240);

        //create the ship sprite
        shuttle = new Sprite(Content, spriteBatch);
        shuttle.Load("shuttle");
        shuttle.scale = 0.2f;

        orbitRadius = 200.0f;
        orbitAngle = 0.0f;
    }

    protected override void Update(GameTime gameTime)
    {
        if (GamePad.GetState(PlayerIndex.One).Buttons.Back ==
            ButtonState.Pressed)
            this.Exit();

        //remember position for orientation
        oldPos = shuttle.position;

        //keep angle within 0-360 degs
        orbitAngle += 1.0f;
        if (orbitAngle > 360.0f)
            orbitAngle -= 360.0f;
```

```
        //calculate shuttle position
        float x = 400 + (float)Math.Cos(MathHelper.ToRadians(orbitAngle))
            * orbitRadius;
        float y = 240 + (float)Math.Sin(MathHelper.ToRadians(orbitAngle))
            * orbitRadius;

        //move the position
        shuttle.position = new Vector2(x, y);

        //point shuttle's nose in the right direction
        float angle = TargetAngle(shuttle.position, oldPos);

        //subtract 180 degrees to reverse the direction
        angle = MathHelper.WrapAngle(angle - MathHelper.ToRadians(180));

        //adjust for artwork pointing up
        angle += MathHelper.ToRadians(90);

        //update shuttle's rotation
        shuttle.rotation = angle;

        base.Update(gameTime);
    }

    protected override void Draw(GameTime gameTime)
    {
        GraphicsDevice.Clear(Color.Black);
        spriteBatch.Begin();

        planet.Draw();
        shuttle.Draw();

        string text = "Angle: " + shuttle.rotation.ToString("N4");
        spriteBatch.DrawString(font, text, new Vector2(200, 440),
            Color.White);

        text = "Radius: " + orbitRadius.ToString("N0");
        spriteBatch.DrawString(font, text, new Vector2(450, 440),
            Color.White);

        spriteBatch.End();
        base.Draw(gameTime);
    }


    float TargetAngle(Vector2 p1, Vector2 p2)
    {
        return TargetAngle(p1.X, p1.Y, p2.X, p2.Y);
    }

    float TargetAngle(double x1,double y1,double x2,double y2)
    {
        double deltaX = (x2-x1);
        double deltaY = (y2-y1);
        return (float)Math.Atan2(deltaY,deltaX);
    }
}
```

Summary

That concludes our hour on rocket science. Given that a WP7 device is several orders of magnitude faster than the computers on the Apollo spacecraft that landed men on the moon, I think there's some validity to doing this on a computer phone.

Q&A

Q. *Is the space shuttle really orbiting the planet in the orbiting spaceship program?*

A. Not really. It is just rotating around a center point that happens to be at the center of the planet sprite. It's kind of a trick that wouldn't work if the scene were moving.

Q. *The helicopter demo program looks as though it could be made into a game pretty easily. Is this a good starting point for a game?*

A. Certainly! By just making a flat "road" along the bottom of the screen, you could have soldiers and tanks and jeeps move along the road and let the player shoot at them while dodging enemy bullets.

Workshop

Quiz

1. What are the names of the trig functions used to calculate angular velocity?

2. What trig function calculates the angle to a target?

3. What XNA function converts a radian angle to degrees?

Answers

1. Sine and cosine

2. Arctangent

3. `Math.ToDegrees()`

Exercises

There's so much potential with the two examples in this chapter that I can think of a half dozen games that we could design from them very easily. But we spent a lot of time already with the orbiting space shuttle demo, and not much time on the helicopter demo, so let's spend more time with the latter. Modify the helicopter demo so that it is possible to move the helicopter sprite forward (right) and backward (left) on the screen. Add an enemy helicopter that flies in the opposite direction, and make it possible for the player to shoot the enemy down. But also make it so that the player must dodge the enemy helicopter because they will crash if they collide.

HOUR 10

When Objects Collide

What You'll Learn in This Hour:

▶ **Boundary collision detection**
▶ **Radial collision detection**
▶ **Assessing the damage**

Thus far, we have learned a lot about drawing things on the small but high-resolution screen of WP7 devices. Drawing is only the first step in making a game. There must be some way for objects to interact, to affect each other during gameplay. This interaction usually involves bumping into each other, which might be a rocket hitting an alien ship, a soldier jumping on top of a crate, a plumber bonking evil turtles, a blue hedgehog grabbing coins, a yellow mouth eating dots. The list goes on and on. In every case, there is a situation in which one sprite "touches" another, triggering some event. Detecting when that occurs is not automatic, not built into XNA. We have to write the code to detect sprite collisions on our own. XNA does provide a very easy-to-use method to help do just that, however. The focus of this hour is not just on detecting collisions, but on learning what to do afterward—collision handling or response.

Boundary Collision Detection

The first type of collision test we'll examine uses the boundaries of two rectangles for the test condition. Also called "bounding box" collision detection, this technique is simple and fast, which makes it ideal in situations in which a *lot* of objects are interacting on the screen at once. Not as precise as the radial technique (coming up next), boundary collision detection does return adequate results for a high-speed arcade game. Interestingly, this is also useful in a graphical user interface (GUI), comparing the boundary of the mouse cursor with GUI objects for highlighting and selection purposes. On the WP7, however, we can't actually track mouse *movement* because a "mouse" does not even exist on Windows Phone, only touch points.

By the
~~Way~~ We will learn to program a simple GUI with buttons and sliders in Hour 20, "Creating a Graphical User Interface."

XNA provides a useful struct called `Rectangle`. Among the many methods in this struct is `Intersects()`, which accepts a single parameter—another `Rectangle`. The return value of `Intersects()` is just a `bool` (true/false). The trick to using `Rectangle.Intersects()` effectively is creating a bounding rectangle around a sprite at its current location on the screen, taking into account the sprite's width and height. When we get into animation a couple of hours from now, we'll have to adapt this code to take into account the width and height of individual frames. In the meantime, we can use the width and height of the whole texture since we're just working with simple static sprite images at this point. Figure 10.1 illustrates the boundary around a sprite image.

FIGURE 10.1
The image dimensions are used as the boundary.

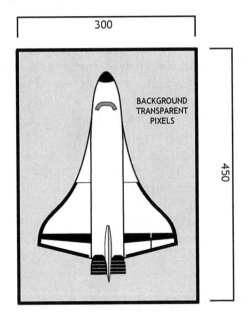

As you can see in this illustration, boundary collision does not require that the image have an equal width and height, since the bounding rectangle can handle a nonuniform aspect ratio. However, it is usually better to store game artwork in square images for best results.

Accounting for Pivot

Remember that `Sprite.position` references the *pivot point* of the object, also known as the *origin*. Normally, the origin is at the center of the sprite. If the origin is changed from the center of the sprite, the boundary will return an incorrect result! Therefore, if you change the origin, it's up to you to take that into account when calculating boundaries. The Sprite class does not account for such changes. The calculation for the boundary might be done like so at this point:

```
int halfw = image.Width / 2;
int halfh = image.Height / 2;
return new Rectangle(
    (int)position.X - halfw,
    (int)position.Y - halfh,
    image.Width,
    image.Height);
```

Accounting for Scaling

That should work nicely, all things being equal. But another important factor that must be considered is *scaling*. Has the scale been changed from 1.0, or full image size? If so, that will affect the boundary of the sprite, and we have to account for that or else false results will come back while the game is running, causing a sprite to collide when it clearly did not touch another sprite (due to scaling errors). When the boundary is calculated, not only the origin must be accounted for, but the scaling as well, which adds a bit of complexity to the Boundary() method. Not to worry, though—it's calculated by the method for us. Here is a new version that takes into account the scaling factor:

```
int halfw = (int)( (float)(image.Width / 2) * scaleV.X );
int halfh = (int)( (float)(image.Height / 2) * scaleV.Y );
return new Rectangle(
    (int)position.X - halfw,
    (int)position.Y - halfh,
    halfw * 2,
    halfh * 2);
```

What is happening in this code is that the width and height are each divided by two, and the scaling is multiplied by these halfw and halfh values to arrive at scaled dimensions, which are then multiplied by two to get the full width and height when returning the Rectangle.

Sprite Class Changes

To simplify the code, we can add a new method to the Sprite class that will return the boundary of a sprite at its current location on the screen. While we're at it, it's time to give Sprite a new home in its own source code file. The new file will be called Sprite.cs. The namespace is a consideration, because the class needs a home. I propose just calling it GameLibrary, and in any program that uses Sprite, a simple using statement will import it.

The new version of this class includes the Boundary() method discussed earlier. An additional new method is also needed for debugging purposes. Every class has the capability to override the ToString() method and return any string value. We can override ToString() and have it return information about the sprite. This string can be logged to a text file if desired, but it is easier to just print it on the screen. The code in ToString() is quite messy due to all the formatting codes used, but the result looks nice when printed. It can be very helpful to add a ToString() to a custom class for this purpose, for quick debugging. For example, it is helpful to see the position and boundary of a sprite to verify whether collision is working correctly. See the demo coming up shortly to see an example of this in action. Our Sprite class, the source code for which is shown in Listing 10.1, sure has grown since its humble beginning!

LISTING 10.1   Revised source code for the Sprite class.

```
public class Sprite
{
    private ContentManager p_content;
    private SpriteBatch p_spriteBatch;
    public Texture2D image;
    public Vector2 position;
    public Vector2 velocityLinear;
    public Color color;
    public float rotation;
    public float velocityAngular;
    public Vector2 scaleV;
    public Vector2 origin;
    public bool alive;
    public bool visible;

    public Sprite(ContentManager content, SpriteBatch spriteBatch)
    {
        p_content = content;
        p_spriteBatch = spriteBatch;
        image = null;
        position = Vector2.Zero;
        velocityLinear = Vector2.Zero;
        color = Color.White;
        rotation = 0.0f;
        velocityAngular = 0.0f;
        scaleV = new Vector2(1.0f);
        origin = Vector2.Zero;
        alive = true;
        visible = true;
    }

    public float scale
    {
        get { return scaleV.X; }
        set
        {
            scaleV.X = value;
            scaleV.Y = value;
```

```
        }
}

public bool Load(string assetName)
{
    try
    {
        image = p_content.Load<Texture2D>(assetName);
        origin = new Vector2(image.Width / 2, image.Height / 2);
    }
    catch (Exception) { return false; }
    return true;
}

public void Draw()
{
    p_spriteBatch.Draw(image, position, null, color, rotation,
        origin, scaleV, SpriteEffects.None, 0.0f);
}

public void Move()
{
    position += velocityLinear;
}

public void Rotate()
{
    rotation += velocityAngular;
    if (rotation > Math.PI * 2)
        rotation -= (float)Math.PI * 2;
    else if (rotation < 0.0f)
        rotation = (float)Math.PI * 2 - rotation;
}

public Rectangle Boundary()
{
    int halfw = (int)( (float)(image.Width / 2) * scaleV.X );
    int halfh = (int)( (float)(image.Height / 2) * scaleV.Y );

    return new Rectangle(
        (int)position.X - halfw,
        (int)position.Y - halfh,
        halfw * 2,
        halfh * 2);
}

public override string ToString()
{
    string s = "Texture {W:" + image.Width.ToString() +
        " H:" + image.Height.ToString() + "}\n" +
        "Position {X:" + position.X.ToString("N2") + " Y:" +
            position.Y.ToString("N2") + "}\n" +
        "Lin Vel " + velocityLinear.ToString() + "\n" +
        "Ang Vel {" + velocityAngular.ToString("N2") + "}\n" +
        "Scaling " + scaleV.ToString() + "\n" +
        "Rotation " + rotation.ToString() + "\n" +
        "Pivot " + origin.ToString() + "\n";
    Rectangle B = Boundary();
    s += "Boundary {X:" + B.X.ToString() + " Y:" +
```

```
            B.Y.ToString() + " W:" + B.Width.ToString() +
            " H:" + B.Height.ToString() + "}\n";

        return s;
    }
}
```

When animation support is added to the `Sprite` class, we will have to remember to update the `Sprite.Boundary()` method to take into account the width and height of a single *frame* rather than using the width and height of the whole image as is currently being done. Frame animation is covered in Hour 14, "Sprite Frame Animation."

Boundary Collision Demo

Let's put the new `Sprite` method to use in an example. This example has four asteroids moving across the screen, and our spaceship pilot must cross the asteroid belt without getting hit by an asteroid. This example is automated—there's no user input. So just watch it run this time. The source code is found within Listing 10.2, while Figure 10.2 shows a screenshot of the program running. When the ship collides with an asteroid, it simply stops until the asteroid goes on by. But to give the ship more survivability, additional intelligence code has to be added.

FIGURE 10.2
The ship tries to dodge asteroids as it crosses the asteroid field.

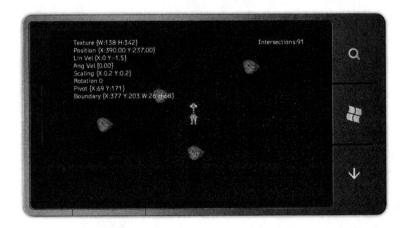

When the demo is completed later in the hour, it will also have dodging capability. If an asteroid is directly above or below the ship when a "grazing" collision occurs, the ship can simply stop to avoid being destroyed. But if an asteroid is coming from the left or right, destruction is imminent! When this happens, the pilot has to use emergency thrusters to quickly move forward to get out of the way of the asteroid. This is also automated, so again, just watch it run, as input is ignored. We'll start by just having the ship stop when a collision occurs, and add the capability to speed up in the section coming up on collision response.

Note that the using statements are included here just to show that GameLibrary must be included (the namespace containing the Sprite class), but they will again be omitted in future listings.

LISTING 10.2   Source code for the boundary collision demo program.

```
using System;
using System.Collections.Generic;
using System.Linq;
using Microsoft.Xna.Framework;
using Microsoft.Xna.Framework.Audio;
using Microsoft.Xna.Framework.Content;
using Microsoft.Xna.Framework.GamerServices;
using Microsoft.Xna.Framework.Graphics;
using Microsoft.Xna.Framework.Input;
using Microsoft.Xna.Framework.Input.Touch;
using Microsoft.Xna.Framework.Media;
using GameLibrary;

namespace Bounding_Box_Collision
{
    public class Game1 : Microsoft.Xna.Framework.Game
    {
        GraphicsDeviceManager graphics;
        SpriteBatch spriteBatch;
        Random rand;
        Viewport screen;
        SpriteFont font;
        Sprite[] asteroids;
        Sprite ship;
        const float SHIP_VEL = -1.5f;
        int collisions = 0;
        int escapes = 0;

        public Game1()
        {
            graphics = new GraphicsDeviceManager(this);
            Content.RootDirectory = "Content";
            TargetElapsedTime = TimeSpan.FromTicks(333333);
        }

        protected override void Initialize()
        {
            base.Initialize();
        }

        protected override void LoadContent()
        {
            spriteBatch = new SpriteBatch(GraphicsDevice);
            screen = GraphicsDevice.Viewport;
            rand = new Random();
            font = Content.Load<SpriteFont>("WascoSans");
```

```
        //create asteroids
        asteroids = new Sprite[4];
        for (int n=0; n<4; n++)
        {
            asteroids[n] = new Sprite(Content, spriteBatch);
            asteroids[n].Load("asteroid");
            asteroids[n].position.Y = (n+1) * 90;
            asteroids[n].position.X = (float)rand.Next(0, 760);
            int factor = rand.Next(2, 12);
            asteroids[n].velocityLinear.X = (float)
                ((double)factor * rand.NextDouble());
        }

        //create ship
        ship = new Sprite(Content, spriteBatch);
        ship.Load("ship");
        ship.position = new Vector2(390, screen.Height);
        ship.scale = 0.2f;
        ship.velocityLinear.Y = SHIP_VEL;
    }

    protected override void Update(GameTime gameTime)
    {
        if (GamePad.GetState(PlayerIndex.One).Buttons.Back ==
            ButtonState.Pressed)
            this.Exit();

        //move asteroids
        foreach (Sprite ast in asteroids)
        {
            ast.Move();
            if (ast.position.X < 0 - ast.image.Width)
                ast.position.X = screen.Width;
            else if (ast.position.X > screen.Width)
                ast.position.X = 0 - ast.image.Width;
        }

        //move ship
        ship.Move();
        if (ship.position.Y < 0)
        {
            ship.position.Y = screen.Height;
            escapes++;
        }

        //look for collision
        int hit = 0;
        foreach (Sprite ast in asteroids)
        {
            if (BoundaryCollision(ship.Boundary(), ast.Boundary()))
            {
                //oh no, asteroid collision is imminent!
                EvasiveManeuver(ast);
                collisions++;
                hit++;
                break;
            }
```

```
            //if no collision, resume course
            if (hit == 0)
                ship.velocityLinear.Y = SHIP_VEL;
        }

        base.Update(gameTime);
    }

    protected override void Draw(GameTime gameTime)
    {
        GraphicsDevice.Clear(Color.CornflowerBlue);
        spriteBatch.Begin();

        foreach (Sprite ast in asteroids)
            ast.Draw();

        ship.Draw();

        string text = "Collisions:" + collisions.ToString();
        spriteBatch.DrawString(font, text, new Vector2(600, 0),
            Color.White);

        text = "Escapes:" + escapes.ToString();
        spriteBatch.DrawString(font, text, new Vector2(600, 25),
            Color.White);

        spriteBatch.DrawString(font, ship.ToString(), new Vector2(0, 0),
            Color.White);

        spriteBatch.End();
        base.Draw(gameTime);
    }

    void EvasiveManeuver(Sprite ast)
    {
        //for now, just stop the ship
        ship.velocityLinear.Y = 0.0f;
    }

    bool BoundaryCollision(Rectangle A, Rectangle B)
    {
        return A.Intersects(B);
    }
    }
}
```

Radial Collision Detection

The term "radial" refers to rays or radii (plural for radius), implying that this form
of collision detection uses the radii of objects. Another common term is "distance" or
"spherical" collision testing. In some cases, a bounding sphere is used to perform 3D
collision testing of meshes in a rendered scene, the 3D version of a bounding circle.
(Likewise, a bounding cube represents the 3D version of rectangular boundary

collision testing.) Although radial collision can be done with an image that has an unbalanced aspect ratio (of width to height), best results will be had when the image has uniform dimensions. The first figure here, Figure 10.3, shows how a bounding circle will not correspond to the image's width and height correctly, and this radius would have to be set manually.

FIGURE 10.3
A bounding circle around a nonsquare image.

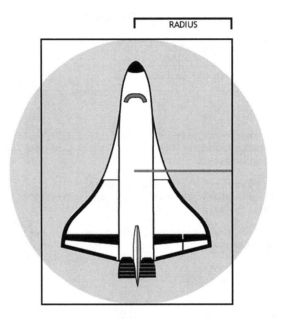

RADIUS

But if the image's width and height are uniform, as illustrated in Figure 10.4, then the width or height of the image can be used for the radius, simplifying everything. The beauty of radial collision testing is that only a single float is needed—the radius, along with a method to calculate the distance between two objects. This illustration also shows the importance of reducing the amount of empty space in an image. The transparent background pixels in this illustration (the area within the box) should be as close to the edges of the visible pixels of the shuttle as possible to improve collision results. The radius and distance factors will never be perfect, so reducing the overall radii of both sprites is often necessary. I have found in testing that 80% produces good results. Due to the shape of some images, reducing the radius by 50% might even be helpful, especially in a high-speed arcade-style game in which the velocity would exceed the collision error anyway.

Here is a method that will be helpful when radial collision detection is being used:

```
bool RadialCollision(Vector2 A, Vector2 B, float radius1, float radius2)
{
    double diffX = A.X - B.X;
```

```
    double diffY = A.Y - B.Y;
    double dist = Math.Sqrt(Math.Pow(diffX, 2) + Math.Pow(diffY, 2));
    return (dist < radius1 + radius2);
}
```

An overload with `Sprite` properties will make using the method even more useful in a game:

```
bool RadialCollision(Sprite A, Sprite B)
{
    float radius1 = A.image.Width / 2;
    float radius2 = B.image.Width / 2;
    return RadialCollision(A.position, B.position, radius1, radius2);
}
```

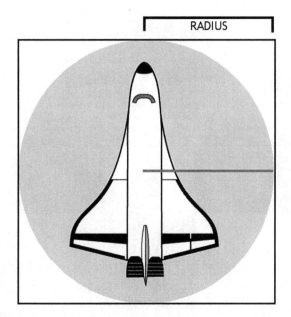

FIGURE 10.4
The bounding circle shows the radius at all points from the center.

To test radial collision, just make a change to the Boundary Collision program so that `RadialCollision()` is called instead of `BoundaryCollision()` in the program's `Update()` method.

Assessing the Damage

We now have two algorithms to test for sprite collisions: boundary and radial. Detecting collisions is the first half of the overall collision-handling code in a game. The second half involves *responding* to the collision event in a meaningful way.

There are as many ways to respond to the collision are there are games in the computer networks of the world—that is, there is no fixed "right" or "wrong" way to do this; it's a matter of gameplay. I will share one rather generic way to respond to collision events by figuring out where the offending sprite is located in relation to the main sprite.

First, we already know that a collision occurred, so this is post-collision response, not predictive response. The question is not whether a collision occurred, but where the offending sprite is located. Remember that the *center* of a sprite represents its position. So if we create four virtual boxes around our main sprite, and then use those to test for collision with the offender, we can get a general idea of where it is located: above, below, left, or right, as Figure 10.5 shows.

FIGURE 10.5
Four collision
response boxes
are used to
quickly deter-
mine colliding
object position.

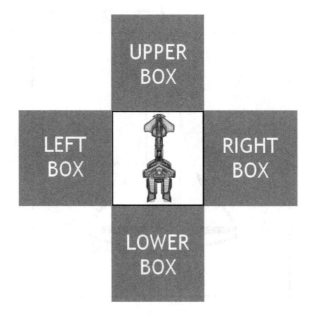

There will be cases in which the offender is within two of these virtual boxes at the same time, but we aren't concerned with perfect results, just a general result that is "good enough" for a game. If you are doing a slow-paced game in which pixel-perfect collision is important, it would be vital to write more precise collision response code, perhaps a combination of boundary and radial collision values hand-coded for each sprite's unique artwork. It might even be helpful to separate appendages into separate sprites and move them in relation to the main body, then perform collision testing on each item of the overall "game object." Figure 10.6 shows a screenshot of the new boundary collision example, which now has some collision-avoidance intelligence built in. The source code for the program is contained in Listing 10.3.

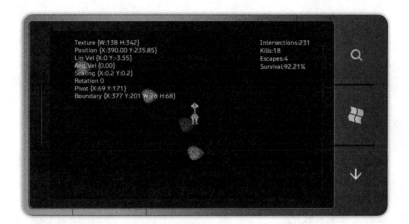

FIGURE 10.6
The ship
now has a
rudimentary
intelligence
to avoid
collisions.

LISTING 10.3   Source code for the *new* boundary collision program with collision-avoidance A.I.

```
public class Game1 : Microsoft.Xna.Framework.Game
{
    GraphicsDeviceManager graphics;
    SpriteBatch spriteBatch;
    Random rand;
    Viewport screen;
    SpriteFont font;
    Sprite[] asteroids;
    Sprite ship;
    int collisions = 0;
    int escapes = 0;
    int kills = 0;
    int hit = 0;
    const float SHIP_VEL = 1.5f;
    const float SHIP_ACCEL = 0.2f;
    const float ESCAPE_VEL = 2.5f;

    public Game1()
    {
        graphics = new GraphicsDeviceManager(this);
        Content.RootDirectory = "Content";
        TargetElapsedTime = TimeSpan.FromTicks(333333);
    }

    protected override void Initialize()
    {
        base.Initialize();
    }

    protected override void LoadContent()
    {
        spriteBatch = new SpriteBatch(GraphicsDevice);
        screen = GraphicsDevice.Viewport;
        rand = new Random();
        font = Content.Load<SpriteFont>("WascoSans");
```

```
//create asteroids
asteroids = new Sprite[4];
for (int n=0; n<4; n++)
{
    asteroids[n] = new Sprite(Content, spriteBatch);
    asteroids[n].Load("asteroid");
    asteroids[n].position.Y = (n+1) * 90;
    asteroids[n].position.X = (float)rand.Next(0, 760);
    int factor = rand.Next(2, 12);
    asteroids[n].velocityLinear.X = (float)
        ((double)factor * rand.NextDouble());
}

//create ship
ship = new Sprite(Content, spriteBatch);
ship.Load("ship");
ship.position = new Vector2(390, screen.Height);
ship.scale = 0.2f;
ship.velocityLinear.Y = -SHIP_VEL;
}

protected override void Update(GameTime gameTime)
{
    if (GamePad.GetState(PlayerIndex.One).Buttons.Back ==
        ButtonState.Pressed)
        this.Exit();

    //move asteroids
    foreach (Sprite ast in asteroids)
    {
        ast.Move();
        if (ast.position.X < 0 - ast.image.Width)
            ast.position.X = screen.Width;
        else if (ast.position.X > screen.Width)
            ast.position.X = 0 - ast.image.Width;
    }

    //move ship
    ship.Move();
    if (ship.position.Y < 0)
    {
        ship.position.Y = screen.Height;
        escapes++;
    }

    //look for collision
    foreach (Sprite ast in asteroids)
    {
        if (RadialCollision(ship, ast))
        {
            //oh no, asteroid collision is imminent!
            EvasiveManeuver(ast);
            collisions++;
            hit++;
        }
    }
```

```
    //accelerate
    if (ship.velocityLinear.Y >= -SHIP_VEL)
    {
        ship.velocityLinear.Y -= SHIP_ACCEL;
        if (ship.velocityLinear.Y < -SHIP_VEL)
            ship.velocityLinear.Y = -SHIP_VEL;
    }
    else if (ship.velocityLinear.Y < SHIP_VEL)
    {
        ship.velocityLinear.Y += SHIP_ACCEL;
        if (ship.velocityLinear.Y > SHIP_VEL)
            ship.velocityLinear.Y = SHIP_VEL;
    }

    base.Update(gameTime);
}

protected override void Draw(GameTime gameTime)
{
    GraphicsDevice.Clear(Color.Black);
    spriteBatch.Begin();

    foreach (Sprite ast in asteroids)
    {
        ast.Draw();
        ast.color = Color.White;
    }

    ship.Draw();

    string text = "Intersections:" + collisions.ToString();
    spriteBatch.DrawString(font, text, new Vector2(600, 0), Color.White);

    text = "Kills:" + kills.ToString();
    spriteBatch.DrawString(font, text, new Vector2(600, 25), Color.White);

    text = "Escapes:" + escapes.ToString();
    spriteBatch.DrawString(font, text, new Vector2(600, 50), Color.White);

    float survival = 100.0f - (100.0f / ((float)collisions
        / (float)kills));
    text = "Survival:" + survival.ToString("N2") + "%";
    spriteBatch.DrawString(font, text, new Vector2(600, 75), Color.White);

    spriteBatch.DrawString(font, ship.ToString(), new Vector2(0, 0),
        Color.White);

    spriteBatch.End();
    base.Draw(gameTime);
}

void EvasiveManeuver(Sprite ast)
{
    ast.color = Color.Red;

    //shortcuts for ship
    int SW = (int)(float)(ship.image.Width * ship.scale);
    int SH = (int)(float)(ship.image.Height * ship.scale);
```

```
        int SX = (int)ship.position.X - SW/2;
        int SY = (int)ship.position.Y - SH/2;

        //create boundary boxes around the ship
        Rectangle[] boxes = new Rectangle[4];
        boxes[0] = ship.Boundary(); //upper
        boxes[0].Y -= SH;
        boxes[1] = ship.Boundary(); //lower
        boxes[1].Y += SH;
        boxes[2] = ship.Boundary(); //left
        boxes[2].X -= SW;
        boxes[3] = ship.Boundary(); //right
        boxes[3].X += SW;

        if (boxes[0].Intersects(ast.Boundary()))
            ship.velocityLinear.Y = SHIP_VEL * ESCAPE_VEL;
        else if (boxes[1].Intersects(ast.Boundary()))
            ship.velocityLinear.Y = -SHIP_VEL * ESCAPE_VEL;
        else if (boxes[2].Intersects(ast.Boundary()))
            ship.velocityLinear.Y = -SHIP_VEL * ESCAPE_VEL;
        else if (boxes[3].Intersects(ast.Boundary()))
            ship.velocityLinear.Y = -SHIP_VEL * ESCAPE_VEL;

        //check for a "kill," intersection with small inner box
        Rectangle kill = ship.Boundary();
        int shrinkh = kill.Width / 4;
        int shrinkv = kill.Height / 4;
        kill.Inflate(-shrinkh, -shrinkv);
        if (kill.Intersects(ast.Boundary()))
            kills++;
    }

    bool BoundaryCollision(Rectangle A, Rectangle B)
    {
        return A.Intersects(B);
    }

    bool RadialCollision(Sprite A, Sprite B)
    {
        float radius1 = A.image.Width / 2;
        float radius2 = B.image.Width / 2;
        return RadialCollision(A.position, B.position, radius1, radius2);
    }

    bool RadialCollision(Vector2 A, Vector2 B, float radius1, float radius2)
    {
        double diffX = A.X - B.X;
        double diffY = A.Y - B.Y;
        double dist = Math.Sqrt(Math.Pow(diffX, 2) + Math.Pow(diffY, 2));
        return (dist < radius1 + radius2);
    }
}
```

This is perhaps our longest sample program so far, even taking into account that that Sprite class is now found in a different source code file. Game A.I. is a challenging subject. By studying the way the algorithm responds to asteroid collisions, you could use this technique for any number of game scenarios to improve gameplay and/or increase the difficulty by making your A.I. sprites more intelligent.

Summary

We learned about collision detection via boundary and radial collision methods, and used these algorithms to study collision response in gameplay code. When a collision algorithm is available, it really opens up our ability to make a game for the first time. As we saw in the final example of this hour, the level of response to collisions can be basic or advanced, rudimentary or quite intelligent, as the spaceship in this example demonstrated.

Q&A

Q. *The A.I. code does not always get the ship completely out of the way of an asteroid. Is there a way to fine-tune the collision response code so that it never gets hit?*

A. Actually, no; because there are several asteroid sprites on the screen, moving at different velocities, it's not possible to make perfect predictions. But if the algorithm were to look *left* and *right* as well as *up* and *down*, it might be possible to improve the dodging capability of the sprite.

Q. *The statistical numbers on the top right in the demo are interesting. Would it be possible to add more ships and have them compete to see which one gets across the screen without getting destroyed, or perhaps play against the player?*

A. Absolutely! This is another example of gameplay that could be adapted for a real game with player input.

Workshop

Quiz

1. What shape is involved in bounding rectangle collision detection?
2. What shape is involved in radial collision detection?
3. What XNA function makes radial collision detection possible?

Answers

1. Rectangle

2. Circle

3. None; we had to calculate distance on our own!

Exercises

While watching the ship speed up, slow down, or go into reverse in response to the asteroid collisions, did you think of any ways to improve the intelligence of the asteroid-avoidance algorithm? I think adding response boxes to the four corners (in addition to the boxes in the four facing directions) would dramatically improve the response of the ship. Going from four to eight response boxes would prevent the ship from "stuttering" when an asteroid comes up from the side and the ship responds; then the asteroid triggers the upper or lower box. With boxes added to the corners, an immediate forward or backward response could be programmed into the program, greatly increasing the survival rate. See what you can do to improve survival with your own ideas!

A second exercise might be more interesting if you prefer a more active game, and less of a passive demo. Instead of improving the A.I., add user input support to make this a game instead of just a demo.

HOUR 11

Managing Lots of Sprites

What You'll Learn in This Hour:

- ▶ Robot trash collectors
- ▶ Building the example
- ▶ Simulating group dynamics

We have developed a lot of capabilities within the realm of sprite programming up to this point, but we still have quite a bit more work to do before attempting to create a serious game. At this point, you have learned more than enough to make a *simple* game. That wouldn't be a problem at this point, and if you wanted to take a break now, as we near the halfway point in the book, to work on a simple game of your own design, now would be a good time to practice your skills up to this point.

We are going to learn about managing a large number of game objects, represented as sprites in this case. Some use the term *entities* to refer to a game object, so we would be working with an *entity manager* in that case. Although every game will be programmed differently to meet its design goals, there are some common programming patterns that tend to emerge in every game, no matter whether it's as simple as Pong or as complex as World of Warcraft. These patterns are so common that they were collected into game libraries in the early years of game development, and later into what are today called *game engines*. We don't have time to build a game engine for Windows Phone, but we can at least dabble in it and learn how a large number of game objects can be managed efficiently.

Robot Trash Collectors

Our example in this hour is a simulation of robot trash collectors. The robots are represented as white circles, and the trash items as red squares. The robot cleaners will look for the closest trash item and move toward it, getting rid of the trash when it is touched. Figure 11.1 shows the simulation running with just one robot.

FIGURE 11.1
Simulation of
robotic trash
collectors with
population
control A.I.

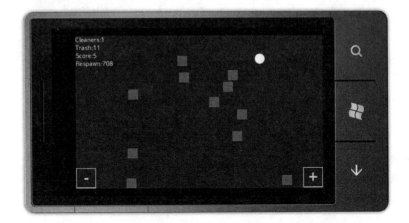

To make the simulation more interesting, it has the capability to automatically manage the amount of trash produced based on the number of cleaners present. A minus button at the bottom left removes cleaners, and its complementary plus button at the lower right adds new cleaners. As long as there is trash remaining, new trash is added rather slowly. But if the number of cleaners increases and the trash goes down, more trash is added more quickly to keep the cleaners busy. Figure 11.2 shows the simulation with five cleaners. Note the respawn time.

FIGURE 11.2
Five robot
cleaners are
present, which
increases the
trash rate.

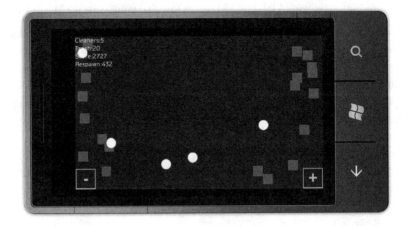

An algorithm of two trash items to one robot cleaner is used to adjust the speed. If there is fewer than twice the number of trash items compared to the cleaners, the speed is increased (by speeding up the respawn time). By watching the simulation run over time, you can see that a balance is maintained as long as the numbers are reasonable. Adding up to 100 or more robot cleaners causes the trash production to shift into high gear to keep up! See Figure 11.3 for an example.

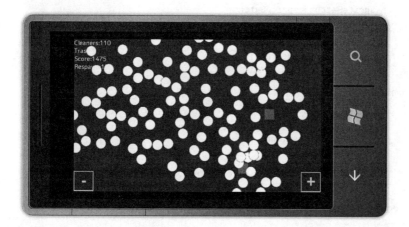

FIGURE 11.3
The robot cleaner population is out of control!

> Don't let the primitive artwork dissuade you from studying the example in this hour. The code shared here will be extremely valuable in your own future game projects.

By the Way

Building the Example

The simulation project this hour has a few asset requirements that you can source from the resource files for this hour, or just make yourself. The button image is just a 64×64 square. The robots are represented by a 32×32 white circle with alpha transparency around the edges. The trash is represented by a 32×32 red square. You are free to use different images if you want, perhaps even little robot and trash images! You can also change the theme of the art; how about insects and food?

Button Class

A helper class is needed to handle the buttons used to increase and decrease the number of robots. The Button class (see Listing 11.1) inherits from Sprite, so it will have all of Sprite's capabilities and then some.

LISTING 11.1 Source Code for the Button Class

```
public class Button : Sprite
{
    public string text;
    private SpriteBatch p_spriteBatch;
    private SpriteFont p_font;
```

```
public Button(ContentManager content, SpriteBatch spriteBatch,
    SpriteFont font) :
    base(content, spriteBatch)
{
    p_spriteBatch = spriteBatch;
    p_font = font;
    Load("button");
    text = "";
    color = Color.LightGreen;
}

public void Draw()
{
    base.Draw();
    Vector2 size = p_font.MeasureString(text);
    Vector2 pos = position;
    pos.X -= size.X / 2;
    pos.Y -= size.Y / 2;
    p_spriteBatch.DrawString(p_font, text, pos, color);
}

public bool Tapped(Vector2 pos)
{
    Rectangle rect = new Rectangle((int)pos.X, (int)pos.Y, 1, 1);
    return Boundary().Intersects(rect);
}
}
}
```

As you can see from the code, a constructor requires ContentManager and SpriteBatch parameters (which are just passed directly to the Sprite constructor), as well as a third parameter, SpriteFont, so that the button can print text on its own. Draw() calculates the size of the text and tries to center it. The font being used in this example is Wasco Sans Bold 36-point, but you are welcome to use a different font if you want. The Tapped() method receives as a parameter the position of a click/tap and checks to see whether it (the button) was tapped, returning true or false.

> This Button class is covered in more detail, along with several more classes, in the "GUI hour"—look forward to Hour 20, "Creating a Graphical User Interface."

Main Source Code

Listing 11.2 contains the main source code for the Entity Grouping Demo program. We'll go over the new helper methods after this.

LISTING 11.2   Source Code for the Entity Grouping Demo Program

```
public class Game1 : Microsoft.Xna.Framework.Game
{
    GraphicsDeviceManager graphics;
    SpriteBatch spriteBatch;
    TouchLocation oldTouch;
    Random rand;
    SpriteFont font, buttonFont;
```

```
Button plus, minus;
List<Sprite> cleaners;
Texture2D circleImage;
List<Sprite> trash;
Texture2D trashImage;
int lastTime = 0;
int target = -1;
int respawn = 500;
int score = 0;

public Game1()
{
    graphics = new GraphicsDeviceManager(this);
    Content.RootDirectory = "Content";
    TargetElapsedTime = TimeSpan.FromTicks(333333);
    oldTouch = new TouchLocation();
}

protected override void Initialize()
{
    base.Initialize();
}

protected override void LoadContent()
{
    rand = new Random();
    spriteBatch = new SpriteBatch(GraphicsDevice);
    font = Content.Load<SpriteFont>("WascoSans");
    buttonFont = Content.Load<SpriteFont>("ButtonFont");

    //create minus button
    minus = new Button(Content, spriteBatch, buttonFont);
    minus.position = new Vector2(32, 480-32);
    minus.text = "-";

    //create plus button
    plus = new Button(Content, spriteBatch, buttonFont);
    plus.position = new Vector2(800 - 32, 480 - 32);
    plus.text = "+";

    //create cleaners group
    cleaners = new List<Sprite>();
    circleImage = Content.Load<Texture2D>("circle");
    AddCleaner();

    //create trash group
    trash = new List<Sprite>();
    trashImage = Content.Load<Texture2D>("trash");
    AddTrash();
}

protected override void Update(GameTime gameTime)
{
    if (GamePad.GetState(PlayerIndex.One).Buttons.Back ==
        ButtonState.Pressed)
        this.Exit();

    //get state of touch input
    TouchCollection touchInput = TouchPanel.GetState();
```

```
if (touchInput.Count > 0)
{
    TouchLocation touch = touchInput[0];

    if (touch.State == TouchLocationState.Pressed &&
        oldTouch.State == TouchLocationState.Released)
    {
        if (minus.Tapped(touch.Position))
            RemoveCleaner();
        if (plus.Tapped(touch.Position))
            AddCleaner();
    }
    oldTouch = touch;
}

//add new trash item periodically
if ((int)gameTime.TotalGameTime.TotalMilliseconds >
    lastTime + respawn)
{
    lastTime = (int)gameTime.TotalGameTime.TotalMilliseconds;
    AddTrash();
}

if (trash.Count > cleaners.Count * 2)
{
    respawn += 1;
    if (respawn > 1000)
        respawn = 1000;
}
else
{
    respawn -= 1;
    if (respawn < 10)
        respawn = 10;
}

//move the cleaners
for (int n = 0; n < cleaners.Count; n++)
{
    //find trash to pick up
    target = FindNearestTrash(cleaners[n].position);
    if (target > -1)
    {
        float angle = TargetAngle(cleaners[n].position,
            trash[target].position);
        cleaners[n].velocityLinear = Velocity(angle, 2.0f);
        cleaners[n].Move();
    }

    //look for collision with trash
    CollectTrash(cleaners[n].position);

    //look for collision with other cleaners
    for (int c = 0; c < cleaners.Count; c++)
    {
        if (n != c)
        {
```

```
                while (cleaners[n].Boundary().Intersects(
                    cleaners[c].Boundary()))
                {
                    cleaners[c].velocityLinear.X += 0.001f;
                    cleaners[c].velocityLinear.Y += 0.001f;
                    cleaners[c].Move();
                }
            }
        }
    }

    base.Update(gameTime);
}

protected override void Draw(GameTime gameTime)
{
    GraphicsDevice.Clear(Color.DarkBlue);
    spriteBatch.Begin();

    minus.Draw();
    plus.Draw();

    foreach (Sprite spr in trash)
        spr.Draw();

    foreach (Sprite spr in cleaners)
        spr.Draw();

    spriteBatch.DrawString(font,
        "Cleaners:"+cleaners.Count.ToString(),
        Vector2.Zero, Color.White);
    spriteBatch.DrawString(font, "Trash:"+trash.Count.ToString(),
        new Vector2(0,25), Color.White);
    spriteBatch.DrawString(font, "Score:" + score.ToString(),
        new Vector2(0, 50), Color.White);
    spriteBatch.DrawString(font, "Respawn:" + respawn.ToString(),
        new Vector2(0, 75), Color.White);

    spriteBatch.End();
    base.Draw(gameTime);
}
```

Main Simulation Functionality Code

The "meat and potatoes" code that drives the simulation is coming up next, in
Listing 11.3. Here we find helper methods that look for the nearest trash items, move
the robots toward the trash, add new robots, remove robots, and calculate distance
and velocity. Some of these methods, like AddCleaner() and RemoveCleaner(),
could have been just coded directly where they are called in the program, but this
approach is *much* cleaner and reusable.

LISTING 11.3   Entity Grouping Demo Program (Continued)

```
void RemoveCleaner()
{
    if (cleaners.Count > 0)
        cleaners.RemoveAt(0);
}

    void AddCleaner()
    {
        Sprite obj = new Sprite(Content, spriteBatch);
        obj.image = circleImage;
        obj.position = new Vector2((float)rand.Next(0, 760),
            (float)rand.Next(0, 450));
        cleaners.Add(obj);
    }

    void AddTrash()
    {
        Sprite obj = new Sprite(Content, spriteBatch);
        obj.image = trashImage;
        obj.position = new Vector2((float)rand.Next(0, 760),
            (float)rand.Next(0, 450));
        trash.Add(obj);
    }

    int FindNearestTrash(Vector2 pos)
    {
        int target = -1;
        float closest = 9999;

        if (trash.Count == 0) return -1;

        for (int n = 0; n < trash.Count; n++)
        {
            float dist = Distance(pos, trash[n].position);
            if (dist < closest)
            {
                closest = dist;
                target = n;
            }
        }
        return target;
    }

    void CollectTrash(Vector2 pos)
    {
        if (trash.Count == 0) return;

        for (int n = 0; n < trash.Count; n++)
        {
            float dist = Distance(pos, trash[n].position);
            if (dist < 8)
            {
                score++;
                trash.RemoveAt(n);
                break;
            }
        }
    }
```

```
float Distance(Vector2 A, Vector2 B)
{
    double diffX = A.X - B.X;
    double diffY = A.Y - B.Y;
    double dist = Math.Sqrt(Math.Pow(diffX, 2) + Math.Pow(diffY, 2));
    return (float)dist;
}

float TargetAngle(Vector2 p1, Vector2 p2)
{
    return TargetAngle(p1.X, p1.Y, p2.X, p2.Y);
}

float TargetAngle(double x1, double y1, double x2, double y2)
{
    double deltaX = (x2 - x1);
    double deltaY = (y2 - y1);
    return (float)Math.Atan2(deltaY, deltaX);
}

Vector2 Velocity(float angle, float acceleration)
{
    double x = Math.Cos(angle) * acceleration;
    double y = Math.Sin(angle) * acceleration;
    return new Vector2((float)x, (float)y);
}
}
```

Simulating Group Dynamics

The key to this simulation example is a pair of linked lists called *cleaners* and *trash*. A linked list is a managed collection for a single type of data, like our Sprite class. In C#, the list is defined with the data type (Sprite) as a template in brackets:

```
List<Sprite> cleaners;
```

The list is created in LoadContent():

```
cleaners = new List<Sprite>();
```

At this point, the list is ready to be filled with Sprite objects. Each object is a separate, complete Sprite object with its own properties and methods. A new object is added to the list with the Add() method. This code creates a new Sprite object and adds it to the list:

```
Sprite sprite = new Sprite(Content, spriteBatch);
sprite.position = new Vector2(0, 0);
cleaners.Add(sprite);
```

Testing revealed that the simulation locks up when there are more than about 250 robots, at which point it is difficult to click the minus button to reduce the population.

Watch Out!

You can add as many objects to the list as you want, using a for loop, or by reading data in from a level file, or by any other means, and the list will grow as needed to contain all the objects being added. When objects have been added to the list, they can be forgotten to a certain degree. It's up to *us* to make sure we can identify each object inside the list later if we want to use a specific object. For instance, if all the objects for a game are stored in a list like this, and you want to highlight the player's character, then there must be a way to uniquely identify that sprite among all the others. This can be done by adding an identifier to the Sprite class, such as an ID number or name string. We aren't doing that in this simulation because every object has equal treatment.

Using List Objects

There will be at least two different points where all the objects in the list must be accessed—from Update() and Draw(). That is, again, the very least number of times, while you might need to access the list elsewhere to test for collisions or for other purposes. There are two ways to iterate the list, using a for loop or using a foreach iterator.

A property of List provides the number of items it contains, called Count. For example:

```
for (int n = 0; n < cleaners.Count; n++)
{
    //reference cleaners[n]
}
```

Another way to access a list is with a foreach loop such as this:

```
foreach (Sprite sprite in cleaners)
{
    //reference sprite
}
```

▼   **Try It Yourself**

Creating and Using a List

A List is like an array, but it is much easier to use. Let's learn how to create a List container for other objects.

1. Define the new List variable in the program's global variables section. In the brackets, you will define the type of data that the List will contain— which can be *anything*, such as Sprite or int or string.

   ```
   List<string> groceries;
   ```

2. Create or initialize the `List` variable, again with the data type in brackets. Plus, don't forget the parentheses at the end! The parentheses mean this is a function—or rather, method—call, the constructor method to be precise.

```
groceries = new List<string>();
```

3. Add items to the list like so:

```
groceries.Add("butter");
groceries.Add("milk");
groceries.Add("bread");
```

4. Access the items in the list using either a `for` loop with the `groceries.count` property, or a `foreach` loop with the `groceries` object.

```
foreach (string item in groceries)
{
    // ... do something with the item here
}
```

Iteration Techniques Compared

There are distinct advantages to both iteration mechanisms, depending on programming needs. The numeric `for` loop is helpful when you want to find the index position of a certain object in the list and then reference it later with indexers (`[ ]`). For instance, you might keep track of a "clicked" object with a number variable, and then just index inside the list with that variable, like so:

```
cleaners[clicked].Move();
```

The `foreach` loop is easier to use if you just want to do a quick update of every object, and is commonly used to update the position or draw the object. Of course, there are many other purposes for a `foreach` iteration, and this is just one example. In the simulation project, all the robot cleaners are drawn with just two lines of code:

```
foreach (Sprite spr in cleaners)
    spr.Draw();
```

> Very complex-*appearing* A.I. behaviors can seem to derive from surprisingly simple algorithms. When it comes down to analysis, simple rules determine human behavior in social environments too!

Did you Know?

But in another part of the project, an index `for` loop is used to find the nearest trash. This snippet of code from the `FindNearestTrash()` method looks for the closest trash item by calculating the distance to every item in the trash list, keeping track of the *index* of the closest one with an `int` variable called `closest`. That specific `trash` item can then be found by indexing into `trash` with the variable.

```
for (int n = 0; n < trash.Count; n++)
{
    float dist = Distance(pos, trash[n].position);
    if (dist < closest)
    {
        closest = dist;
        target = n;
    }
}
```

That's all there is to it! In the final analysis, we use the distance calculation for many, many things in an ordinary video game!

Summary

This hour was primarily concerned with creating a group of sprites in order to update and draw them as a group. While studying that basic premise for the hour, we developed an interesting simulation with ramifications for game A.I. that can be studied and improved on. The basic code presented in this hour is found at the core of most game engines in one form or another.

Q&A

Q. *Would it be possible to cause the "robots" in the game to collide with each other rather than just moving over the top of each other?*

A. Yes, that can be done, but it adds a strain to the program due to the way in which many robots will head toward a single trash item. An interesting modification might be to cause the robots to go after only the trash that is not already being targeted.

Q. *Can the simple white circles and red boxes be replaced with better artwork?*

A. Yes indeed. Just look at the circle.png and trash.png files and replace them with your own. But I recommend keeping the size of each image at 32×32 pixels.

Workshop

Quiz

1. How do we determine when two objects are close to each other?

2. What XNA function do we use in order to move one object toward another?

3. How do we determine when two objects are touching?

Answers

1. By using the `Distance()` function

2. `Math.Atan2()`

3. By using collision detection

Exercises

The simulation produces some interesting results when robot cleaners collide with each other. Perusing the code reveals a `while` loop that causes one robot to jump out of the way when it collides with another, to quickly resolve collision problems. Try removing this code so that robots can collide with each other without incident, and run the simulation to see what happens. What eventually happens to most or all of the robot sprites?

HOUR 12

Sprite Color Animation

What You'll Learn in This Hour:

- ▶ **Base animation**
- ▶ **The main animation class**
- ▶ **Color animation**
- ▶ **Solid color animation**
- ▶ **Color cycling**
- ▶ **Color bouncing**

Color animation is a subject not often addressed, possibly because the possibilities
are not often given much attention in the design of a game, or the designer is not
aware of the value of this technique. Animating color refers to cycling the colors in
a game object to produce interesting special effects. The simplest example is a game
object that fades out of existence, perhaps the *only* color animation that has truly
seen widespread use over the years to represent an object that is going away or has
been *killed* or *removed*, depending on the theme of the game. The capabilities of
SpriteBatch include the capability to draw a texture with any RGBA color, and any
component (red, green, blue, alpha) of the color can be changed at any time. The
trick is to learn how to transform the colors based on time at a desired rate, and
then to define properties for the animation that cause it to flip-flop back and forth,
wrap around (to create a "blink" effect), follow a sine wave pattern, and so forth.
We will study these possibilities with sample code and write a base Animation class
that will work with Sprite and transform animation in the next hour. This will give
you solid exposure to a very good example of object-oriented programming.

Getting Started with Color Animation

We will begin with a new Animation class that can transform the color of a sprite as
the first "visual" form of animation. Basic transforms will be added in the following

hour to this new class so that translation, rotation, scaling, and velocity can be used as animation parameters. Then, the `Animation` class will be expanded further in Hour 14, "Sprite Frame Animation," to include frame animation based on custom artwork.

The first important point to consider when building an animation system that works *with* the `Sprite` class *without* infiltrating the `Sprite` class—that is, without mucking it up—is to design the animation system in such a way that *transform* or *change values* are used, not the internal properties of `Sprite`. Animation will be a *passive*, nonintrusive helper for `Sprite`, producing transform values that can be used or ignored, as the programmer sees fit. Animation can be integrated inside `Sprite`, or one or more animations can be applied to a sprite in the main program code instead.

The second significant aspect to this animation system is that animation applied to a sprite will not be permanent. A single animation is processed to a conclusion and then removed. What this allows us to do is write "fire and forget" animation code by setting up an animation event, turning it on, and then just watching it work. When completed, the animation object is deleted. Now, it's perfectly fine if you *want* an animation to continue. *You* have control over when and where the animating property is set to `false` (which will cause it to be removed). To make this work in such a "fire and forget" manner, the `Sprite` class will need to be able to handle more than one animation at a time. This calls for a *managed list*.

The Main Animation Class

The primary or base `Animation` class, from which all "functional" animation subclasses will be derived, must have certain methods in place for modifying properties within `Sprite`. If we want to animate the color, a `ModifyColor()` method must be included. If we want to animate the scale, a `ModifyScale()` method is required. There really aren't very many such methods needed in the base `Animation` class, because we need to animate only things that will affect a sprite's appearance or behavior. Remember, our `Sprite` class already has the capability to perform transforms (changing the position, rotation, and scaling). Although it is possible to animate the basic transform properties in `Sprite`, that will be rare. Nevertheless, we still must give the programmer the ability to animate the transforms. Listing 12.1 contains our base `Animation` class.

LISTING 12.1 Animation Class Source Code

```
public class Animation
{
    public bool animating;

    public Animation()
```

```
    {
        animating = false;
    }

    public virtual void Update()
    {
    }

    public virtual Color ModifyColor(Color original)
    {
        return original;
    }

    public virtual Vector2 ModifyPosition(Vector2 original)
    {
        return original;
    }

    public virtual float ModifyRotation(float original)
    {
        return original;
    }

    public virtual float ModifyScale(float original)
    {
        return original;
    }
}
```

Using Animation as a Base Class

Note how the methods in Animation return the passed parameter. This is a default behavior that will just perpetuate any properties that are not modified by a subclass. For instance, if we are doing just color animation, and not changing rotation or any other property, then rotation is completely ignored by the subclass and will have no effect on the animation being processed. We will look at some basic examples of transform animations later in the hour.

A subclass of Animation should override at least one of the ModifyXXX() methods in order to do something useful. Unless at least one of them is modified, no animation will occur and the class will essentially do nothing. On the flip side, more than one type of animation can be performed by the same class! Suppose you want a sprite to move back and forth on the screen while rotating and scaling—this animation system can handle that task. The sprite can then be used for collision testing, and all other aspects of sprite behavior remain intact! Perhaps the simplest functional subclass of Animation might look like this:

```
public class AnimationTemplate : Animation
{
    public AnimationTemplate()
        : base()
```

```
    {
    }

    public void Update()
    {
    }
}
```

You can use this as a template for your own custom animations. Just override any of the Modify*XXX*() methods (such as ModifyColor()) to modify the properties you want to affect a sprite's behavior. The Update() method can be used for general-purpose processing. In the next two hours, we will use Update() as a general-purpose "pump" or "motor" for frame animation and transforms. Note that you can also add any variables you need to your Animation subclass. You can also override the parameter list of the modification methods to produce custom results (such as custom subsets of an existing animation).

Modifications to the `Sprite` Class

The Sprite class will need a few changes to support animation. First, there's the addition of the Animation variable as a private:

```
private Animation p_animation;
```

Next, there's initialization of the variable in the Sprite constructor:

```
p_animation = null;
```

And next, we need a method to set the current animation. We will eventually replace this with a List and support more than one animation at a time, but for now we'll start with first things first!

```
public void SetAnimation(Animation animation)
{
    p_animation = animation;
}
```

Finally, we need a new method to get animation up and running! The following Animate() method will evolve quite a bit over the next two chapters. At this point, we need to work with only one type of animation (color cycling).

```
public void Animate()
{
    if (p_animation != null)
    {
        if (p_animation.animating)
        {
```

```
            this.color = p_animation.ModifyColor(this.color);
        }
    }
}
```

Color Animation

Color animation begins with a solid color that can then be transformed by manipulating the color components (red, green, blue, and alpha). We'll see how to write a basic solid-color class to begin experimenting with color animation before getting into color cycling.

Solid Colors

A solid-color "animation" might seem contradictory, but there actually is a very good use for such a thing. Although it is true that a sprite can be drawn in any desired color, that often requires additional global variables because the `Sprite` class does not keep track of color changes, just the `color` property. To change the color on the fly while a game is running would require globals to keep track of the colors and a conditional variable used to trigger the color change. We can do this more easily with a subclass of `Animation` that works with solid colors.

Let's begin with Listing 12.2, the source code to the new `SolidColor` class, which inherits from `Animation`. There's very little to this class, which makes it a good starting point for our study of color animation coming up.

LISTING 12.2 Source Code for the SolidColor Class

```
public class SolidColor : Animation
{
    public Color color;

    public SolidColor(Color color)
        : base()
    {
        this.color = color;
        animating = true;
    }

    public override Color ModifyColor(Color original)
    {
        return color;
    }
}
```

The Solid Color project is part of the Color Animation Demo solution included with this hour (several projects in the solution share a common content project for convenience). To run this specific project in the solution, right-click the project name and select Debug, Start New Instance. In this manner, any project in a larger solution can be debugged, while F5 will try to run the currently "active" project. Figure 12.1 shows the program running. There are three boxes that move on the screen, and they change color anytime they hit the edge. Simple as that! The source code to the project is found in Listing 12.3.

FIGURE 12.1
Solid color transform as a form of "animation."

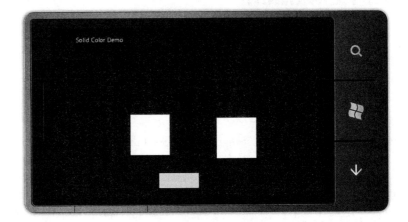

LISTING 12.3   Source Code for the Solid Color Project

```
public class Game1 : Microsoft.Xna.Framework.Game
{
    GraphicsDeviceManager graphics;
    SpriteBatch spriteBatch;
    Random rand;
    SpriteFont font;
    Texture2D shapeImage;
    List<Sprite> shapes;

    public Game1()
    {
        graphics = new GraphicsDeviceManager(this);
        Content.RootDirectory = "Content";
        TargetElapsedTime = TimeSpan.FromTicks(333333);
    }

    protected override void Initialize()
    {
        base.Initialize();
    }

    protected override void LoadContent()
    {
        rand = new Random();
        spriteBatch = new SpriteBatch(GraphicsDevice);
        font = Content.Load<SpriteFont>("WascoSans");

        shapeImage = Content.Load<Texture2D>("box");
```

```
        Sprite box1 = new Sprite(Content, spriteBatch);
        box1.image = shapeImage;
        box1.position = new Vector2(rand.Next(0, 200), rand.Next(0, 380));
        box1.velocityLinear = new Vector2(4.0f, 3.0f);
        box1.origin = new Vector2(64, 64);
        box1.SetAnimation(null);

        Sprite box2 = new Sprite(Content, spriteBatch);
        box2.image = shapeImage;
        box2.position = new Vector2(rand.Next(200, 400), rand.Next(0, 380));
        box2.velocityLinear = new Vector2(4.0f, 3.0f);
        box2.origin = new Vector2(64, 64);
        box2.SetAnimation(null);

        Sprite box3 = new Sprite(Content, spriteBatch);
        box3.image = shapeImage;
        box3.position = new Vector2(rand.Next(400, 600), rand.Next(0, 380));
        box3.velocityLinear = new Vector2(4.0f, 3.0f);
        box3.origin = new Vector2(64, 64);
        box3.SetAnimation(null);

        shapes = new List<Sprite>();
        shapes.Add(box1);
        shapes.Add(box2);
        shapes.Add(box3);
    }

    protected override void Update(GameTime gameTime)
    {
        if (GamePad.GetState(PlayerIndex.One).Buttons.Back ==
            ButtonState.Pressed)
            this.Exit();

        foreach (Sprite spr in shapes)
        {
            spr.Move();

            if (spr.position.X < 0 || spr.position.X > 800 ||
                spr.position.Y < 0 || spr.position.Y > 480)
            {
                spr.SetAnimation(new SolidColor(
                    new Color(rand.Next(255), rand.Next(255),
                        rand.Next(255))));

                if (spr.position.X < -64 || spr.position.X > 800+64)
                    spr.velocityLinear.X *= -1;

                if (spr.position.Y < -64 || spr.position.Y > 480+64)
                    spr.velocityLinear.Y *= -1;
            }
            else
                spr.SetAnimation(new SolidColor(Color.White));
        }

        base.Update(gameTime);
    }
```

```
protected override void Draw(GameTime gameTime)
{
    GraphicsDevice.Clear(Color.Black);
    spriteBatch.Begin();

    foreach (Sprite spr in shapes)
    {
        spr.Animate();
        spr.Draw();
    }

    spriteBatch.DrawString(font, "Solid Color Demo",
        new Vector2(0, 0), Color.White);

    spriteBatch.End();
    base.Draw(gameTime);
}
}
```

Color Cycling

One common color animation involves cycling a color within a range and either
going back and forth between two limits or wrapping around in either direction. A
base CycleColor class will help us get started and then we can write subclasses
from it to do specific color movements. The source code is found in Listing 12.4.

LISTING 12.4   Source Code for the CycleColor Class

```
public class CycleColor : Animation
{
    public int red, green, blue, alpha;

    public CycleColor(int red, int green, int blue, int alpha)
        : base()
    {
        this.red = red;
        this.green = green;
        this.blue = blue;
        this.alpha = alpha;
        animating = true;
    }

    public override Color ModifyColor(Color original)
    {
        Color modified = original;

        if (animating)
        {
            int R = original.R + red;
            int G = original.G + green;
            int B = original.B + blue;
            int A = original.A + alpha;
```

```
        if (R < 0 || R > 255 || G < 0 || G > 255 || B < 0 || B > 255
            || A < 0 || A > 255)
        {
            animating = false;
        }
        modified = new Color(R, G, B, A);
    }
    return modified;
}
}
```

This class will cycle a color from its original values upward or downward based on the color cycling modifiers passed to the CycleColor() constructor until the range is exceeded, at which point animation stops. The modifiers will usually be +1 or -1 for each color component, unless faster color cycling is desired. Let's test it with a quick sample program called Cycle Color Animation (see Listing 12.5).

Three boxes are added: colored red, green, and blue. The boxes fade completely to black based on the CycleColor class's properties, but if different colors were used for each one, they would not fade completely to black, but would just modify the color components to produce different color results. Setting the initial conditions (such as original color) does have an effect and should be considered ahead of time. In the combined Visual Studio solution for this hour, this project is called Cycle Color Animation, and is shown in Figure 12.2.

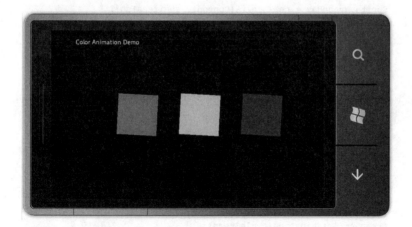

FIGURE 12.2
Demonstrating color cycling with three rotating boxes of different colors.

LISTING 12.5   Source Code to the Cycle Color Animation Project

```
public class Game1 : Microsoft.Xna.Framework.Game
{
    GraphicsDeviceManager graphics;
    SpriteBatch spriteBatch;
    TouchLocation oldTouch;
```

```
SpriteFont font;
Texture2D shapeImage;
List<Sprite> shapes;
CycleColor cycleRed, cycleGreen, cycleBlue;

public Game1()
{
    graphics = new GraphicsDeviceManager(this);
    Content.RootDirectory = "Content";
    TargetElapsedTime = TimeSpan.FromTicks(333333);
}

protected override void Initialize()
{
    base.Initialize();
}

protected override void LoadContent()
{
    spriteBatch = new SpriteBatch(GraphicsDevice);
    font = Content.Load<SpriteFont>("WascoSans");

    shapeImage = Content.Load<Texture2D>("box");

    Sprite redBox = new Sprite(Content, spriteBatch);
    redBox.image = shapeImage;
    redBox.position = new Vector2(200, 240);
    redBox.origin = new Vector2(64, 64);
    redBox.velocityAngular = 0.05f;
    redBox.color = new Color(255, 0, 0);

    Sprite greenBox = new Sprite(Content, spriteBatch);
    greenBox.image = shapeImage;
    greenBox.position = new Vector2(400, 240);
    greenBox.origin = new Vector2(64, 64);
    greenBox.velocityAngular = 0.05f;
    greenBox.color = new Color(0, 255, 0);

    Sprite blueBox = new Sprite(Content, spriteBatch);
    blueBox.image = shapeImage;
    blueBox.position = new Vector2(600, 240);
    blueBox.origin = new Vector2(64, 64);
    blueBox.velocityAngular = 0.05f;
    blueBox.color = new Color(0, 0, 255);

    cycleRed = new CycleColor(-1, 0, 0, 0);
    redBox.SetAnimation(cycleRed);

    cycleGreen = new CycleColor(0, -1, 0, 0);
    greenBox.SetAnimation(cycleGreen);

    cycleBlue = new CycleColor(0, 0, -1, 0);
    blueBox.SetAnimation(cycleBlue);

    shapes = new List<Sprite>();
    shapes.Add(redBox);
```

```csharp
        shapes.Add(greenBox);
        shapes.Add(blueBox);
    }

    protected override void Update(GameTime gameTime)
    {
        if (GamePad.GetState(PlayerIndex.One).Buttons.Back ==
            ButtonState.Pressed)
            this.Exit();

        foreach (Sprite spr in shapes)
        {
            spr.Rotate();
            spr.Move();
        }

        if (!cycleBlue.animating)
        {
            cycleBlue.blue *= -1;
            cycleBlue.animating = true;
        }

        if (!cycleGreen.animating)
        {
            cycleGreen.green *= -1;
            cycleGreen.animating = true;
        }

        if (!cycleRed.animating)
        {
            cycleRed.red *= -1;
            cycleRed.animating = true;
        }

        base.Update(gameTime);
    }

    protected override void Draw(GameTime gameTime)
    {
        GraphicsDevice.Clear(Color.Black);
        spriteBatch.Begin();

        foreach (Sprite spr in shapes)
        {
            spr.Animate();
            spr.Draw();
        }

        spriteBatch.DrawString(font, "Color Animation Demo",
            new Vector2(0, 0), Color.White);

        spriteBatch.End();
        base.Draw(gameTime);
    }
}
```

The examples in this hour are combined into a single Visual Studio solution so that they can all share the same content (a single white box image). To run a specific project in a combined solution, right-click the project and use Debug, Start New Instance. Optionally, you can highlight any one of the projects, set it as the Active Project, and then press F5 to run it.

Color Bouncing

The code in the previous example can be improved upon with a new subclass of CycleColor that automatically "bounces" the color components within a specified range. The new subclass is called CycleColorBounce, as found in Listing 12.6. Since this class does not assume that the color component range will bounce between 0 and 255, there is a min and max property for each color component, defined as integers. Although a more complex data type like Vector4 would clean up the code a bit, I was going for clarity. Now, this Animation subclass does not ever end by setting animating to false, so this animation will continue forever unless an intervention takes place. Another possibility is to have it perform a single bounce forward and backward before ending. Then, if you want to perform the animation again, it can be restarted.

LISTING 12.6   Source Code to the CycleColorBounce Class

```
public class CycleColorBounce : CycleColor
{
    public int rmin, rmax, gmin, gmax, bmin, bmax, amin, amax;

    public CycleColorBounce(int red, int green, int blue, int alpha)
        : base(red,green,blue,alpha)
    {
        rmin = gmin = bmin = amin = 0;
        rmax = gmax = bmax = amax = 255;
    }

    public override Color ModifyColor(Color original)
    {
        Color modified = original;

        if (animating)
        {
            int R = original.R + red;
            int G = original.G + green;
            int B = original.B + blue;
            int A = original.A + alpha;

            if (R < rmin)
            {
                R = rmin;
                red *= -1;
            }
            else if (R > rmax)
```

```
        {
            R = rmax;
            red *= -1;
        }

        if (G < gmin)
        {
            G = gmin;
            green *= -1;
        }
        else if (G > gmax)
        {
            G = gmax;
            green *= -1;
        }

        if (B < bmin)
        {
            B = bmin;
            blue *= -1;
        }
        else if (B > bmax)
        {
            B = bmax;
            blue *= -1;
        }

        if (A < amin)
        {
            A = amin;
            alpha *= -1;
        }
        else if (A > amax)
        {
            A = amax;
            alpha *= -1;
        }

        modified = new Color(R, G, B, A);
    }
    return modified;
    }
}
```

The example for color bouncing is very similar to the previous example, with only minor changes to the variable declarations and initialization of the objects. I opted to turn off rotation of the sprites just to make this example stand apart from the previous one a bit. The source code to the Color Bouncing program that demonstrates this class is found in Listing 12.7.

LISTING 12.7   Source Code to the Color Bouncing Program

```
public class Game1 : Microsoft.Xna.Framework.Game
{
    GraphicsDeviceManager graphics;
    SpriteBatch spriteBatch;
    SpriteFont font;
    Texture2D shapeImage;
    List<Sprite> shapes;
    CycleColorBounce cycleRed, cycleGreen, cycleBlue;

    public Game1()
    {
        graphics = new GraphicsDeviceManager(this);
        Content.RootDirectory = "Content";
        TargetElapsedTime = TimeSpan.FromTicks(333333);
    }

    protected override void Initialize()
    {
        base.Initialize();
    }

    protected override void LoadContent()
    {
        spriteBatch = new SpriteBatch(GraphicsDevice);
        font = Content.Load<SpriteFont>("WascoSans");

        shapeImage = Content.Load<Texture2D>("box");

        Sprite redBox = new Sprite(Content, spriteBatch);
        redBox.image = shapeImage;
        redBox.position = new Vector2(200, 240);
        redBox.origin = new Vector2(64, 64);
        redBox.color = new Color(255, 0, 0);

        Sprite greenBox = new Sprite(Content, spriteBatch);
        greenBox.image = shapeImage;
        greenBox.position = new Vector2(400, 240);
        greenBox.origin = new Vector2(64, 64);
        greenBox.color = new Color(0, 255, 0);

        Sprite blueBox = new Sprite(Content, spriteBatch);
        blueBox.image = shapeImage;
        blueBox.position = new Vector2(600, 240);
        blueBox.origin = new Vector2(64, 64);
        blueBox.color = new Color(0, 0, 255);

        cycleRed = new CycleColorBounce(-5, 0, 0, 0);
        cycleRed.rmin = 100;
        cycleRed.rmax = 200;
        redBox.SetAnimation(cycleRed);

        cycleGreen = new CycleColorBounce(0, -10, 0, 0);
        cycleGreen.gmin = 150;
        cycleGreen.gmax = 255;
        greenBox.SetAnimation(cycleGreen);
```

```
        cycleBlue = new CycleColorBounce(0, 0, -20, 0);
        cycleBlue.bmin = 0;
        cycleBlue.bmax = 255;
        blueBox.SetAnimation(cycleBlue);

        shapes = new List<Sprite>();
        shapes.Add(redBox);
        shapes.Add(greenBox);
        shapes.Add(blueBox);
    }

    protected override void Update(GameTime gameTime)
    {
        if (GamePad.GetState(PlayerIndex.One).Buttons.Back ==
            ButtonState.Pressed)
            this.Exit();

        foreach (Sprite spr in shapes)
        {
            spr.Rotate();
            spr.Move();
        }

        base.Update(gameTime);
    }

    protected override void Draw(GameTime gameTime)
    {
        GraphicsDevice.Clear(Color.Black);
        spriteBatch.Begin();

        foreach (Sprite spr in shapes)
        {
            spr.Animate();
            spr.Draw();
        }

        spriteBatch.DrawString(font, "Color Bouncing Demo",
            new Vector2(0, 0), Color.White);

        spriteBatch.End();
        base.Draw(gameTime);
    }
}
```

This example is included in the Color Animation Demo solution, called Color Bouncing, and is shown in Figure 12.3. Each of the three boxes performs color cycle bouncing at a different rate to demonstrate the versatility of the animation system.

All the color animation being demonstrated in this hour can be applied to sprites with actual game artwork rather than a white shape. These special effects are demonstrated on a simple white box only for illustration, to show what is possible!

FIGURE 12.3
Animating color
components
bouncing
between mini-
mum and maxi-
mum values.

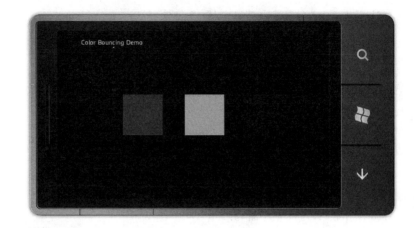

Summary

We have only scratched the surface of sprite animation in this hour, with much
more to come in the following two hours, which cover transform animation (basic
transforms that change the sprite *over time* rather than instantly), and the hour after
that, which covers frame animation.

Q&A

Q. *Is it possible to animate the colors of a bitmap using the classes in this
chapter?*

A. Yes.

Q. *What about causing a bitmapped sprite to fade in and out using colors?*

A. The way to do that is with a color cycle using the alpha channel.

Workshop

Quiz

1. What is the name of the base class used for animation?

2. What is the name of the method used to associate a `Sprite` with an Animation?

3. How is color animation applied to a `Sprite` object?

Answers

1. `Animation`

2. `Sprite.SetAnimation()`

3. One or more `ModifyXXX()` methods apply the changes to `Sprite` properties.

Exercises

The examples in this hour are ripe for the picking by a creative programmer! It goes without saying that you need to create *your own* animation class, a subclass of `Animation`, that performs some change to the color of a sprite over time, as the examples this hour have already shown. Come up with an awesome new technique that would be really useful in a game, such as fading to black followed by an explosion of colors just before the object "dies"—just as a suggestion!

Sprite Transform Animation

What You'll Learn in This Hour:

- ▶ **Transform animations**
- ▶ **Position transforms**
- ▶ **Rotation and scaling transforms**
- ▶ **Combining multiple animations**

The preceding hour saw the introduction of a powerful new Animation class that added color animation effect capabilities to Sprite objects. By subclassing Animation, we can create specific animation effects in reusable classes, such as the CycleColor class that demonstrated color cycling over time. There are many more possibilities with the Animation class that have not been explored yet, so we will spend this hour delving into new aspects of animation that are easy to implement and that produce great results for relatively little effort. Specifically, we'll look at animating the *transforms* that can be applied with existing properties in the Sprite class: position, rotation, and scaling. These properties are important as they are currently implemented in Sprite, so we won't mess up what already works. Instead, variations of the Animation class will set up *modifiers* for these Sprite properties, with changes applied to the Sprite.Animate() method to make it work.

Adding Transform Support to the Animation Class

To perform transforms on a sprite, we need to add some new code to the Sprite.Animate() method. Currently, the method supports only color animation, and we want transforms as well. So, here are the changes:

```
public void Animate()
{
    if (p_animation != null)
```

```
    {
        if (p_animation.animating)
        {
            color = p_animation.ModifyColor(color);
            position = p_animation.ModifyPosition(position);
            rotation = p_animation.ModifyRotation(rotation);
            scaleV = p_animation.ModifyScale(scaleV);
        }
    }
}
```

This is all that is needed to give Animation access to Sprite properties, and we will take full advantage of it!

Position Transforms

When it comes to "animating" the position of a sprite with a custom animation class, we are really getting into custom behaviors, and the term "animation" may not be as appropriate—but it is what it is, so let's just work with it. If you want to use the term "behavior" in the name for your own transform animation classes, that might seem more appropriate. Since we can do anything with the position, a really dumb but technically valid translation "animation" could be to simply position a sprite to one hard-coded location and never let it leave. That's silly but it can be done, because the translation modifier added to the Sprite class makes it possible.

The important thing to remember when writing a translation class is to override the ModifyPosition() method (coming from the base Animation class). Any of these base methods that are not overridden will return the passed parameter back, so that no changes are made. Here is just *one* possible translation class called OrbitalMovement, shown in Listing 13.1. This class inherits from Animation, and exposes a number of properties (which will usually just be passed to the constructor to make initialization simple). ModifyPosition() is where all the work is done. Using some trig, the incoming position is completely ignored, while a calculated orbital position for the object is returned. In other words, it doesn't matter where a Sprite is located; when this method runs, it calculates position based on sine and cosine calculations, using the properties provided.

LISTING 13.1   Source Code for the OrbitalMovement Class

```
public class OrbitalMovement : Animation
{
    public int radius;
    public Vector2 center;
    public double angle;
    public float velocity;
```

```
public OrbitalMovement(Vector2 center, int radius, double angle,
    float velocity)
    : base()
{
    animating = true;
    this.center = center;
    this.radius = radius;
    this.angle = angle;
    this.velocity = velocity;
}

public override Vector2 ModifyPosition(Vector2 original)
{
    Vector2 modified = original;
    angle += velocity;
    modified.X = center.X + (float)(Math.Cos(angle) * radius);
    modified.Y = center.Y + (float)(Math.Sin(angle) * radius);
    return modified;
}
}
```

Figure 13.1 shows the output of the Transform Animation Demo program, which is found in Listing 13.2. There are a lot of asteroids orbiting a black hole in this small simulation! The really great thing about it is that no orbit code is found anywhere in the main program—it's all stuffed in the OrbitalMovement class! Let this be just one example of what you can do on your own with similar results. I don't know about you, but I enjoy producing interesting results with relatively small amounts of code. It is a challenge! Consider how to combine several simple rules to produce interesting results, rather than taking the brute force approach and coding a solution one step at a time. You may be surprised by how this *synergy* of code works. Following is the code for the program so that you can see how the black hole and asteroids are created and drawn.

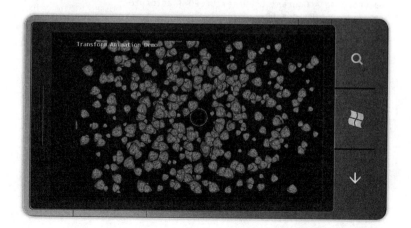

FIGURE 13.1
The Transform Animation Demo uses a custom animation class to simulate an orbit.

LISTING 13.2   Source Code for the Transform Animation Demo Program

```
public class Game1 : Microsoft.Xna.Framework.Game
{
    GraphicsDeviceManager graphics;
    SpriteBatch spriteBatch;
    Random rand;
    SpriteFont font;
    Texture2D asteroidImg;
    List<Sprite> objects;

    public Game1()
    {
        graphics = new GraphicsDeviceManager(this);
        Content.RootDirectory = "Content";
        TargetElapsedTime = TimeSpan.FromTicks(333333);
    }

    protected override void Initialize()
    {
        base.Initialize();
    }

    protected override void LoadContent()
    {
        rand = new Random();
        spriteBatch = new SpriteBatch(GraphicsDevice);
        font = Content.Load<SpriteFont>("WascoSans");

        objects = new List<Sprite>();'

        Sprite blackhole = new Sprite(Content, spriteBatch);
        blackhole.Load("blackhole");
        blackhole.position = new Vector2(400, 240);
        blackhole.scale = 0.5f;
        blackhole.origin = new Vector2(64, 64);
        blackhole.velocityAngular = 1.0f;
        objects.Add(blackhole);

        asteroidImg = Content.Load<Texture2D>("asteroid");
        for (int n = 0; n < 500; n++)
        {
            Sprite ast = new Sprite(Content, spriteBatch);
            ast.image = asteroidImg;
            ast.origin = new Vector2(32, 32);
            ast.scale = 0.25f + (float)(rand.NextDouble() * 0.5);
            ast.velocityAngular = (float)(rand.NextDouble() * 0.1);
            Vector2 pos = new Vector2(380 + rand.Next(40),
                220 + rand.Next(40));
            double angle = rand.NextDouble() * 6.0;
            int radius = rand.Next(60, 400);
            float velocity = (float)(rand.NextDouble() * 0.01 *
                ((400-radius) * 0.1) );
            ast.SetAnimation(new OrbitalMovement(pos, radius,
                angle, velocity));
```

```
            objects.Add(ast);
        }
    }

    protected override void Update(GameTime gameTime)
    {
        if (GamePad.GetState(PlayerIndex.One).Buttons.Back ==
            ButtonState.Pressed)
            this.Exit();

        foreach (Sprite spr in objects)
        {
            spr.Move();
            spr.Rotate();
        }

        base.Update(gameTime);
    }

    protected override void Draw(GameTime gameTime)
    {
        GraphicsDevice.Clear(Color.Black);
        spriteBatch.Begin();

        foreach (Sprite spr in objects)
        {
            spr.Animate();
            spr.Draw();
        }

        spriteBatch.DrawString(font, "Transform Animation Demo",
            new Vector2(0, 0), Color.White);

        spriteBatch.End();
        base.Draw(gameTime);
    }
}
```

Rotation and Scaling Transforms

We don't need a custom Animation subclass just to rotate a Sprite object, so what
is the purpose of a so-called rotation animation? Don't think of rotation in terms of
absolute rotation value being set and used to draw. Consider rotation instead in
terms of *rotation over time*. We can transform an animation in small increments over
time for interesting results. For example, a sprite could rotate back and forth
between 180 degrees to look like it's wobbling, or it could rotate around at one-second increments like the hand of a clock. It's all based on the code in your own
Animation subclass. To demonstrate, I've created an analog clock example. The
clock will be based around a class called ClockHand, found in Listing 13.3.

LISTING 13.3   Source Code for the ClockHand Class

```
public class ClockHand : Animation
{
    public int direction;

    public ClockHand(int direction) //0 to 59
        : base()
    {''
        animating = true;
        this.direction = direction;
    }

    public override float ModifyRotation(float original)
    {
        float angle = (float)(direction / 60.0f) *
            (float)(2.0f * Math.PI);
        return angle;
    }
}
```

This class is on the simple side so it can be used for hours, minutes, and seconds. Assuming you supply the project with an arrow for the "clock hands," the ClockHand.direction property represents the time value. For minutes and seconds, this comes to a value from 0 to 59. For hours, we can use the same range by just multiplying hours by 5 (because 60 / 12 = 5). The time values are passed to ClockHand.direction at regular intervals in the program's Update() method:

```
hours.direction = DateTime.Now.Hour * 5;
minutes.direction = DateTime.Now.Minute;
seconds.direction = DateTime.Now.Second;
```

Figure 13.2 shows the output of the Rotate/Scale Animation Demo, but we can just call it the "Clock Demo" for short. This example does scale the clock-hand sprites during initialization, but the scale factor is not being actively used in this example. Given the ease with which rotation was modified in this example, I'm sure you will see how easy scaling would be as well. The source code is found in Listing 13.4.

LISTING 13.4   Source Code for the Clock Demo Program

```
public class Game1 : Microsoft.Xna.Framework.Game''
{
    GraphicsDeviceManager graphics;
    SpriteBatch spriteBatch;
    Random rand;
    SpriteFont font;
    List<Sprite> objects;
    ClockHand hours, minutes, seconds;

    public Game1()
    {
        graphics = new GraphicsDeviceManager(this);
        Content.RootDirectory = "Content";
```

```
        TargetElapsedTime = TimeSpan.FromTicks(333333);
    }

    protected override void Initialize()
    {
        base.Initialize();
    }

    protected override void LoadContent()
    {
        rand = new Random();
        spriteBatch = new SpriteBatch(GraphicsDevice);
        font = Content.Load<SpriteFont>("WascoSans");

        objects = new List<Sprite>();

        Sprite clock = new Sprite(Content, spriteBatch);
        clock.Load("clock");
        clock.position = new Vector2(400, 240);
        objects.Add(clock);

        hours = new ClockHand(0);
        minutes = new ClockHand(0);
        seconds = new ClockHand(0); ''

        Sprite hourHand = new Sprite(Content, spriteBatch);
        hourHand.Load("arrow200");
        hourHand.position = new Vector2(400, 240);
        hourHand.origin = new Vector2(30, 199);
        hourHand.scaleV = new Vector2(1.5f, 0.7f);
        hourHand.color = new Color(250, 50, 250);
        hourHand.SetAnimation(hours);
        objects.Add(hourHand);

        Sprite minuteHand = new Sprite(Content, spriteBatch);
        minuteHand.Load("arrow200");
        minuteHand.position = new Vector2(400, 240);
        minuteHand.origin = new Vector2(30, 199);
        minuteHand.scaleV = new Vector2(1.0f, 0.9f);
        minuteHand.color = new Color(250, 100, 150);
        minuteHand.SetAnimation(minutes);
        objects.Add(minuteHand);

        Sprite secondHand = new Sprite(Content, spriteBatch);
        secondHand.Load("arrow200");
        secondHand.position = new Vector2(400, 240);
        secondHand.origin = new Vector2(30, 199);
        secondHand.scaleV = new Vector2(0.25f, 1.0f);
        secondHand.color = new Color(120, 80, 150);
        secondHand.SetAnimation(seconds);
        objects.Add(secondHand);
    }

    protected override void Update(GameTime gameTime)
    {
        if (GamePad.GetState(PlayerIndex.One).Buttons.Back ==
            ButtonState.Pressed)
            this.Exit();
```

```
        foreach (Sprite spr in objects)
        {
            spr.Rotate();
            spr.Move();
        }

        hours.direction = DateTime.Now.Hour * 5;
        minutes.direction = DateTime.Now.Minute;
        seconds.direction = DateTime.Now.Second;

        base.Update(gameTime);
    }''

    protected override void Draw(GameTime gameTime)
    {
        GraphicsDevice.Clear(Color.Black);
        spriteBatch.Begin();

        foreach (Sprite spr in objects)
        {
            spr.Animate();
            spr.Draw();
        }

        spriteBatch.DrawString(font, "Rotate/Scale Animation Demo",
            new Vector2(0, 0), Color.White);

        spriteBatch.End();
        base.Draw(gameTime);
    }
}''
```

FIGURE 13.2
The Clock Demo actually shows how to use an animation class that modifies rotation.

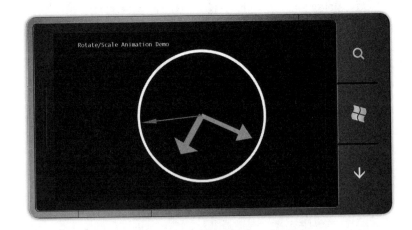

Code Consistency

An interesting thing has happened since we started using the `Animation` class and all of its children. Have you noticed that much of the source code in our examples changes very little from one project to the next? Oh, there are often different variables in use, but `LoadContent()` seems to be where most of the code is being written at this point. Have you really noticed much of a change to `Update()` or `Draw()` in quite some time? This is a *good sign*! When standard code begins to remain unchanged, that means we have replaced the core logic of the program with a state-driven, property-based game engine. Sure, it's a very, *very* simple game engine, but that is the path we are now on. The end result is some *very* solid code, easy to debug, easy to modify, easy to understand. Strive for this type of code in your own projects!

Combining Multiple Animations

We have quite a bit of good animation code now with the ability to add new effects fairly easily using the techniques learned in the preceding two chapters. The next step is quite revolutionary: doing more than one animation at a time! The current animation system will apply a behavior to a game sprite using a single method, `Sprite.SetAnimation()`. This is going to be replaced with a more powerful mechanism that will support many animations stored in a list.

Although it is technically possible to remove an animation from the list, we're not to be concerned with seldom-used features like that. Our sprite animation system currently supports just one animation, but it can be replaced at any time with the `SetAnimation()` method just mentioned. The same will be true when multiple animation support is added, because the list container will have public scope.

Remember the 80/20 rule! Focus most of your efforts on writing code that will be used 80% of the time, not on features rarely used (unless you have time to kill).

Sprite Class Modifications

Try It Yourself ▼

Adding Multiple Animation Support

We need to make a few changes to the `Sprite` class to support multiple animations.

1. Remove the old `Animation` variable, `p_animation`, and replace it with a `List`:

```
//private Animation p_animation;
public List<Animation> animations;
```

2. Completely remove the SetAnimation() method, which is no longer used:

```
//public void SetAnimation(Animation animation)
//{
//      p_animation = animation;
//}
```

3. Make the following changes to the Animate() method. This is the most dramatic change to the class required at this time, adding support for multiple animations. Now, when an animation has completed (by setting the animating property to false), it is actually *removed*!

```
public void Animate()
{
    if (animations.Count == 0) return;
    foreach (Animation anim in animations)
    {
        if (anim.animating)
        {
            color = anim.ModifyColor(color);
            position = anim.ModifyPosition(position);
            rotation = anim.ModifyRotation(rotation);
            scaleV = anim.ModifyScale(scaleV);
        }
        else
        {
            animations.Remove(anim);
            return;
        }
    }
}
```

New Animations

To support the upcoming example, here are a couple of new animations to examine. They are called Spin and Throb, affecting the rotation and scaling, respectively. First up is the Spin class, which does a 360-degree spin and then stops. Note that this class overrides only ModifyRotation(), but none of the other modification methods. The source code is found in Listing 13.5.

LISTING 13.5   Source Code for the Spin Class

```
public class Spin : Animation
{
    private float angleDist, velocity;

    public Spin(float velocity)
        : base()
    {
        animating = true;
```

```
            this.velocity = velocity;
            angleDist = 0.0f;
        }

        public override float ModifyRotation(float original)
        {
            if (animating)
            {
                float fullCircle = (float)(2.0 * Math.PI);
                angleDist += velocity;
                if (angleDist > fullCircle)
                    animating = false;

                original += velocity;
            }
            return original;
        }
    }
}t
```

Next up is the Throb class, which performs a scaling "throb" of a sprite by cycling between a start and an end scale value. This class implements only ModifyScale(), because it does not need to touch any other property. The source code is found in Listing 13.6.

LISTING 13.6 Source Code for the Throb Class

```
public class Throb : Animation
{
    public float startScale, endScale, speed;
    private bool p_started;

    public Throb(float startScale, float endScale, float speed)
        : base()
    {t
        p_started = false;
        animating = true;
        this.startScale = startScale;
        this.endScale = endScale;
        this.speed = speed;
    }

    public override Vector2 ModifyScale(Vector2 original)
    {
        if (!animating) return original;
        Vector2 modified = original;
        if (!p_started)
        {
            modified.X = startScale;
            modified.Y = startScale;
            p_started = true;
        }
        modified.X += speed;
        modified.Y += speed;
        if (modified.X >= endScale)
            speed *= -1;
```

```
        else if (modified.X <= startScale)
            animating = false;

        return modified;
    }
}t
```

Multiple Animation Demo

With all of these enhancements, we can now do multiple animations per sprite. Remember, the behavior of the animations is entirely up to *you*, so if you don't like how an animation is automatically removed when it is done, then change it! Figure 13.3 shows the sample program. The Throb animation is automatically renewed anytime the animations have all completed. Also, you can tap the screen to add a Spin animation. The fun thing about this demo is that you can tap the screen repeatedly to give the sprite a *superfast* spin! That is, you can do so until each Spin has finished its 360-degree rotation and is removed. Listing 13.7 has the source code.

FIGURE 13.3
Testing multiple animations with the Spin and Throb animations simultaneously.

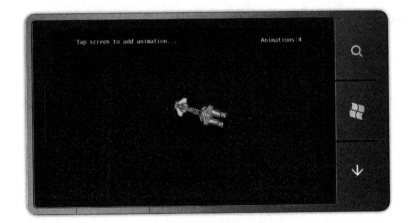

LISTING 13.7   Source Code for the Multiple Animation Demo Program

```
public class Game1 : Microsoft.Xna.Framework.Game
{
    GraphicsDeviceManager graphics;
    SpriteBatch spriteBatch;
    TouchLocation oldTouch;
    Random rand;
    SpriteFont font;
    Sprite ship;
```

```
public Game1()
{
    graphics = new GraphicsDeviceManager(this);
    Content.RootDirectory = "Content";
    TargetElapsedTime = TimeSpan.FromTicks(333333);
    oldTouch = new TouchLocation();
}

protected override void Initialize()
{
    base.Initialize();
}

protected override void LoadContent()
{
    rand = new Random();
    spriteBatch = new SpriteBatch(GraphicsDevice);
    font = Content.Load<SpriteFont>("WascoSans");

    ship = new Sprite(Content, spriteBatch);
    ship.Load("ship");
    ship.position = new Vector2(400, 240);
    ship.rotation = (float)rand.NextDouble();

    ship.animations.Add(new Spin(0.1f));
    ship.animations.Add(new Throb(0.5f, 3.0f, 0.2f));
}f'

protected override void Update(GameTime gameTime)
{
    if (GamePad.GetState(PlayerIndex.One).Buttons.Back ==
        ButtonState.Pressed)
        this.Exit();

    //get state of touch input
    TouchCollection touchInput = TouchPanel.GetState();
    if (touchInput.Count > 0)
    {
        TouchLocation touch = touchInput[0];
        if (touch.State == TouchLocationState.Pressed &&
            oldTouch.State == TouchLocationState.Released)
        {
            ship.animations.Add(new Spin(0.1f));
        }
        oldTouch = touch;
    }

    ship.Rotate();
    ship.Move();

    base.Update(gameTime);
}

protected override void Draw(GameTime gameTime)
{
    GraphicsDevice.Clear(Color.Black);
    spriteBatch.Begin();
```

```
        ship.Animate();

        //reset throb
        if (ship.animations.Count == 0)
            ship.animations.Add(new Throb(0.5f, 3.0f, 0.2f));

        ship.Draw();

        int anims = ship.animations.Count;
        spriteBatch.DrawString(font, "Tap screen to add animation...",
            new Vector2(0,0), Color.White);
        spriteBatch.DrawString(font, "Animations:" + anims.ToString(),
            new Vector2(600,0), Color.White);

        spriteBatch.End();
        base.Draw(gameTime);
    }f'
}
```

Summary

This hour was awesome! We now have an extremely versatile sprite animation system in place, and haven't even touched on frame animation yet, which is normally the *sole emphasis* of all animation. There's so much we can do with just simple artwork without frame animation; imagine what we can do *with* frame animation! Great, that's the subject of the next hour.

Q&A

Q. *What are the three primary transforms that can be changed with custom animations? What other properties should be included?*

A. Position, rotation, and scaling. And that's open for discussion.

Q. *Would it be possible to make an "animation chain" in which one completed animation triggers the start of another? Explain how that might work.*

A. Yes. Answers will vary.

Workshop

Quiz

1. What does the `Sprite` class use to make multiple animations possible?

2. Which update method in `Animation` makes changes to the position of a sprite?

3. Which `Animation` method makes changes to animation frames?

Answers

1. A `List` variable

2. `ModifyPosition()`

3. None; that hasn't been done yet!x

Exercises

There are so many possibilities with the examples in this hour that it's hard to decide where to begin! It goes without saying that you should create your own new animation class and try it out in combination with *other* animations at the same time. See what interesting combinations you can come up with! What about combining a Spin with a `ReverseSpin` at the same time?

HOUR 14

Sprite Frame Animation

What You'll Learn in This Hour:

- ▶ **Drawing animation frames**
- ▶ **Preparing the animation**
- ▶ **Calculating frame position**
- ▶ **Animation over time**

We have finally arrived at the sprite *frame animation* hour, after talking about it for so long. This is an important subject that is really not at all related to color or transform animations that have been developed over the past two hours, but we're going to make them work together anyway! To reiterate, a sprite is a 2D representation of a game entity that usually must interact with the player in some way. A car or house might be rendered in 2D and interact with the player by simply getting in the way, stopping the player by way of collision physics, which we studied back in Hour 10, "When Objects Collide."

Sprite animation is made possible with SpriteBatch.Draw(), which we have already been using quite extensively. Drawing a sprite is not the issue—we can already do that. Until now, however, our sprites have been based around a single image loaded as a texture and drawn whole. This is called *rasterization*, converting the color data in the image buffer into pixel colors on the screen. We need to add animation support to our existing Sprite class, and also make animation work with the existing color and transform "animations" that were covered in the past two hours. The end result will be frame animation with the same color and transform effects!

Drawing Animation Frames

Let's dig into the nitty-gritty of sprite animation. Most beginners create an animation sequence by loading each frame from a separate bitmap file and storing the frames in an array or a list. This approach has the distinct disadvantage of requiring many files for even a basic animation for a walking character or some other game object, which often involves 50 to 100 or more frames. Although it can be done, that is a slow and error-prone way to handle animation. Instead, it is preferable to use an animation *sheet*.

Preparing the Animation

A sprite animation sheet is a single bitmap containing many frames arranged in rows and columns, as shown in Figure 14.1. In this sprite sheet (of an animated asteroid), there are eight columns across and 64 frames overall. The animation here was rendered from a 3D model, which is why it looks so great when animated on the screen! One question that might come up is, where do you get animations? Most game art is created by a professional artist specifically for one game, and then it is never used again (usually because the game studio owns the assets). There are, however, several good sources of free artwork online, such as Reiner's Tilesets (http://www.reinerstilesets.de).

FIGURE 14.1
Sprite sheet of animation frames for an asteroid.

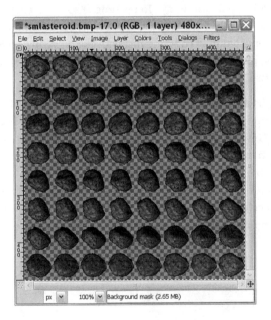

SpriteBatch doesn't care whether your sprite's source image uses a color key or an alpha channel for transparency; it just renders the image. If you have an image with an alpha channel, like a TGA or PNG, then it will be rendered with any existing alpha, with translucent blending of the background. This is the technique used to render a sprite with transparency in XNA. Looking at sprite functionality at a lower level, you can tell the sprite renderer (SpriteBatch) what color you want to use when drawing the image, which was the focus of the preceding two hours on performing color and transform animations.

The bitmap file should have an alpha channel if you want to use transparency (which is almost always the case). Most artists prefer to define their own translucent pixels for best results rather than leaving it to chance in the hands of a programmer. The main reason to use alpha rather than color-key transparency is better quality. An alpha channel can define pixels with shades of translucency. In contrast, a color key is an all-or-nothing, on/off setting with a solid edge, because such an image will have discrete pixels. You can do alpha blending at runtime to produce special effects (such as a particle emitter), but for maximum quality, it's best to prepare artwork in advance. See Figure 14.2.

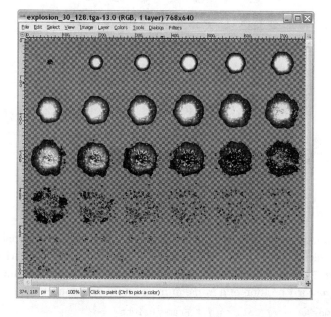

FIGURE 14.2
A sprite animation sheet of an explosion showing the alpha channel.

Rather than using a black border around a color-keyed sprite (the old-school way of highlighting a sprite), an artist will usually blend a border around a sprite's edges using an alpha level for partial translucency. To do that, you must use a file format that supports 32-bit RGBA images. TGA and PNG files both support an alpha channel and XNA supports them. The PNG format is a good choice that you may consider using most of the time because it has wide support among all graphic editing tools.

Calculating Frame Position

Assuming that we have an animation sheet like the asteroid animation shown in Figure 14.2, we can begin exploring ways to draw a single frame. This will require some changes to the Sprite class, which currently just uses the dimensions of the loaded image. That will have to change to reflect the dimensions of a single frame, not the whole image. To calculate the position of a frame in the sheet, we have to know the width and height of a single frame. Then, beginning at the upper left, we can calculate how to move right and down the correct number of frames. Figure 14.3 shows a typical sheet with the columns and rows labeled for easy reference.

FIGURE 14.3
This animation sheet has eight columns and eight rows, for 64 total frames.

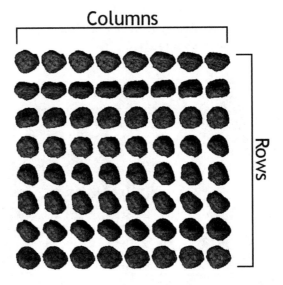

The more important of the two is the row calculation, so we'll do that one first. To make this calculation, you need to know how many frames there are across from left to right. These are the columns. (See Figure 14.4.) Here is the formula for calculating the *row* or *Y* position of a frame number on the sprite sheet:

```
Y = ( Frame_Number / Columns ) * Frame_Height
```

To calculate the *column* or *X* position of a frame number on the sprite sheet, a similar-*looking* calculation is done, but the result is quite different:

```
X = ( Frame_Number % Columns ) * Frame_Width
```

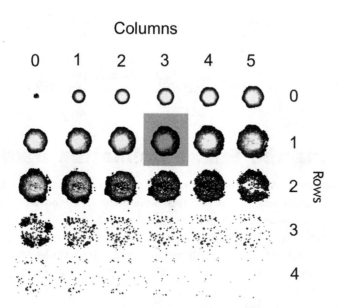

FIGURE 14.4
Calculating the position of a frame in the animation sheet.

Note that the math operator is not division. The percent symbol (%) is the *modulus operator* in C#. Modulus is similar to division, but instead of returning the quotient (or answer), it returns the *remainder*! Why do we care about the *remainder*? That represents the X position of the frame! Here's the answer: because X is the *extra* or *leftover* amount after the division. Recall that the formula for calculating Y gave us a distinct *integer* quotient. We want to use the same variables, but modulus rather than division gives us the *partial column* in the row, which represents the X value.

Drawing One Frame

Equipping ourselves with these formulas, we can write the code to draw a frame from a sprite sheet onto the screen. First, we'll create a `Rectangle` to represent the source frame:

```
Rectangle source = new Rectangle();
source.X = (frame % columns) * width;
source.Y = (frame / columns) * height;
source.Width = width;
source.Height = height;
```

Next, we'll use the `Rectangle` when calling `SpriteBatch.Draw()`, using one of the overloads of the method that allows use of a source rectangle. We can retain the existing *rotation*, *origin*, and *scale* parameters while still drawing just a single frame.

```
spriteBatch.Draw( image,           //source Texture2D
                  position,        //destination position
```

```
source,               //source Rectangle
Color.White,          //target color
rotation,             //rotation value
origin,               //pivot for rotation
scale,                //scale factor
SpriteEffects.None,   //flip or mirror effects
0.0f );               //z-index order
```

Creating the Frame Animation Demo

The only way to really get experience with animation is to practice by writing code. One fairly common mistake that results in an animated sprite not showing up is to forget the frame size property. This must be set after a bitmap file is loaded or the image property is set to an outside Texture2D object. The Sprite.size property is a Vector2 that must be set to the width and height of a single frame. Forgetting to do this *after* loading the bitmap will result in the animation not showing up correctly.

Sprite Class Changes

Some rather dramatic changes must be made to the Sprite class to support frame animation. Now, the reason for most of the changes involves the sprite sheet image. Previously, the whole image was used, for drawing, for calculating scale, and so on. Now, that code has to be changed to account for the size of just one frame, not the whole image.

▼ **Try It Yourself**

Modifying the Sprite Class

1. First up, we have some new variables in the Sprite class. These can be added to the top of the class with the other variables:

   ```
   private double startTime;
   public Vector2 size;
   public int columns, frame, totalFrames;
   ```

2. In the Sprite constructor, the new variables are initialized after all the others. The columns and totalFrames variables are *crucial* to drawing simple sprites when no animation is being used. In other words, they're needed to preserve compatibility with code that used the Sprite class before this point. By setting columns to 1, we tell the Draw() method to treat the image as if there is just one column. Likewise, setting totalFrames to 1 ensures that just that one frame is drawn, even if no animation is used. A flag will be used in the Draw()

method just to make sure null errors don't occur, but these initialized values should take care of that as well.

```
size.X = size.Y = 0;
columns = 1;
frame = 0;
totalFrames = 1;
startTime = 0;
```

A "null error" is an error that occurs when some code tries to use a variable that is *null*, which means, it is *nothing*. Trying to use *nothing* in code causes an error because the compiler doesn't know what to do with it.

Did you Know?

3. Next up are two helper properties that make using Sprite a bit easier, by exposing the X and Y properties of position. This is a convenience rather than a required change, but it is very helpful in the long term.

```
public float X
{
    get
    {
        return position.X;
    }
    set
    {
        position.X = value;
    }
}

public float Y
{
    get
    {
        return position.Y;
    }
    set
    {
        position.Y = value;
    }
}
```

4. Next, we need to review the Load() method again for reference, just to note what is being initialized at this point. Pay special attention to origin and size, because they are *involved* in a single frame being drawn correctly. Notice that origin is initialized with the *full size* of the image. When using a sprite sheet, origin *must* be reset after the image is loaded for drawing to work correctly!

```
public bool Load(string assetName)
{
    try
    {
        image = p_content.Load<Texture2D>(assetName);
        origin = new Vector2(image.Width / 2, image.Height / 2);
    }
    catch (Exception) { return false; }

    size.X = image.Width;
    size.Y = image.Height;

    return true;
}
```

5. Next, make the required changes to the Sprite.Draw() method. Quite a dramatic change has come over Draw(), transforming it into a fully featured animation rendering routine with support for single images or sprite sheet animations. This is a frame animation workhorse—this is where all the "good stuff" is happening.

```
public void Draw()
{
    if (!visible) return;

    if (totalFrames > 1)
    {
        Rectangle source = new Rectangle();
        source.X = (frame % columns) * (int)size.X;
        source.Y = (frame / columns) * (int)size.Y;
        source.Width = (int)size.X;
        source.Height = (int)size.Y;
        p_spriteBatch.Draw(image, position, source, color,
            rotation, origin, scale, SpriteEffects.None, 0.0f);
    }
    else
    {
        p_spriteBatch.Draw(image, position, null, color, rotation,
            origin, scaleV, SpriteEffects.None, 0.0f);
    }
}
```

6. Next, make a minor improvement to the Rotate() method to speed it up. If no rotation is happening, the calculations are skipped.

```
public void Rotate()
{
    if (velocityAngular != 0.0f)
    {
        rotation += velocityAngular;
        if (rotation > Math.PI * 2)
```

```
            rotation -= (float)Math.PI * 2;
        else if (rotation < 0.0f)
            rotation = (float)Math.PI * 2 - rotation;
    }
}
```

7. Next, we must make minor modifications to the Boundary() method to account for the size of a single frame, rather than using the whole image. The old lines have been commented out; note the new calculations for halfw and halfh.

```
public Rectangle Boundary()
{
    //int halfw = (int)((float)(image.Width / 2) * scaleV.X);
    //int halfh = (int)((float)(image.Height / 2) * scaleV.Y);
    int halfw = (int)((float)(size.X / 2) * scaleV.X);
    int halfh = (int)((float)(size.Y / 2) * scaleV.Y);

    return new Rectangle(
        (int)position.X - halfw,
        (int)position.Y - halfh,
        halfw * 2,
        halfh * 2);
}
```

8. Next, we'll add two new overloads of Animate() to support frame animation. It might be less confusing to call these FrameAnimate() if you want, because they share the same name as the previous version of Animate() that did color and transform animations. The difference between those and frame animation is that the latter requires parameters, either the elapsed time or the actual frame range, time, and animation speed. First, let's review the existing method (no changes required):

```
public void Animate()
{
    if (animations.Count == 0) return;
    foreach (Animation anim in animations)
    {
        if (anim.animating)
        {
            color = anim.ModifyColor(color);
            position = anim.ModifyPosition(position);
            rotation = anim.ModifyRotation(rotation);
            scaleV = anim.ModifyScale(scaleV);
        }
        else
        {
            animations.Remove(anim);
            return;
        }
    }
}
```

Okay, now here are the new methods for frame animation that you can add to the source code. The elapsedTime parameter helps the animation code to run at the correct speed. Note that the simple version calls the more complex version with default values for convenience. If you want to draw just a subset of an animation set, this second version of Animate() will do that.

```
public void Animate(double elapsedTime)
{
    Animate(0, totalFrames-1, elapsedTime, 30);
}

public void Animate(int startframe, int endframe, double elapsedTime,
    double speed)
{
    if (totalFrames <= 1) return;

    startTime += elapsedTime;
    if (startTime > speed)
    {
        startTime = 0;
        if (++frame > endframe) frame = startframe;
    }
}
```

That concludes the changes to the Sprite class, so now we can go into the example.

Sample Program

The example for this hour draws a bunch of animated asteroid sprites that move across the screen (in the usual landscape mode). But this is no simple demo—there is rudimentary gameplay. A small spaceship has been added. Tap above the ship to move it up, or below the ship to move it down, and avoid the asteroids! (See Figure 14.5.)

LISTING 14.1   Source Code for the Frame Animation Demo Program

```
public class Game1 : Microsoft.Xna.Framework.Game
{
    GraphicsDeviceManager graphics;
    SpriteBatch spriteBatch;
    TouchLocation oldTouch;
    Random rand;
    SpriteFont font;
    List<Sprite> objects;
    Sprite fighter;
    int score = 0;
    int hits = 0;
```

```
public Game1()
{
    graphics = new GraphicsDeviceManager(this);
    Content.RootDirectory = "Content";
    TargetElapsedTime = TimeSpan.FromTicks(333333);
    oldTouch = new TouchLocation();
}

protected override void Initialize()
{
    base.Initialize();
}

protected override void LoadContent()
{
    rand = new Random();
    spriteBatch = new SpriteBatch(GraphicsDevice);
    font = Content.Load<SpriteFont>("WascoSans");

    //create object list
    objects = new List<Sprite>();

    //create fighter sprite
    fighter = new Sprite(Content, spriteBatch);
    fighter.Load("fighter");
    fighter.position = new Vector2(40, 240);
    fighter.rotation = MathHelper.ToRadians(90);

    //create asteroid sprites
    for (int n = 0; n < 20; n++)
    {
        Sprite ast = new Sprite(Content, spriteBatch);
        ast.Load("asteroid");
        ast.size = new Vector2(60, 60);
        ast.origin = new Vector2(30, 30);
        float x = 800 + (float)rand.Next(800);
        float y = (float)rand.Next(480);
        ast.position = new Vector2(x, y);
        ast.columns = 8;
        ast.totalFrames = 64;
        ast.frame = rand.Next(64);
        x = (float)(rand.NextDouble() * rand.Next(1, 10));
        y = 0;
        ast.velocityLinear = new Vector2(-x, y);
        objects.Add(ast);
    }
}

protected override void Update(GameTime gameTime)
{
    if (GamePad.GetState(PlayerIndex.One).Buttons.Back ==
        ButtonState.Pressed)
        this.Exit();

    //get state of touch input
    TouchCollection touchInput = TouchPanel.GetState();
    if (touchInput.Count > 0)
    {
```

```
        TouchLocation touch = touchInput[0];
        if (touch.State == TouchLocationState.Pressed)
        {
            if (touch.Position.Y < fighter.Y )
            {
                fighter.velocityLinear.Y -= 1.0f;
            }
            else if (touch.Position.Y >= fighter.Y)
            {
                fighter.velocityLinear.Y += 1.0f;
            }
        }
        oldTouch = touch;
    }

    //gradually reduce velocity
    if (fighter.velocityLinear.Y < 0)
        fighter.velocityLinear.Y += 0.05f;
    else if (fighter.velocityLinear.Y > 0)
        fighter.velocityLinear.Y -= 0.05f;

    //keep fighter in screen bounds
    if (fighter.Y < -32)
    {
        fighter.Y = -32;
        fighter.velocityLinear.Y = 0;
    }
    else if (fighter.Y > 480-32)
    {
        fighter.Y = 480-32;
        fighter.velocityLinear.Y = 0;
    }

    fighter.Move();

    //update all objects
    foreach (Sprite spr in objects)
    {
        spr.Rotate();
        spr.Move();

        //wrap asteroids around screen
        if (spr.X < -60)
        {
            spr.X = 800;
            score++;
        }

        //look for collision with fighter
        if (fighter.Boundary().Intersects(spr.Boundary()))
        {
            hits++;
            spr.X = 800;
        }
    }

    base.Update(gameTime);
```

```
    }

    protected override void Draw(GameTime gameTime)
    {
        GraphicsDevice.Clear(Color.Black);
        spriteBatch.Begin();

        foreach (Sprite spr in objects)
        {
            spr.Animate(gameTime.ElapsedGameTime.Milliseconds);
            spr.Draw();
        }

        fighter.Draw();

        spriteBatch.DrawString(font, "Score:" + score.ToString() +
            ", Hits:" + hits.ToString(), Vector2.Zero, Color.White);

        spriteBatch.End();
        base.Draw(gameTime);
    }
}
```

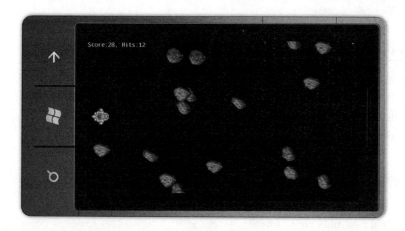

FIGURE 14.5
The Frame Animation Demo is a mini-game of dodging the asteroids.

Summary

This hour added a very important new tool to our WP7 programming toolbox: the ability to do frame animation! This is the traditional "true" animation that one usually thinks of when hearing the word "animation," but it has been somewhat confused by the code written in the preceding two hours. We can use this awesome new Sprite class to make a very complex game already. But there are yet more techniques we can develop to expand these capabilities even further!

Q&A

Q. *If a sprite does not appear where it should, even when hard-coded to a specific X,Y location, what is the most likely cause of the problem?*

A. First, check the image for null, and then verify that the origin has been set.

Q. *When my sprite is animating, it seems to fold up (or to the left) and look sort of like a flip book rather than an animation. What's wrong?*

A. That is a very common problem. The solution is to check the width and height of the frames in your sprite sheet image, because your code is probably off by one pixel.

Workshop

Quiz

1. What name did we give to an image containing rows and columns of animation frames?

2. What are the two most significant properties involved in calculating the source animation frame?

3. When drawing a sprite with rotation, should the angle be in radians or degrees?

Answers

1. A "sprite sheet"

2. Columns and current frame

3. Radians

Exercises

The animation example in this hour supports rudimentary user input so that the ship can be moved up or down to dodge the asteroids. This is almost a complete game in its own right. See what *you* can do with this initial gameplay and make a complete game out of it! It would be cool if the ship would explode when hit instead of just adding to the "hit" tally. The asteroids also just wrap around when they hit the ship. Instead, the asteroids should be randomized when they reemerge from the other side so that they appear to the player as completely new obstacles in a larger asteroid field. If you are feeling really creative, we could borrow the Millennium Falcon and add some TIE fighters and TIE bombers, but that would require an expensive license from Lucasfilm. *Officially*, that is.

HOUR 15

Transforming Frame Animations

What You'll Learn in This Hour:

▶ **Drawing frames with color mods**
▶ **Pivot optimization**
▶ **Revisiting** `CycleColorBounce`
▶ **Drawing frames with transform mods**
▶ **Custom frame animation**
▶ **Animation update**
▶ **Animation Mods Demo**

Now we will pause from all the intense fundamental code building to *use* the `Sprite` class and make any modifications needed to put it into production, so to speak. The class now supports color animation, transform animations (that is, movement, rotation, and scaling over time), and frame animation. But what we have not tested yet is a combination of the three together. Are there any issues that arise when we're performing a transform on just one frame of animation? We will look into just that and more in this hour. To differentiate between the two types of "animation," I will use the word "modifications" or "mods" when referring to color and transform changes applied to a sprite, and reserve the word "animation" solely for frame animation from now on. "Transforming" also refers to the basic changes made to a sprite that defines its behavior in a game, which is also addressed in this hour.

Drawing Frames with Color Mods

We will first test the frame animation system with color modifications (developed back in Hour 12, "Sprite Color Animation"), then get into transform mods, and then create a new frame animation mod system as well.

Pivot Optimization

The sprite's pivot point used for rotation, called *origin*, is a potentially serious source of difficulty and head scratching. When recurring events or calculations can be automated, they should be. Anytime the sprite *frame size* is changed, the origin should be modified along with it. This calls for either a method or a property. Presently, both `size` and `origin` are defined as public `Vector2` variables in `Sprite`:

```
public Vector2 size;
public Vector2 origin;
```

We want to make a change so that it doesn't wreck any previous code that relies on the `Sprite` class, although those prior examples could just use an earlier version of the class if necessary. Perhaps the easiest way to do this is with a property, with `size` made private. This will require several changes in the `Sprite` class, as `size` is used quite a bit.

▼ **Try It Yourself**

Sprite Class Modifications to Support, Well, Modifications

We will make changes to the `Sprite` class from the preceding chapter to support color and transform animation of a sprite with *frame animation* support.

1. First, we'll make a variable change in `Sprite`:

   ```
   //public Vector2 size;
   private Vector2 p_size;
   ```

2. Next, we'll take care of initialization in the constructor:

   ```
   //size.X = size.Y = 0;
   size = Vector2.Zero;
   ```

3. Now we'll work on the new property, with the changes made to the pivot/origin being done automatically:

   ```
   public Vector2 size
   {
       get { return p_size; }
       set
       {
           p_size = value;
           origin = new Vector2(p_size.X / 2, p_size.Y / 2);
       }
   }
   ```

4. One of the additional locations in the class where size is used is in Load(), which must be modified as follows. Note that with the property now being used, the new line of code causes origin to be changed as well! Now we're already starting to see the benefit of this property right inside the Sprite class, and it will be equally helpful outside. Now, we can still manually change the origin whenever needed (for instance, recall the clock example from Hour 13, which needed to set the origin for the clock hands manually for it to rotate correctly). Just remember that changing size automatically changes the pivot point (origin).

```
public bool Load(string assetName)
{
    try
    {
        image = p_content.Load<Texture2D>(assetName);
        origin = new Vector2(image.Width / 2, image.Height / 2);
    }
    catch (Exception) { return false; }

    //size.X = image.Width;
    //size.Y = image.Height;
    size = new Vector2(image.Width, image.Height);

    return true;
}
```

▲

Revisiting CycleColorBounce

The CycleColor class was introduced back during Hour 12 as a way to fade any color in a desired direction, going to fully red, or full whiteout, or fade to black, or any combination in between. A subclass was then developed, called CycleColorBounce, that could do the same color transforms, but would not automatically stop animating when the limits were reached. Instead, it would continue to cycle. We also considered a class called SolidColor that did no real color changes, but that would be helpful in some cases when just a solid color is needed without changing the base Sprite.color property manually. In other words, without creating an additional "old color" style property in the class, SolidColor allowed a sprite to change color temporarily and then return.

Despite the relative simplicity of color modification *in principle*, it turns out that—ironically—our color mod classes are the most complex. Here again in Listing 15.1 are the Animation subclasses for reference, since we are using them in the example. For a complete explanation, refer to Hour 12 for details. Just remember that the color parameters passed to the constructor are the *change values*, not the color components.

LISTING 15.1   Review of CycleColor Class for Reference (Not New Code)

```
public class CycleColor : Animation
{
    public int red, green, blue, alpha;

    public CycleColor(int red, int green, int blue, int alpha)
        : base()
    {
        this.red = red;
        this.green = green;
        this.blue = blue;
        this.alpha = alpha;
        animating = true;
    }

    public override Color ModifyColor(Color original)
    {
        Color modified = original;

        if (animating)
        {
            int R = original.R + red;
            int G = original.G + green;
            int B = original.B + blue;
            int A = original.A + alpha;

            if (R < 0 || R > 255 || G < 0 || G > 255 ||
                B < 0 || B > 255 || A < 0 || A > 255)
            {
                animating = false;
            }
            modified = new Color(R, G, B, A);
        }
        return modified;
    }
}

public class CycleColorBounce : CycleColor
{
    public int rmin, rmax, gmin, gmax, bmin, bmax, amin, amax;

    public CycleColorBounce(int red, int green, int blue, int alpha)
        : base(red,green,blue,alpha)
    {
        rmin = gmin = bmin = amin = 0;
        rmax = gmax = bmax = amax = 255;
    }

    public override Color ModifyColor(Color original)
    {
        Color modified = original;

        if (animating)
        {
            int R = original.R + red;
            int G = original.G + green;
            int B = original.B + blue;
            int A = original.A + alpha;
```

```
            if (R < rmin)
            {
                R = rmin;
                red *= -1;
            }
            else if (R > rmax)
            {
                R = rmax;
                red *= -1;
            }

            if (G < gmin)
            {
                G = gmin;
                green *= -1;
            }
            else if (G > gmax)
            {
                G = gmax;
                green *= -1;
            }

            if (B < bmin)
            {
                B = bmin;
                blue *= -1;
            }
            else if (B > bmax)
            {
                B = bmax;
                blue *= -1;
            }

            if (A < amin)
            {
                A = amin;
                alpha *= -1;
            }
            else if (A > amax)
            {
                A = amax;
                alpha *= -1;
            }

            modified = new Color(R, G, B, A);
        }
        return modified;
    }
}
```

Listing 15.2 shows some source code showing how we will test color modification in the upcoming example; we will delay going into the example until the next section, which features a combined example.

LISTING 15.2   Sample Source Code Demonstrating the Latest Sprite Changes

```
//create skeleton sprite
skelly = new Sprite(Content, spriteBatch);
skelly.Load("skeleton_attack");
skelly.position = new Vector2(425, 240);
skelly.size = new Vector2(96,96);
skelly.scale = 2.0f;
skelly.columns = 10;
skelly.totalFrames = 80;
skelly.animations.Add(new CycleColorBounce(1, 2, 2, 0));
objects.Add(skelly);
```

We haven't tried to do anything this complex yet. The question is, will it work—will color and frame animations work correctly "out of the box" or will changes be needed?

The particular sprite sheet used for the color mod example is shown in Figure 15.1. As you can see, it is an animated skeleton with a sword (courtesy of Reiner Prokein via his website, http://www.reinerstilesets.de). We will see this awesome skeleton sprite in the upcoming example.

FIGURE 15.1
Animated skeleton warrior used as an example with color modification.

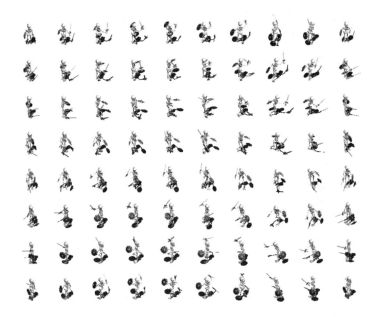

Drawing Frames with Transform Mods

Now we will test the frame animation system with transform modifications (developed back in Hour 13, "Sprite Transform Animation"). Color modification is rather trivial compared to transform modifications, which involve gradually affecting movement, rotation, or scaling over time, very much in parallel with how frame animation changes the image over time. When we're dealing with transforms, though, the image size and position are *crucial* for these mods to work correctly. If an image is loaded in from a bitmap file that has dimensions of 1024×1024, and then transforms are applied to the sprite based on this image size, most likely the sprite will not even show up on the WP7 screen, because frame animation is also being done, and the image is being thrown out of the range of the screen, in all likelihood. So, the initial setup of the sprite's properties is essential to make transformed frame animation work correctly.

Figure 15.2 shows the sprite sheet for the animated swordsman also featured in the example (also courtesy of Reiner Prokein, http://www.reinerstilesets.de).

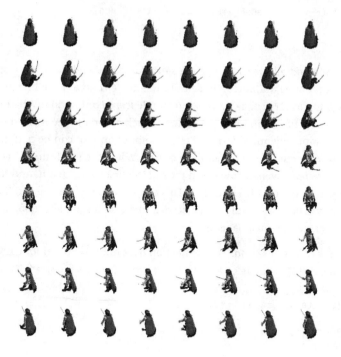

FIGURE 15.2
Animated swordsman used to demo two combined animations.

Custom Frame Animation

We have been using the simple version of the `Sprite.Animate()` method so far, passing just the time value to cause the animation to run at a consistent frame rate. But there is a second version of `Sprite.Animate()` that is called from this first one,

giving us the ability to fine-tune or manually intervene in the way the animation
runs. Here are the two methods again for reference (covered in the preceding hour):

```
public void Animate(double elapsedTime)
{
    Animate(0, totalFrames-1, elapsedTime, 30);
}

public void Animate(int startFrame, int endFrame,
    double elapsedTime, double speed)
{
    if (totalFrames <= 1) return;

    startTime += elapsedTime;
    if (startTime > speed)
    {
        startTime = 0;
        if (++frame > endFrame) frame = startFrame;
    }
}
```

The second method allows us to pass the start frame and end frame for a specific
range of frames to be animated. By default, the first Animate() method just draws
all frames (0 to totalFrames-1). This is a simple *looped* animation: When the last
frame is reached, the animation system loops back around to the first frame again.
But there are more advanced forms of frame animation that can be performed as
well, such as a frame *bounce* rather than a loop: When the last frame is reached, the
animation *direction* reverses downward toward the first frame again, and then
reverses again in the positive direction. This can be actually quite useful if the artwork has only half of the total frames needed to create a complete loop, and instead
the bounce technique must be used.

Now we come to the dilemma: The game loop does not have room for custom, manual method calls! Here is the code in Update() that updates the sprite list:

```
//update all objects
foreach (Sprite spr in objects)
{
    spr.Rotate();
    spr.Move();
}
```

And here is the code in Draw() that animates and draws all the sprites:

```
foreach (Sprite spr in objects)
{
    spr.Animate(); //mods
    spr.Animate(gameTime.ElapsedGameTime.Milliseconds); //frames
    spr.Draw();
}
```

It is true that we *can* jump into these foreach loops and make manual changes to a specific sprite in the list. Or we can just leave a sprite out of the list and handle it separately. That works and there's nothing wrong with that approach. But it kind of defeats the benefits of having an automated game loop, in which sprites are updated and drawn automatically based on *properties*. This describes a *data-driven* game loop, and it is simply unmatched in versatility and power when it comes to building a complex game. In other words, we *want* this to work correctly; we really don't want to bypass it. If a new feature is needed, it's better to work that into the loop than to make exceptions.

What we need is a new *modification* method in the Animation class. Do you see where we're going with this?

Updating the Animation Class

The Sprite class will retain the two new Animate() methods from the preceding hour, and that form of frame animation can be used when it will suffice. But we will now add a more versatile frame animation system that uses the Animation class, fully merging the functionality of color and transform animation with frame animation. This calls for some changes to the Animation class, but no changes to the Sprite class are needed because it already supports multiple animations.

Add the following new method called ModifyFrame() to the Animation class as shown:

```
public class Animation
{
    . . . some portions skipped
    public virtual int ModifyFrame(int current)
    {
        return current;
    }
}
```

New Modifications to the Sprite Class

To make the new frame animation work with Sprite, some things must be modified.

1. A new variable, frameDir, must be added to the class:

   ```
   public int columns, frame, totalFrames, frameDir;
   ```

2. It is initialized in the constructor:

```
columns = 1;
frame = 0;
totalFrames = 1;
frameDir = 1;
```

3. The `Animate()` method can be updated like so (note the line in bold). Remember, this call to `ModifyFrame()` is the default or base method call, and the current frame is passed as the sole parameter. Any class that inherits from Animate and overrides `ModifyFrame()` will have the animation range set to specific values.

```
public void Animate()
{
    if (animations.Count == 0) return;

    foreach (Animation anim in animations)
    {
        if (anim.animating)
        {
            color = anim.ModifyColor(color);
            position = anim.ModifyPosition(position);
            rotation = anim.ModifyRotation(rotation);
            scaleV = anim.ModifyScale(scaleV);
            frame = anim.ModifyFrame(frame);
        }
        else
        {
            animations.Remove(anim);
            return;
        }
    }
}
```

New Animation Subclass Examples

Strangely enough, *that's it!* That's all we had to do to add frame animation support to the Animation class. Now we can create custom subclasses that inherit from Animation to create any kind of special frame animation we need. Listing 15.3 gives two sample animations involving frame modifications that you can study as a reference.

LISTING 15.3   New Animations

```
public class FrameLoop : Animation
{
    public FrameLoop(int start, int end, int current, int direction)
        : base()
    {
```

```
        animating = true;
    }

    public override int ModifyFrame(int start, int end, int current,
        int direction)
    {
        current += direction;
        if (current > end)
            current = start;
        else if (current < start)
            current = end;

        return current;
    }
}

public class FrameBounce : Animation
{
    public FrameBounce(int start, int end, int current, int direction)
        : base()
    {
        animating = true;
    }

    public override int ModifyFrame(int start, int end, int current,
        int direction)
    {
        current += direction;
        if (current > end)
        {
            direction *= -1;
            current = end;
        }
        else if (current < start)
        {
            direction *= -1;
            current = start;
        }

        return current;
    }
}
```

> **By the Way**
>
> If you want frame animation to continue to function as it did before, one option is to automatically add a FrameLoop object to the animation list when a sprite is created (from the Sprite constructor). But it's probably better to just work with the more advanced system now in place.

The FrameLoop class duplicates the existing functionality of parameterized Sprite.Animate(), which updates frame animation. Those two methods could now be removed since FrameLoop replicates that functionality, but I will just leave them alone since they might be useful. Next, the FrameBounce class handles the situation in which an animation will go from start frame to end frame, and then reverse direction down toward start frame again, rather than looping.

Figure 15.3 shows an animated dragon that will also be used in the example.

FIGURE 15.3
Animated dragon used to demo `OrbitalMovement` and `FrameBounce`.

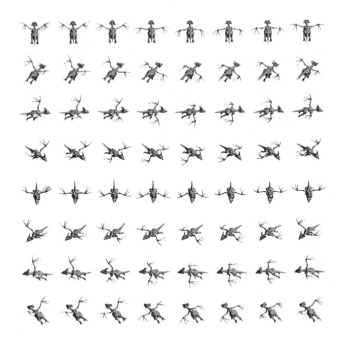

As of the preceding hour, we had an updated `Draw()` that handles sprite frame animation like so:

```
foreach (Sprite spr in objects)
{
    spr.Animate(); //mods
    spr.Animate(gameTime.ElapsedGameTime.Milliseconds); //frames
    spr.Draw();
}
```

The second line in the method, the second call to `Animate()`, can now be removed, after `FrameLoop` or `FrameBounce` has been added as an animation. But if you do remove that line, you *must* be sure to add `FrameLoop` or `FrameBounce` (or some variation thereof) to the animation list after a sprite has been created. For instance:

```
//create dragon sprite
dragon = new Sprite(Content, spriteBatch);
dragon.Load("dragon");
dragon.animations.Add(new FrameLoop(48, 56, 48, 1));
```

Animation Mods Demo

We need a complete example to demonstrate how the new improvements to the animation system work. Figure 15.4 shows the final output of the demo for this hour. On the left is the swordsman character animated with `FrameLoop` and `ThrobBounce`.

The New ThrobBounce Class

The ThrobBounce class inherits from Throb and perpetuates the "throb" animation by overriding the animating property (making it continue when the animation normally ends). For reference, the original Throb class is shown here in Listing 15.4 as well since it is inherited.

LISTING 15.4   New ThrobBounce Class (Throb Repeated for Reference)

```
public class Throb : Animation
{
    public float startScale, endScale, speed;
    private bool p_started;

    public Throb(float startScale, float endScale, float speed)
        : base()
    {
        p_started = false;
        animating = true;
        this.startScale = startScale;
        this.endScale = endScale;
        this.speed = speed;
    }

    public override Vector2 ModifyScale(Vector2 original)
    {
        if (!animating) return original;

        Vector2 modified = original;

        if (!p_started)
        {
            modified.X = startScale;
            modified.Y = startScale;
            p_started = true;
        }
```

```
        modified.X += speed;
        modified.Y += speed;

        if (modified.X >= endScale)
            speed *= -1;
        else if (modified.X <= startScale)
            animating = false;

        return modified;
    }
}

public class ThrobBounce : Throb
{
    public ThrobBounce(float startScale, float endScale, float speed)
        : base(startScale, endScale, speed)
    {
    }

    public override Vector2 ModifyScale(Vector2 original)
    {
        //keep it going
        Vector2 scale = base.ModifyScale(original);
        if (!animating)
        {
            animating = true;
            speed *= -1;
        }
        return scale;
    }
}
```

The Animation Mods Demo Source Code

Here in Listing 15.5 is the complete source code for the Animation Mods Demo that wraps up all the techniques of this hour in one short example.

LISTING 15.5   Source Code for the Animation Mods Demo Program

```
public class Game1 : Microsoft.Xna.Framework.Game
{
    GraphicsDeviceManager graphics;
    SpriteBatch spriteBatch;
    TouchLocation oldTouch;
    Random rand;
    SpriteFont font;
    List<Sprite> objects;
    Sprite swordsman, skelly, dragon;

    public Game1()
    {
        graphics = new GraphicsDeviceManager(this);
        Content.RootDirectory = "Content";
        TargetElapsedTime = TimeSpan.FromTicks(333333);
        oldTouch = new TouchLocation();
    }
```

```
protected override void Initialize()
{
    base.Initialize();
}

protected override void LoadContent()
{
    rand = new Random();
    spriteBatch = new SpriteBatch(GraphicsDevice);
    font = Content.Load<SpriteFont>("WascoSans");

    //create object list
    objects = new List<Sprite>();

    //create swordsman sprite
    swordsman = new Sprite(Content, spriteBatch);
    swordsman.Load("swordsman_walking");
    swordsman.position = new Vector2(150, 240);
    swordsman.size = new Vector2(96, 96);
    swordsman.columns = 8;
    swordsman.totalFrames = 64;
    swordsman.animations.Add(new FrameLoop(0, 63, 1));
    swordsman.animations.Add(new ThrobBounce(0.5f, 4.0f, 0.1f));
    objects.Add(swordsman);

    //create skeleton sprite
    skelly = new Sprite(Content, spriteBatch);
    skelly.Load("skeleton_attack");
    skelly.position = new Vector2(425, 240);
    skelly.size = new Vector2(96,96);
    skelly.scale = 2.0f;
    skelly.columns = 10;
    skelly.totalFrames = 80;
    skelly.animations.Add(new FrameLoop(0, 79, 1));
    skelly.animations.Add(new CycleColorBounce(1, 2, 2, 0));
    objects.Add(skelly);

    //create dragon sprite
    dragon = new Sprite(Content, spriteBatch);
    dragon.Load("dragon");
    dragon.position = new Vector2(700, 240);
    dragon.size = new Vector2(128, 128);
    dragon.scale = 1.5f;
    dragon.columns = 8;
    dragon.totalFrames = 64;
    dragon.animations.Add(new FrameBounce(48, 55, 1));
    dragon.animations.Add(new OrbitalMovement(
        dragon.position, 50, 0, 0.1f));
    objects.Add(dragon);
}

protected override void Update(GameTime gameTime)
{
    if (GamePad.GetState(PlayerIndex.One).Buttons.Back ==
        ButtonState.Pressed)
        this.Exit();
```

```
    //update all objects
    foreach (Sprite spr in objects)
    {
        spr.Rotate();
        spr.Move();
    }

    base.Update(gameTime);
}

protected override void Draw(GameTime gameTime)
{
    GraphicsDevice.Clear(Color.Black);
    spriteBatch.Begin();

    foreach (Sprite spr in objects)
    {
        spr.Animate();
        spr.Draw();
    }

    spriteBatch.DrawString(font, "", Vector2.Zero, Color.White);

    spriteBatch.End();
    base.Draw(gameTime);
}
}
```

Summary

The sprite animation system is now completely functional, with lots of room for growth and with support for custom Animation subclasses. In a professional game, these subclasses would be programmed by designers with Lua script code, allowing designers to make their own custom animations, and the job of the programmers essentially being done at this point with regard to the Animation and Sprite classes. But we aren't getting into scripting, so feel free to create your own *awesome* new animation classes to see what interesting effects you can come up with! In the following hour, we will study *one last* subject related to sprites: z-index ordering. This will allow our sprites to draw over each other with some having higher priority than others.

Q&A

Q. *What is the difference between color animation, transform animation, and frame animation?*

A. These are different topics. The new system created in this chapter might be called *animated frame animation*, since the "frame animation" occurs due to the sprite sheet image drawing code, whereas the Animation mods that can be applied are related to color and transform animation via the Animation class. It is an unfortunate and combustible group of terms.

Q. *I didn't realize there was so much that could be done with sprite animation. What's next?*

A. That's up to you! Create some new animations!

Workshop

Quiz

1. What is the name of the Animation method that affects sprite frames?

2. Which Animation subclass helps with looping frame animation?

3. Which Animation subclass helps with bouncing frame animation?

Answers

1. ModifyFrame()

2. FrameLoop

3. FrameBounce

Exercises

Your exercise for this chapter is to create your own new frame animation class that does something interesting with the sprites in the chapter example! Here is a suggestion: Make it possible for the user to move the hero character up, down, left, or right, and make him perform the walk animation in the right direction while moving.

HOUR 16

Drawing with Z-Index Ordering

What You'll Learn in This Hour:

▶ **Prioritized drawing**
▶ `Sprite` **class changes**
▶ `SpriteBatch` **changes**
▶ **Z-Index Demo**

This will be the final hour of discussing sprite programming, because we have tackled the subject thoroughly throughout Part II, "Sprite Programming," with many detailed examples. It goes without saying that one cannot build a commercial-quality game as a book example, but we will at least have the tools available to build such a game with a focus on 2D gameplay. There is much to be said about a fully rendered 3D game, even on the small platform of the WP7, but rather than making a half-baked attempt at both, this book is going fully into the depths of 2D sprite-based programming, which is where most programmers new to the platform will want to start anyway. Beyond these concepts and techniques, any XNA book that covers 3D rendering will also work on WP7 (although custom shaders are not supported on this hand-held device).

Prioritized Drawing

We already have the ability to perform prioritized "z-index" drawing of a sprite image with the `SpriteBatch.Draw()` method, and we *have* been using the z-index parameter all along, just set to a value of zero. This effectively gave every sprite the same priority. When that is the case, priority will be based entirely on the order at which sprites are drawn (in gameplay code). `SpriteBatch.Draw()` has the capability to automatically prioritize the drawing of some sprites over the top of other sprites using this z-index buffer.

What does "z-index" mean, you may be wondering? When doing 2D sprite programming, we deal only with the X and Y coordinates on the screen. The Z coordinate, then, is the position of the sprite in relation to other sprites that overlap each other. The range for the z-index goes from 0.0 to 1.0. So, a sprite with a z-index priority of 0.6 will draw *over* a sprite with a z-index priority of 0.3. Note that 1.0 is the highest, and 0.0 is the lowest.

Sprite Class Changes

▼ **Try It Yourself**

Adding Z-Buffering to the Sprite Class

A very minor change is required to enable z-index drawing in our `Sprite` class. We'll go over those changes here.

1. Add a `zindex` variable to the class:

   ```
   public float zindex;
   ```

2. In the `Sprite` class constructor, initialize the new variable:

   ```
   zindex = 0.0f;
   ```

3. Replace the hard-coded zero with the `zindex` variable in the `SpriteBatch.Draw()` calls inside `Sprite.Draw()` (there are two of them):

   ```
   public void Draw()
   {
       if (!visible) return;
       if (totalFrames > 1)
       {
           Rectangle source = new Rectangle();
           source.X = (frame % columns) * (int)size.X;
           source.Y = (frame / columns) * (int)size.Y;
           source.Width = (int)size.X;
           source.Height = (int)size.Y;
           p_spriteBatch.Draw(image, position, source, color,
               rotation, origin, scale, SpriteEffects.None, zindex);
       }
       else
       {
           p_spriteBatch.Draw(image, position, null, color, rotation,
               origin, scaleV, SpriteEffects.None, zindex);
       }
   }
   ```

▲

Adding Rendering Support for Z-Buffering

To use a z-buffer for prioritized drawing, a change must be made to the call to
SpriteBatch.Begin(), which gets drawing started in the main program code. No
change is made to SpriteBatch.End(). There are actually *five* overloads of
SpriteBatch.Begin()! The version we want requires just two parameters:
SpriteSortMode and BlendState. Table 16.1 shows the SpriteSortMode enumera-
tion values.

TABLE 16.1 SpriteSortMode Enumeration

Item	Description
Deferred	Sprites are drawn when End is called in one batch.
Immediate	Sprites will be drawn with each Draw call.
Texture	Sprites are sorted by texture prior to drawing.
BackToFront	Sprites are sorted by depth in back-to-front order prior to drawing.
FrontToBack	Sprites are sorted by depth in front-to-back order prior to drawing.

The default sorting mode is Deferred, which is what SpriteBatch uses when the
default Begin() is called. For z-index ordering, we will want to use either
BackToFront or FrontToBack. There is very little difference between these two
except the weight direction of each sprite's z-index.

When using BackToFront, smaller z-index values have higher priority, with 0.0
being drawn over other sprites within the range up to 1.0.

When using FrontToBack, the opposite is true: Larger z-index values (such as 1.0)
are treated with higher priority than lower values (such as 0.0).

It works best if you just choose one and stick with it to avoid confusion. If you think
of a z-index value of 1.0 being "higher" in the screen depth, use FrontToBack. If 0.0
seems to have a higher priority, use BackToFront.

In our example, we will use FrontToBack, with larger values for the z-index having
higher priority.

Z-Index Demo

To demonstrate the effect z-index ordering has on a scene, I have prepared an example that draws a screen full of sprites and then moves a larger sprite across the screen. Based on the z-index value of each sprite, the larger sprite will appear either over or under the other sprites. In this example, the screen is filled with animated asteroid sprites, and the larger sprite is an image of a shuttle. Figure 16.1 shows the demo with the shuttle sprite drawn on top of the first half of the asteroids.

FIGURE 16.1
The shuttle appears over the first half of the rows.

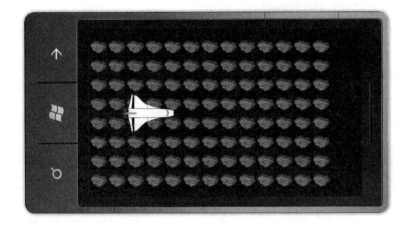

Figure 16.2 shows the shuttle sprite farther across the screen, where it appears under the second half of the rows of asteroid sprites (which have a higher z-index than the shuttle sprite).

FIGURE 16.2
The shuttle appears under the second half of the rows.

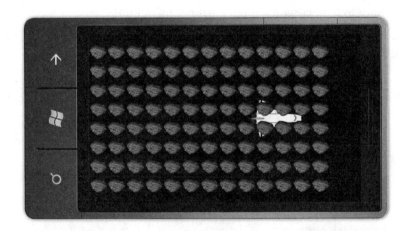

Wrapping Around the Screen Edge

To assist with this demo, a new `Animation` subclass has been written to automatically wrap a sprite around the edges of the screen. This completely eliminates any gameplay code that would otherwise have to be added to the `Update()` method. This is called synergy—when a combination of simple things produces awesome results! We're starting to see that happen with our sprite and animation code now. Wrapping around the edges of the screen might be considered more of a *behavior* than an *animation*.

```
public class WrapBoundary : Animation
{
    Rectangle boundary;

    public WrapBoundary(Rectangle boundary)
        : base()
    {
        animating = true;
        this.boundary = boundary;
    }

    public override Vector2 ModifyPosition(Vector2 original)
    {
        Vector2 pos = original;

        if (pos.X < boundary.Left)
            pos.X = boundary.Right;
        else if (pos.X > boundary.Right)
            pos.X = boundary.Left;

        if (pos.Y < boundary.Top)
            pos.Y = boundary.Bottom;
        else if (pos.Y > boundary.Bottom)
            pos.Y = boundary.Top;

        return pos;
    }
}
```

Z-Index Demo Source Code

Listing 16.1 contains the source code for the Z-Index Demo. Note the code highlighted in bold—these lines are relevant to our discussion of z-buffering.

LISTING 16.1   Source Code for the Z-Index Demo

```
public class Game1 : Microsoft.Xna.Framework.Game
{
    GraphicsDeviceManager graphics;
    SpriteBatch spriteBatch;
    TouchLocation oldTouch;
```

```
Random rand;
SpriteFont font;
List<Sprite> objects;
Texture2D asteroidImage;

public Game1()
{
    graphics = new GraphicsDeviceManager(this);
    Content.RootDirectory = "Content";
    TargetElapsedTime = TimeSpan.FromTicks(333333);
    oldTouch = new TouchLocation();
}

protected override void Initialize()
{
    base.Initialize();
}

protected override void LoadContent()
{
    rand = new Random();
    spriteBatch = new SpriteBatch(GraphicsDevice);
    font = Content.Load<SpriteFont>("WascoSans");

    //create object list
    objects = new List<Sprite>();

    //create shuttle sprite
    Sprite shuttle = new Sprite(Content, spriteBatch);
    shuttle.Load("shuttle");
    shuttle.scale = 0.4f;
    shuttle.position = new Vector2(0, 240);
    shuttle.rotation = MathHelper.ToRadians(90);
    shuttle.velocityLinear = new Vector2(4, 0);
    Rectangle bounds = new Rectangle(-80, 0, 800 + 180, 480);
    shuttle.animations.Add(new WrapBoundary(bounds));
    shuttle.zindex = 0.5f;
    objects.Add(shuttle);

    //load asteroid image
    asteroidImage = Content.Load<Texture2D>("asteroid");

    //create asteroid sprites with increasing z-index
    for (int row = 0; row < 13; row++)
    {
        float zindex = row / 12.0f;
        for (int col = 0; col < 8; col++)
        {
            Sprite spr = new Sprite(Content, spriteBatch);
            spr.image = asteroidImage;
            spr.columns = 8;
            spr.totalFrames = 64;
            spr.animations.Add(new FrameLoop(0, 63, 1));
            spr.position = new Vector2(30 + 60 * row, 30 + col * 60);
            spr.size = new Vector2(60, 60);
            spr.zindex = zindex;
            objects.Add(spr);
        }
```

```
        }
    }

    protected override void Update(GameTime gameTime)
    {
        if (GamePad.GetState(PlayerIndex.One).Buttons.Back ==
            ButtonState.Pressed)
            this.Exit();

        foreach (Sprite spr in objects)
        {
            spr.Rotate();
            spr.Move();
        }

        base.Update(gameTime);
    }

    protected override void Draw(GameTime gameTime)
    {
        GraphicsDevice.Clear(Color.Black);
        spriteBatch.Begin(SpriteSortMode.FrontToBack, BlendState.AlphaBlend);

        foreach (Sprite spr in objects)
        {
            spr.Animate();
            spr.Draw();
        }

        spriteBatch.End();
        base.Draw(gameTime);
    }
}
```

Summary

This hour added z-index ordering support to the Sprite class and demonstrated how the z-index value of a sprite affects its priority in the scene when drawn over or under other sprites. When you're using a z-index, it does not matter when sprites are drawn in terms of Sprite.Draw() calls; they will be ordered according to their z-index value. In the example shared in this hour, we used a z-index ordering of FrontToBack, which causes sprites with a higher z-index to have higher priority.

Q&A

Q. *What about using z-buffering to make characters seem to walk under bridges and tunnels?*

A. That's a very good use for this technique!

Q. *In a scrolling shoot-em-up with airplanes, how could z-buffering be used to make clouds always appear over the top of all other sprites, no matter what their z-index value is?*

A. Remember, sprites are drawn in batches! You can always start up a second or third `SpriteBatch.Begin()` and `SpriteBatch.End()` pair for drawing independently of the z-buffering used previously. Just keep in mind that each pair of calls adds overhead to the rendering system, which will slow down the game.

Workshop

Quiz

1. What parameter must be passed to `SpriteBatch.Begin()` to enable z-buffering with front-to-back ordering?

2. Similarly, what parameter causes sprite drawing to be deferred?

3. For the second parameter, which blending state uses the alpha channel if an image has one?

Answers

1. `SpriteSortMode.FrontToBack`

2. `SpriteSortMode.Deferred`

3. `BlendState.AlphaBlend`

Exercises

Try the following modification to the Z-Index Demo presented in this chapter. For every asteroid sprite on the screen, give it a random z-index value from 0.0 to 1.0, and then run the program as before so that the ship moves across the screen. Keep the ship at a middle value of 0.5. How does the randomness affect the appearance of the asteroid field? Next, what if the asteroids were slowly moving in random directions?

PART III

Gameplay

HOUR 17

Using Location Services (GPS)

What You'll Learn in This Hour:

- ▶ **GPS 101**
- ▶ **Windows Phone location services**
- ▶ **Simulating position changes**
- ▶ **Creating the Geo Position Demo**

In this hour, we will learn about the location services available to our XNA programs from the Windows Phone's GPS receiver. GPS stands for Global Positioning System. Originally developed by the U.S. Department of Defense, GPS is now so widely used that many people and services have come to rely on GPS for their livelihoods. WP7 has a GPS receiver, so location information is available in the hardware. However, we cannot tap into the GPS using the WP7 emulator because, well, it's an *emulator*—a GPS receiver is required to pick up GPS data, so there's no hardware workaround. We can, however, write some code to *simulate* GPS data, via the location services provided by the libraries in XNA. If you have a physical WP7 device for development, you will be able to test real location coordinates. Otherwise, simulating the coordinates works pretty well too.

GPS 101

Let's spend a few minutes to just learn the basics of GPS, in order to better use it in our code. What GPS boils down to—the nitty-gritty—are two floating-point numbers representing the X and Y position on the Earth. The X value has traditionally been called *longitude*, and the Y value has been known as the *latitude*. From a game programming perspective, this is an easier way to grasp the terms, but a naval veteran would scoff at the overly simplistic way this is being presented. We'll gloss over issues of precision in order to grasp the concepts first.

Longitude represents the "X" or horizontal coordinate on the surface of the Earth, running east or west from the zero point.

Latitude represents the "Y" or vertical coordinate on the surface of the Earth, running north or south from the zero point.

The origin (0,0) is located about 400 miles off the western coast of Africa, southwest of Nigeria and south of Ghana. From that origin point, longitude increases to the right (east), and decreases to the left (west); latitude increases up (north), and decreases down (south). In other words, it is oriented exactly like the Cartesian coordinate system we've been using all along for our trig-heavy examples. This makes translating GPS coordinates for the purpose of making a *reality game* a cinch!

To help make sense of the coordinate system, Table 17.1 shows the *approximate* latitude and longitude values of several major cities in the world, formatted in a way that makes sense to game programmers (such that longitude comes before latitude—remember, we aren't navigating here). Note that these are far from precise, just rough estimates to present the *general location* of each city. More precise GPS coordinates will include up to six decimal places of increasing precision, down to just 10 feet or less in granularity.

TABLE 17.1   GPS Data for Major Cities

City	Longitude	Latitude
Atlanta	-84	34
Beijing	116	40
Berlin	13	53
London	0	51
Los Angeles	-118	34
Mexico City	-99	19
Moscow	38	56
New York	-74	41
Paris	2	49
Phoenix	-112	33
Rome	12	42
Sacramento	-121	38
Tokyo	-140	36
Washington, D.C.	-77	39

> If you want to learn more about latitude and longitude coordinates, there is an interactive world map available online at http://itouchmap.com/latlong.html.

Windows Phone Location Services

XNA provides us with a geographic location service in a library located in a namespace called `System.Device.Location`. This library is not included in the project's references by default, so we must add it to use this library in our program.

Try It Yourself

Adding the Location Services Library

1. Right-click References in the Solution Explorer, and then choose Add Reference.

2. In the dialog box that comes up, there is a list with the .NET tab already in view, as shown in Figure 17.1. Select System.Device from the list and click the OK button.

3. The geographic location services library is in a namespace called `System.Device.Location`, which must be added with a using statement to any program that needs these services:

```
using System.Device.Location;
```

Using the Location Services

To read the current device's GPS location, we create an object using the `GeoCoordinateWatcher` class:

```
GeoCoordinateWatcherSim watcher;
```

It is okay to create the `watcher` object in `Initialize()` or `LoadContent()`, or in response to a user event:

```
watcher = new GeoCoordinateWatcher(GeoPositionAccuracy.Default);
```

At this point, the object is created but is not yet receiving any GPS data. We have to create an event handler to handle position status change events. The trigger that causes such an event is movement of the device, which can be fine-tuned with the `MovementThreshold` property:

```
watcher.MovementThreshold = 20;
```

FIGURE 17.1
Adding a refer-
ence to the
System.Device
library.

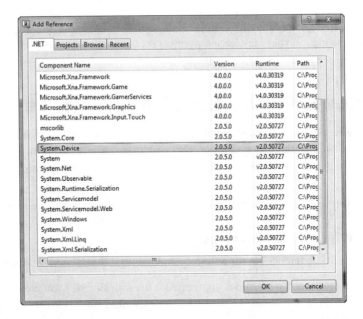

The first event we'll tap into is StatusChanged. A new event method will need to be created to correspond with the name of the method passed to this new event object. In this case, the example is using a string called statusText, which can be printed out from the main Draw() call. Optionally, a programmer-defined status could be set here and used elsewhere in the game:

```
watcher.StatusChanged += new EventHandler
    <GeoPositionStatusChangedEventArgs>(watcher_StatusChanged);

void watcher_StatusChanged(object sender,
GeoPositionStatusChangedEventArgs e)
{
    switch (e.Status)
    {
        case GeoPositionStatus.Disabled:
            statusText += "Location service has been disabled\n";
            break;
        case GeoPositionStatus.Initializing:
            statusText += "Location service is initializing\n";
            break;
        case GeoPositionStatus.NoData:
            statusText += "Location service is not returning any data\n";
            break;
        case GeoPositionStatus.Ready:
            statusText += "Location service is receiving data\n";
            break;
    }
}
```

The actual movement of the GPS device triggers position change events that we can tap into with the PositionChanged event. A similar event method will have to be created for this event as well. In this example, a GeoCoordinate variable called coord is set using the passed parameter that contains the GPS location data:

```
watcher.PositionChanged += new EventHandler
    <GeoPositionChangedEventArgs<GeoCoordinate>>(watcher_PositionChanged);

void watcher_PositionChanged(object sender,
GeoPositionChangedEventArgs<GeoCoordinate> e)
{
    coord = e.Position.Location;
}
```

Simulating Position Changes

The WP7 emulator does not have a GPS receiver, and even if your PC has one, the emulator doesn't know how to use it—the emulator is a self-contained system that only uses the networking of your PC to simulate connectivity. I say "simulate" because in a real WP7 device, that Internet connection would come through the airwaves, presumably G3 or G4, depending on what the service provider supports.

There is a workaround for the limitation. If you want to create a game that uses location services, it's a given you must be able to test it extensively, and even with a real WP7 device, testing GPS code can be a challenge. So, even with hardware, it may be preferred to develop this code with a GPS simulation rather than the real thing. With a simulation, you can define the location data yourself and write the gameplay code to respond to location data in a predictable way. Only the final testing stages of the game would need to be done "in the field."

So, a question arises: How do we simulate GPS data?

The solution is to write a class that inherits from GeoLocationWatcher and then *fill in* data events with a timer that generates real-time updates via GeoLocation events. Voilà!

GeoLocationSim

There are three classes involved in the geographic location simulator. The first is GeoLocationSim, which inherits directly from GeoCoordinateWatcher, the main GPS class in XNA. There are quite a few properties, events, and methods defined in this abstract class that are required to pass this off as a legitimate GeoLocation class so that it works with normal GeoLocation code, but we don't need all of that for testing purposes. Nevertheless, they are all required. In the sample project for this hour, I have added all three classes in a source file called GeoLocationSim.cs. First, take a look at Listing 17.1, the code for the sim class.

LISTING 17.1   Base GeoLocation Simulation Class

```
abstract public class GeoLocationSim : GeoCoordinateWatcher
{
    private GeoPosition<GeoCoordinate> current;
    private Timer timer;

    public GeoLocationSim()
    {
        current = new GeoPosition<GeoCoordinate>();
        Status = GeoPositionStatus.Initializing;
        RaiseStatusChanged();
    }

    private void RaiseStatusChanged()
    {
        GeoPositionStatusChangedEventArgs args =
            new GeoPositionStatusChangedEventArgs(Status);
        if (StatusChanged != null)
        {
            StatusChanged(this, args);
        }
    }

    private void RaisePositionChanged()
    {
        GeoPositionChangedEventArgs<GeoCoordinate> args =
            new GeoPositionChangedEventArgs<GeoCoordinate>(current);
        if (PositionChanged != null)
            PositionChanged(this, args);
    }

    public void OnTimerCallback(object state)
    {
        try
        {
            if (Status == GeoPositionStatus.Initializing)
            {
                Status = GeoPositionStatus.NoData;
                RaiseStatusChanged();
            }
            StartGetCurrentPosition();
            TimeSpan next = GetNextInterval();
            timer.Change(next, next);
        }
        catch (Exception)
        {
            throw;
        }
    }

    protected void UpdateLocation(double longitude, double latitude)
    {
        GeoCoordinate location = new GeoCoordinate(latitude, longitude);
```

```csharp
    if (!location.Equals(current.Location))
    {
        current = new GeoPosition<GeoCoordinate>(
            DateTimeOffset.Now, location);
        if (Status != GeoPositionStatus.Ready)
        {
            Status = GeoPositionStatus.Ready;
            RaiseStatusChanged();
        }
        RaisePositionChanged();
    }
}

abstract protected TimeSpan GetNextInterval();
abstract protected void StartGetCurrentPosition();

//override base property
public GeoPositionPermission Permission
{
    get { return GeoPositionPermission.Granted; }
}

//override base property
public GeoPosition<GeoCoordinate> Position
{
    get { return current; }
}

//override base event
public event EventHandler<GeoPositionChangedEventArgs
    <GeoCoordinate>> PositionChanged;

//override base method
public void Start(bool suppressPermissionPrompt)
{
    Start();
}

//override base method
public void Start()
{
    TimeSpan span = GetNextInterval();
    timer = new Timer(OnTimerCallback, null, span, span);
}

//override base property
public GeoPositionStatus Status
{
    get;
    protected set;
}

//override base event
public event EventHandler
    <GeoPositionStatusChangedEventArgs> StatusChanged;

//override base method
public void Stop()
```

```
    {
        timer.Change(Timeout.Infinite, Timeout.Infinite);
        Status = GeoPositionStatus.Disabled;
        RaiseStatusChanged();
    }

    //override base method
    public bool TryStart(bool suppressPermissionPrompt, TimeSpan timeout)
    {
        Start();
        return true;
    }
}
```

Filling in GPS Data with Timing

SampleGeoCoord is a helper class that is used to fill in GPS position data *with* timing. Each position coordinate corresponds to a one-second interval at which the position update event is triggered. So, this class supplies longitude, latitude, and time.

```
public class SampleGeoCoord
{
    public double Longitude { get; set; }
    public double Latitude { get; set; }
    public TimeSpan Time { get; set; }

    public SampleGeoCoord(double Longitude, double Latitude, int seconds)
    {
        this.Longitude = Longitude;
        this.Latitude = Latitude;
        this.Time = new TimeSpan(0, 0, seconds);
    }
}
```

GeoCoordinateWatcherSim

The GeoCoordinateWatcherSim is our main workhorse simulation class, inheriting directly from GeoLocationSim. This class puts the GeoLocationSim properties, methods, and events to work *using* data populated within an array of SampleGeoCoord objects. In the example coming up that uses this class, I've centered the coordinates around Los Angeles, with 60 seconds of random locations within a radius of about 100 miles around the city coordinates (-118, 34). Listing 17.2 contains the code for the GeoCoordinateWatcherSim class.

LISTING 17.2   Usable GeoCoordinateWatcherSim Worker Class

```
public class GeoCoordinateWatcherSim : GeoLocationSim
{
    List<SampleGeoCoord> events;
    int currentEventId;
```

```
Random rand = new Random();

public GeoCoordinateWatcherSim(GeoPositionAccuracy accuracy)
{
    currentEventId = 0;
    events = new List<SampleGeoCoord>();

    //create random coordinates in Los Angeles
    for (int n = 1; n < 60; n++)
    {
        double Long = -118 - rand.Next(2) - rand.NextDouble();
        double Lat = 33 + rand.Next(2) + rand.NextDouble();
        events.Add(new SampleGeoCoord(Long, Lat, n));
    }
}

private SampleGeoCoord Current
{
    get
    {
        return events[currentEventId % events.Count];
    }
}

protected override void StartGetCurrentPosition()
{
    this.UpdateLocation(Current.Longitude, Current.Latitude);
    currentEventId++;
}

protected override TimeSpan GetNextInterval()
{
    return Current.Time;
}
}
```

Creating the Geo Position Demo

Let's write a program to demonstrate the GeoCoordinateWatcherSim class in action.
The example requires only a font, because it just prints out the longitude and latitude of the geographical coordinate data and the status of the watcher. The code for
the Geo Position Demo program is found in Listing 17.3, and Figure 17.2 shows the
program running. Note that this example will work on a WP7 device without the
simulated data with a single line change, from

```
watcher = new GeoCoordinateWatcherSim(...);
```

to

```
watcher = new GeoCoordinateWatcher(...);
```

FIGURE 17.2
The Geo Position Demo simulates GPS movement.

LISTING 17.3   The Geo Position Demo Program

```
public class Game1 : Microsoft.Xna.Framework.Game
{
    GraphicsDeviceManager graphics;
    SpriteBatch spriteBatch;
    TouchLocation oldTouch;
    Random rand;
    SpriteFont font;
    string statusText = "";
    GeoCoordinateWatcherSim watcher = null;
    GeoCoordinate coord = null;

    public Game1()
    {
        graphics = new GraphicsDeviceManager(this);
        Content.RootDirectory = "Content";
        TargetElapsedTime = TimeSpan.FromTicks(333333);
        oldTouch = new TouchLocation();
    }

    protected override void Initialize()
    {
        base.Initialize();
        StartGeoLocation();
    }

    protected override void LoadContent()
    {
        rand = new Random();
        spriteBatch = new SpriteBatch(GraphicsDevice);
        font = Content.Load<SpriteFont>("WascoSans");
    }

    protected override void UnloadContent()
    {
        base.UnloadContent();
        watcher.Stop();
    }
```

```csharp
    protected override void Update(GameTime gameTime)
    {
        if (GamePad.GetState(PlayerIndex.One).Buttons.Back ==
            ButtonState.Pressed)
            this.Exit();

        base.Update(gameTime);
    }

    protected override void Draw(GameTime gameTime)
    {
        GraphicsDevice.Clear(Color.Black);
        spriteBatch.Begin(SpriteSortMode.FrontToBack,
            BlendState.AlphaBlend);

        spriteBatch.DrawString(font, "Latitude: " +
            coord.Latitude.ToString("0.000"),
            new Vector2(100, 10), Color.White);

        spriteBatch.DrawString(font, "Longitude: " +
            coord.Longitude.ToString("0.000"),
            new Vector2(100, 30), Color.White);

        spriteBatch.DrawString(font, statusText,
            new Vector2(100, 100), Color.White);

        spriteBatch.End();
        base.Draw(gameTime);
    }

    void StartGeoLocation()
    {
        coord = new GeoCoordinate();

        //try to create geo coordinate watcher
        if (watcher == null)
        {
            statusText += "Starting location service...\n";
            watcher = new GeoCoordinateWatcherSim(
                GeoPositionAccuracy.Default);
            watcher.MovementThreshold = 20;
            watcher.StatusChanged += new EventHandler
                <GeoPositionStatusChangedEventArgs>(
                watcher_StatusChanged);
            watcher.PositionChanged += new EventHandler
                <GeoPositionChangedEventArgs<GeoCoordinate>>
                (watcher_PositionChanged);
            watcher.Start();
        }
    }

    void watcher_StatusChanged(object sender,
        GeoPositionStatusChangedEventArgs e)
    {
        switch (e.Status)
        {
            case GeoPositionStatus.Disabled:
                statusText += "Location service has been disabled\n";
                break;
```

```
            case GeoPositionStatus.Initializing:
                statusText += "Location service is initializing\n";
                break;

            case GeoPositionStatus.NoData:
                statusText += "Location service is not returning any data\n";
                break;

            case GeoPositionStatus.Ready:
                statusText += "Location service is receiving data\n";
                break;
        }
    }

    void watcher_PositionChanged(object sender,
        GeoPositionChangedEventArgs<GeoCoordinate> e)
    {
        coord = e.Position.Location;
    }
}
```

Summary

There are many uses for GPS tracking, not to mention potential multiplayer games, but one thing to keep in mind is that GPS only provides location data, but there's no transmitting of that data. After the location is received, that's it—it's data, and it's not transmitted anywhere. GPS is read-only. So, if you have in mind a game, there must still be a network infrastructure connecting all the players, wherein each player will transmit his or her GPS location to the other players over the network. The WP7 platform supports Xbox Live for networking, so that is likely the next subject to study if you're interested in making a networked game.

Q&A

Q. *How would you make a multiplayer game using GPS data to track the players?*

A. Either one of the players or a separate dedicated server must communicate the GPS data from each player in order to send that position data to all the other players.

Q. *Is it possible to calculate the distance in code between two users carrying WP7 devices?*

A. Yes, it is possible, by treating longitude and latitude as X and Y, respectively, and then using the usual distance function to calculate distance between two users. Converting the coordinates into usable units of measure will require some research into GPS unit measurements, though.

Workshop

Quiz

1. What is the name of the library reference that must be added to a project to support GPS?

2. What XNA class do we use to read data from a built-in GPS receiver?

3. Which library namespace must be included in a program using GPS services?

Answers

1. System.Device

2. GeoCoordinateWatcher

3. System.Device.Location

Exercises

Using the website http://itouchmap.com/latlong.html, find your hometown's longitude and latitude coordinates and plug them in to the GeoCoordinateWatcherSim class in place of the existing coordinates of Los Angeles so that you can experiment with simulating movement in your current location. It's about as close as we can come to realizing actual GPS location tracking with simulated data.

HOUR 18

Playing Audio

What You'll Learn in This Hour:

- ▶ **Windows Phone audio**
- ▶ **Simple audio playback**
- ▶ **Adding audio content**
- ▶ **Playing an audio clip**
- ▶ **Audio clip length**

This hour covers the loading and playing of audio files on WP7. All the code will be familiar to someone already experienced with XNA, because the same `SoundEffect` code can be used for audio playback in a Windows Phone game. The XNA audio system is found in the `Microsoft.Xna.Framework.Audio` namespace. For audio playback, we use `SoundEffect` and `SoundEffectInstance`. WP7 does not support the Cross-Platform Audio Creation Tool (XACT) or XACT projects, so we have only the simple loading and playback of audio files on WP7.

Getting Started with Windows Phone Audio

The audio system in XNA makes it possible to reproduce sound effects and music in two different ways, but the WP7 platform supports only one of them. First, we can play audio clips directly from audio files loaded at runtime, with support for the most common audio file formats. Second, in XNA, we can use Microsoft's Cross-Platform Audio Creation Tool, also known as XACT, which is more often used for complex games with many audio files. The first approach involves loading and managing audio objects in our own code. The second approach leaves the details largely up to classes provided for working with XACT resources built at compile time and then made available from a container of objects. But we can't use XACT with WP7 projects, so we'll learn about the first and only option instead. We'll cover the audio system in the `Microsoft.Xna.Framework.Audio` namespace with an example of the audio system.

Simple Audio Playback

There is one very easy way to get audio to play in an XNA project: by using the `SoundEffect` class. There is a drawback to using `SoundEffect` assets that really can't be avoided: the tendency for the content project to become cluttered with asset files. Even so, the `SoundEffect` class is convenient and easy to use. A helper class called `SoundEffectInstance` is also used in conjunction with `SoundEffect` for audio playback. `SoundEffect` itself has a `Play()` method, but it is rudimentary. `SoundEffectInstance.Play()` is more capable and versatile.

Adding Audio Content

▼ **Try It Yourself**

Adding Audio Content

Before we can play an audio clip, we have to add it to the content system.

1. First, right-click the Content project in Solution Explorer, choose Add, and then choose Existing Item, as shown in Figure 18.1. This opens the Add Existing File dialog box.

FIGURE 18.1
Adding an existing audio file to the content project.

2. Locate the audio file you want to add to the project. Select the file in the file browser and click the OK button.

▲

Loading an Audio Asset File

The following audio file types can be added to an XNA project for use with the SoundEffect class, but remember that WP7 does not support XACT:

- XAP

- WAV

- WMA

- MP3

You can create an instance of the SoundEffect class with a variable declared in the globals section at the top of the class as follows:

```
SoundEffect clip;
```

The SoundEffect object is created in the usual LoadContent() function where all other asset files are loaded:

```
protected override void LoadContent()
{
    spriteBatch = new SpriteBatch(GraphicsDevice);
    font = Content.Load<SpriteFont>("Arial");
    clip = Content.Load<SoundEffect>("sound_clip");
}
```

Playing an Audio Clip

The audio clip can be played back using the SoundEffect.Play() method. There is a simple version of Play() and an overloaded version, which gives you control over the Volume, Pitch, and Pan properties. The audio clip is played directly from the object like so:

```
clip.Play();
```

Audio Clip Length

There is really only one useful property in the SoundEffect class: Duration. This property gives you the length of the audio clip in seconds. In the Draw() function of your sample program (Simple Audio Demo), you can print out the length of the audio clip.

```
string text = "Clip length: " + clip.Duration.ToString();
spriteBatch.DrawString(font, text, Vector2.Zero, Color.White);
```

When it comes down to playing audio clips in gameplay code, this class is not very helpful at all. What we need is a class with more functionality.

SoundEffectInstance

The SoundEffect class *works*, but not very well on its own. For one thing, a SoundEffect clip played does not work well in a complex audio environment (with music and different sound effects playing at the same time). For that, we need a helper class that can repeat playback with mixing support. That class is called SoundEffectInstance. This is really what we want to use when playing audio clips.

The SoundEffectInstance class enhances the basic functionality of SoundEffect with additional properties and methods that make it more useful in a real-world game. After loading the SoundEffect in LoadContent(), we can create an instance of the SoundEffectInstance class from its CreateInstance() method:

```
SoundEffect clip = Content.Load<SoundEffect>("sound_clip");
SoundEffectInstance clipInst = clip.CreateInstance();
```

This class makes available several useful methods: Play(), Stop(), Pause(), and Resume(). And the Volume, Pitch, and Pan properties have been moved from parameters into real class properties, which we can modify outside of the Play() method. In addition, we can cause an audio clip to loop during playback with the IsLooping property.

MySoundEffect Class

I have prepared a helper class with essentially the sole purpose of just combining a SoundEffect and SoundEffectInstance object with a Load() method. We will use this helper class in the example coming up next. The source code for the class is found in Listing 18.1.

LISTING 18.1   Source Code for the MySoundEffect Class

```
public class MySoundEffect
{
    private ContentManager p_content;
    public SoundEffect effect;
    public SoundEffectInstance instance;

    public MySoundEffect(ContentManager content)
    {
        p_content = content;
        effect = null;
        instance = null;
    }
```

```
    public void Load(string assetName)
    {
        effect = p_content.Load<SoundEffect>(assetName);
        instance = effect.CreateInstance();
    }
}
```

Creating the Audio Demo Program

The Audio Demo program is a complete example of audio for WP7 with some user input features as well, as shown in Figure 18.2. Five buttons are located on the screen that can be touched to play the five audio clips loaded into the program.

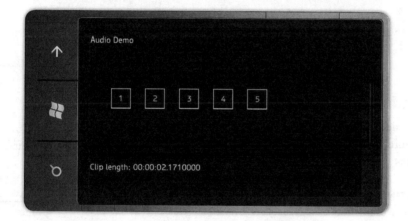

FIGURE 18.2
The Audio Demo program.

Button Class

The audio sample project uses a helper class called Button to draw numbered buttons on the screen that respond to screen touch input events. The Button class requires a bitmap file called button.png that is just a transparent image with a border around its edges. Listing 18.2 contains the source code for the Button class.

LISTING 18.2   The Button Class

```
public class Button : Sprite
{
    public string text;
    private SpriteBatch p_spriteBatch;
    private SpriteFont p_font;

    public Button(ContentManager content, SpriteBatch spriteBatch,
        SpriteFont font) : base(content, spriteBatch)
    {
        p_spriteBatch = spriteBatch;
```

```
        p_font = font;
        Load("button");
        text = "";
        color = Color.LightGreen;
    }

    public void Draw()
    {
        base.Draw();
        Vector2 size = p_font.MeasureString(text);
        Vector2 pos = position;
        pos.X -= size.X / 2;
        pos.Y -= size.Y / 2;
        p_spriteBatch.DrawString(p_font, text, pos, color);
    }

    public bool Tapped(Vector2 pos)
    {
        Rectangle rect = new Rectangle((int)pos.X, (int)pos.Y, 1, 1);
        return Boundary().Intersects(rect);
    }
}
```

Audio Demo Source

The main source code for the Audio Demo project is found in Listing 18.3. The required assets are a button image and five audio files named clip1, clip2, clip3, clip4, and clip5.

LISTING 18.3   Source Code for the Audio Demo Program

```
public class Game1 : Microsoft.Xna.Framework.Game
{
    GraphicsDeviceManager graphics;
    SpriteBatch spriteBatch;
    TouchLocation oldTouch;
    SpriteFont font;

    Button[] buttons;

    MySoundEffect[] sounds;
    int current = -1;

    public Game1()
    {
        graphics = new GraphicsDeviceManager(this);
        Content.RootDirectory = "Content";
        TargetElapsedTime = TimeSpan.FromTicks(333333);
        oldTouch = new TouchLocation();
    }
```

```
protected override void Initialize()
{
    base.Initialize();
    this.IsMouseVisible = true;
}

protected override void LoadContent()
{
    spriteBatch = new SpriteBatch(GraphicsDevice);
    font = Content.Load<SpriteFont>("WascoSans");

    //create buttons
    buttons = new Button[5];
    for (int n = 0; n < 5; n++)
    {
        buttons[n] = new Button(Content, spriteBatch, font);
        buttons[n].text = (n+1).ToString();
        buttons[n].position = new Vector2(100 + 110 * n, 200);
    }

    //create sound clips
    sounds = new MySoundEffect[5];
    for (int n = 0; n < 5; n++)
    {
        sounds[n] = new MySoundEffect(Content);
        sounds[n].Load("Audio//clip" + (n+1).ToString());
    }
}

protected override void Update(GameTime gameTime)
{
    if (GamePad.GetState(PlayerIndex.One).Buttons.Back ==
        ButtonState.Pressed)
        this.Exit();

    TouchCollection touchInput = TouchPanel.GetState();
    if (touchInput.Count > 0)
    {
        TouchLocation touch = touchInput[0];
        if (touch.State == TouchLocationState.Pressed)
        {
            current = -1;
            int n = 0;
            foreach (Button b in buttons)
            {
                int x = (int)touch.Position.X;
                int y = (int)touch.Position.Y;
                if (b.Boundary().Contains(x,y))
                {
                    current = n;
                    sounds[current].instance.Play();
                    break;
                }
                n++;
            }
        }
        oldTouch = touch;
    }
```

```
        base.Update(gameTime);
    }

    protected override void Draw(GameTime gameTime)
    {
        GraphicsDevice.Clear(Color.Black);
        spriteBatch.Begin(SpriteSortMode.FrontToBack,
            BlendState.AlphaBlend);

        spriteBatch.DrawString(font, "Audio Demo", Vector2.Zero,
            Color.White);

        foreach (Button b in buttons)
        {
            b.Draw();
        }

        if (current > -1)
        {
            string text = "Clip length: " +
                sounds[current].effect.Duration.ToString();
            spriteBatch.DrawString(font, text, new Vector2(0, 400),
                Color.White);
        }

        spriteBatch.End();
        base.Draw(gameTime);
    }
}
```

Summary

We have now fully covered the XNA audio system with an example of how to load and play audio files. The helper class, `MySoundEffect`, can be dropped into any WP7 project and used to more easily handle the audio needs of a game.

Q&A

Q. *What is the difference between the audio file formats WAV, WMA, and MP3?*

A. WAV is usually an uncompressed raw format containing audio samples, most commonly used for short sound effects. WMA and MP3 are both compressed audio formats suitable for music.

Q. *Without support for XACT, is there an optional way to organize sound files in a project?*

A. One recommendation is to put all audio assets inside a separate folder in the Content project, such as `.\audio` or `.\sound`.

Workshop

Quiz

1. What is the name of the XNA class used to load an audio file?

2. What is the name of the XNA helper class with additional audio playback features?

3. What is the name of the property that makes an audio clip play with looping?

Answers

1. `SoundEffect`

2. `SoundEffectInstance`

3. `IsLooping`

Exercises

Locate some sound effects of your own and replace the five existing clips with different ones. Try a longer-duration music file that will keep playing while you try playing other sound effects with the music.

Reading and Writing Files Using Storage

What You'll Learn in This Hour:

▶ Windows Phone isolated storage
▶ Saving a data file
▶ Loading a data file
▶ Storage Demo example

This hour covers the storage system on WP7 in the context of reading and writing files for saved games and for game settings (such as user options). The XNA Framework makes it possible to read and write files using the System.IO. IsolatedStorage library. The storage memory on the WP7 is not changeable in code, and we can't peruse the file system. All we can do is read and write files of a variety of types (most notably, XML files). We will focus on saved game data in this hour, but any type of data can be used. The IsolatedStorage library is unique on WP7, not shared by other XNA platforms (Windows and Xbox 360). Isolated storage is just as the name implies, accessible only to the application that is using it. The focus of this hour is on learning how to save game data, such as a high score list, and then read it back again. You will be able to test this with the WP7 emulator by running the example, saving data, and closing the program, then running it again and just loading the data.

Using Windows Phone Isolated Storage

XNA potentially supports many storage devices across all the game systems it targets, but on the WP7, there is only one type: isolated storage. Any type of game asset can be imported into the Content Manager through an existing or user-created content importer, and this is the preferred way to read game data that does not change. For data that might change, such as generated data files or user-created game levels, or saved games, we can access the file system to stream data to our game from isolated storage. Any type of data file can be opened and written to or read from using `Storage.IO` classes, which we will learn about here. Since XML is recognized as a resource file by Content Manager, we will use XML for our example in this hour. XML has the benefit of being versatile and human readable at the same time. But binary and text files can be used as well.

Saving a Data File

We will first learn to create a new file in isolated storage and then read the data back out of the file afterward. The first thing that must be done is to add the library `System.Xml.Serialization` to the project via the references. The Serialization library makes it very easy to convert a class or struct into a file and read it back again without our having to decode the file manually (by setting individual properties one at a time). Let's add it to the project.

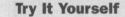

Try It Yourself

Adding XML Support to the Project

1. Right-click References in the Content project and choose Add Reference from the pop-up context menu.

2. Locate the library called `System.Xml.Serialization` in the list, as shown in Figure 19.1.

FIGURE 19.1
The
`System.Xml.`
`Serialization`
library.

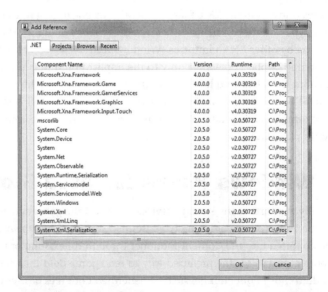

Now that the reference is set, we can use XML files in the project more easily.

Isolated Storage

To access a file in isolated storage, we have to create a file object using the `IsolatedStorageFile` class:

```
IsolatedStorageFile storage =
    IsolatedStorageFile.GetUserStoreForApplication();
```

`IsolatedStorageFile.GetUserStoreForApplication()` is a rather verbose method that creates the new storage object with linkage to the application's (or game's) private storage area, making it available for accessing files, directories, and so on. If the object doesn't need to be made global to the project, a shorthand declaration can be used:

```
var storage = IsolatedStorageFile.GetUserStoreForApplication();
```

Creating a New Directory

Next, a *required* step must be taken: A directory must be created for the application to store files in. The private or isolated storage area has room for dictionary-style key/value data as well as SQL database tables, so we can't just toss files in there like one large file system—we have to create a directory. If you don't create a directory first, an exception error will occur when you try to create a new file. We will use the storage object to create a directory. The `IsolatedStorageFile` class has a method called `DirectoryExists()` that returns `true` if a passed directory exists. `CreateDirectory()` is used to create a new directory. So, if the directory doesn't already exist, we want to create it:

```
const string directory = "StorageDemo";
if (!storage.DirectoryExists(directory))
    storage.CreateDirectory(directory);
```

Creating a New File

Now, we can create a file inside the directory. First, we have to check to see whether the file exists. WP7 does not support the `FileMode.CreateNew` option, which is supposed to overwrite a file if it already exists. Trying to do this generates an exception error, even though it works on Windows and Xbox 360. So, we have to delete the file first before creating it again. Usually this is not a problem because savegame data tends to be rather simple for most games. If you are working on a large, complex game, like an RPG, and there's a lot of data, of course the game might support multiple savegame files, and you'll have a mini file manager built into the game. But we're just learning the ropes here, so we'll do it the simple way to get it working. We use the `FileExists()` and `DeleteFile()` methods to get rid of the old save file:

```
const string filename = directory + "\\savegame.dat";
if (storage.FileExists(filename))
    storage.DeleteFile(filename);
```

Now we're ready to create a new savegame file and write data to it. This is done with the `IsolatedStorageFileStream()` class:

```
var fstream = new IsolatedStorageFileStream(
    filename, FileMode.CreateNew, storage);
```

The `FileMode` enumeration has these values:

- ▶ `CreateNew = 1`
- ▶ `Create = 2`
- ▶ `Open = 3`
- ▶ `OpenOrCreate = 4`
- ▶ `Truncate = 5`
- ▶ `Append = 6`

Writing Data to the File with Serialization

Although any type of data file can be created, XML is quite easy to use, and an entire class or struct variable (full of game data) can be written to the file with only a couple lines of code. If you want to just write binary or text data to the file, that will work also at this point, but it's so much easier to use serialization! Here is a simple struct we can use for this example:

```
public struct SaveGameData
{
    public string Name;
    public int Score;
}
```

A new `SaveGameData` variable is created and the two properties are filled with data. This is where you would store actual game data in the properties in order to restore the game to this gameplay state later when the savegame file is loaded:

```
savedata = new SaveGameData();
savedata.Name = "John Doe";
savedata.Score = rand.Next(500, 5000);
```

Now, to write the data to the file, we have to create an XmlSerializer object, and then write the serialized object out to the file:

```
XmlSerializer serializer = new XmlSerializer(typeof(SaveGameData));
serializer.Serialize(fstream, savedata);
```

At this point, the file has been created and data has been written to it that was contained in the savedata struct variable.

Loading a Data File

Loading a serialized XML file is very similar to the writing process. Of course, you may read a simple text or binary file and parse the data if that is more suitable for your needs, but I'm using serialization and XML because it's so easy and likely to be the approach most game developers take with WP7 savegame data. The same storage object is created, but we don't need any of the code to create a directory or delete the existing file (obviously), so the code to load the savegame file is much simpler:

```
var storage = IsolatedStorageFile.GetUserStoreForApplication();
```

Likewise, the IsolatedStorageFileStream object is created in the same way:

```
var fstream = new IsolatedStorageFileStream(
    filename, FileMode.CreateNew, storage);
```

There is a second way to create the fstream file object variable: by creating the object in a using statement and then adding code that uses the object in the bracketed code block:

```
using (var fstream = new IsolatedStorageFileStream(
    filename, FileMode.Open, storage)) { }
```

By the Way

The XmlSerializer object is created in a similar manner:

```
XmlSerializer serializer = new XmlSerializer(typeof(SaveGameData));
```

The only difference really is a call to Deserialize() instead of Serialize(), and this method *returns* our savegame data as an object:

```
data = (SaveGameData)serializer.Deserialize(fstream);
```

Just for curiosity's sake, here is what the XML file looks like that is created by our code. If you were to serialize a more complex data type, like a Vector4, then the parameters within that class or struct would become sub-items in the XML structure.

```
<?xml version="1.0"?>
<SaveGameData xmlns:xsi="http://www.w3.org/2001/XMLSchema-instance"
  xmlns:xsd="http://www.w3.org/2001/XMLSchema">
  <Name>John Doe</Name>
  <Score>1245</Score>
</SaveGameData>
```

Creating the Storage Demo Example

We will go over a complete program that demonstrates how to save data to a save game file and then load it again, based on some rudimentary user input. Two buttons are created and displayed using our familiar Button class (which inherits from Sprite). This class requires a bitmap file called button.png, so be sure that it exists in the content project.

To verify that the example is working, we will want to run the program, save the data, close the program, and then rerun it and choose the load option to see that the data is still there. So, the example should read and write the data only when the user chooses to, not automatically. When the emulator is being used, exiting the program still preserves it in memory, but closing the emulator will erase all traces of the program and data files.

Closing the WP7 emulator will wipe the storage memory, including data files created by our example here, and any programs previously loaded from Visual Studio. But closing the program and rerunning it will reveal an intact file system. This happens because the emulator creates a new emulation state system when it is run, and that is not saved when it closes.

Figure 19.2 shows the output of the Storage Demo program.

FIGURE 19.2
The Storage Demo example shows how to read and write data.

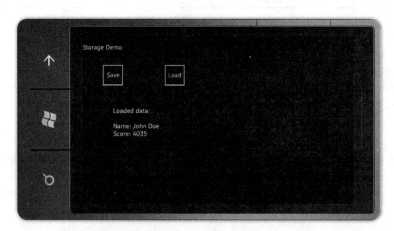

Button Class

Just for the sake of clarity, Listing 19.1 shows the source code for the Button class. We have seen the code before, but it is required by the Storage Demo and is included again for clarity.

LISTING 19.1 Source Code for the Button Class

```
public class Button : Sprite
{
    public string text;
    private SpriteBatch p_spriteBatch;
    private SpriteFont p_font;

    public Button(ContentManager content, SpriteBatch spriteBatch,
        SpriteFont font)
        : base(content, spriteBatch)
    {
        p_spriteBatch = spriteBatch;
        p_font = font;
        Load("button");
        text = "";
        color = Color.LightGreen;
    }

    public void Draw()
    {
        base.Draw();
        Vector2 size = p_font.MeasureString(text);
        Vector2 pos = position;
        pos.X -= size.X / 2;
        pos.Y -= size.Y / 2;
        p_spriteBatch.DrawString(p_font, text, pos, color);
    }

    public bool Tapped(Vector2 pos)
    {
        Rectangle rect = new Rectangle((int)pos.X, (int)pos.Y, 1, 1);
        return Boundary().Intersects(rect);
    }
}
```

Storage Demo Source

Here in Listing 19.2, we have the source code for the Storage Demo program, with the definition of the SaveGameData class as well.

LISTING 19.2 Source Code for the Storage Demo Program

```
public struct SaveGameData
{
    public string Name;
    public int Score;
}
```

```csharp
public class Game1 : Microsoft.Xna.Framework.Game
{
    GraphicsDeviceManager graphics;
    SpriteBatch spriteBatch;
    SpriteFont font;
    Random rand;
    TouchLocation oldTouch;
    Button[] buttons;
    int current = -1;
    bool loaded = false;

    SaveGameData savedata;
    const string directory = "StorageDemo";
    const string filename = directory + "\\savegame.dat";

    public Game1()
    {
        graphics = new GraphicsDeviceManager(this);
        Content.RootDirectory = "Content";
        TargetElapsedTime = TimeSpan.FromTicks(333333);
        oldTouch = new TouchLocation();
        rand = new Random();
    }

    protected override void Initialize()
    {
        base.Initialize();
    }

    protected override void LoadContent()
    {
        spriteBatch = new SpriteBatch(GraphicsDevice);
        font = Content.Load<SpriteFont>("WascoSans");

        //create save button
        buttons = new Button[2];
        buttons[0] = new Button(Content, spriteBatch, font);
        buttons[0].text = "Save";
        buttons[0].position = new Vector2(100, 100);

        //create load button
        buttons[1] = new Button(Content, spriteBatch, font);
        buttons[1].text = "Load";
        buttons[1].position = new Vector2(300, 100);
    }

    protected override void Update(GameTime gameTime)
    {
        if (GamePad.GetState(PlayerIndex.One).Buttons.Back ==
            ButtonState.Pressed)
            this.Exit();

        //get state of touch input
        TouchCollection touchInput = TouchPanel.GetState();
        if (touchInput.Count > 0)
        {
            TouchLocation touch = touchInput[0];
            if (touch.State == TouchLocationState.Pressed)
            {
```

```
                current = -1;
                int n = 0;
                foreach (Button b in buttons)
                {
                    int x = (int)touch.Position.X;
                    int y = (int)touch.Position.Y;
                    if (b.Boundary().Contains(x, y))
                    {
                        current = n;
                        break;
                    }
                    n++;
                }
            }
            oldTouch = touch;
        }

        if (current == 0)
        {
            savedata = new SaveGameData();
            savedata.Name = "John Doe";
            savedata.Score = rand.Next(500, 5000);
            SaveData(savedata);
            loaded = false;
            current = -1;
        }
        else if (current == 1)
        {
            savedata = LoadData();
            loaded = true;
            current = -1;
        }

        base.Update(gameTime);
    }

    protected override void Draw(GameTime gameTime)
    {
        GraphicsDevice.Clear(Color.Black);
        spriteBatch.Begin(SpriteSortMode.FrontToBack,
            BlendState.AlphaBlend);

        print(0, 0, "Storage Demo", Color.White);

        foreach (Button b in buttons)
            b.Draw();

        if (loaded)
        {
            print(100, 200, "Loaded data:\n\n" +
                "Name: " + savedata.Name + "\n" +
                "Score: " + savedata.Score.ToString() + "\n",
                Color.White);
        }

        spriteBatch.End();
        base.Draw(gameTime);
    }
```

```
void print(int x, int y, string text, Color color)
{
    var pos = new Vector2((float)x, (float)y);
    spriteBatch.DrawString(font, text, pos, color);
}

private void SaveData(SaveGameData data)
{
    var storage = IsolatedStorageFile.GetUserStoreForApplication();

    //create directory for data
    if (!storage.DirectoryExists(directory))
        storage.CreateDirectory(directory);

    //delete any existing file
    if (storage.FileExists(filename))
        storage.DeleteFile(filename);


    //create new savegame file
    using (var fstream = new IsolatedStorageFileStream(filename,
        FileMode.CreateNew, storage))
    {
        XmlSerializer serializer = new XmlSerializer(
            typeof(SaveGameData));
        serializer.Serialize(fstream, data);
    }
}

private SaveGameData LoadData()
{
    SaveGameData data;

    var storage = IsolatedStorageFile.GetUserStoreForApplication();
    using (var fstream = new IsolatedStorageFileStream(filename,
        FileMode.Open, storage))
    {
        XmlSerializer serializer = new XmlSerializer(
            typeof(SaveGameData));
        data = (SaveGameData)serializer.Deserialize(fstream);
    }

    return data;
}
}
```

Summary

We now have the ability to create a savegame file and load it again! This greatly enhances the replay value of a game that would otherwise appear to have been freshly installed every time it is run. Use this feature to store game settings, player names, and high score lists, as well as generated game levels and anything else that needs to be remembered by the game for the next time.

Q&A

Q. *Is it possible to use the file I/O code and isolated storage to read the binary data from a game level created with a custom tool and draw the level in a WP7 game?*

A. Yes, we can read and interpret binary data, but if there are bitmap assets required for the level (as is usually the case), that might be an intractable problem. The data *can* be read, though. You might need to study the data file format used by the editor tool in order to read it in XNA.

Q. *Can isolated storage be used to store data used by a custom WP7-based game level editor, which would let users edit their own game levels right on the phone?*

A. Yes, it can!

Workshop

Quiz

1. What is the name of the XML library added to the project as a reference?
2. What is the name of the class used to access isolated storage space?
3. What method returns the isolated storage space for the current application?

Answers

1. `System.XML.Serialization`
2. `IsolatedStorageFile`
3. `GetUserStoreForApplication()`

Exercises

Use the file I/O code presented in this chapter to create a high score list that can be reused with any game project. Put all the code inside a class called `HighScoreList`, and have it automatically pull the current high score list when the object is created. Add methods to change or replace any item in the list and save it back to isolated storage. You can then use this class with your future WP7 games.

HOUR 20

Creating a Graphical User Interface

What You'll Learn in This Hour:

- ▶ **Creating the GUI controls**
- ▶ `Sprite` **class improvements**
- ▶ **GUI base class:** `Control`
- ▶ `Label` **control**
- ▶ `Button` **control**
- ▶ **Horizontal Slider control**
- ▶ **Vertical Slider control**
- ▶ **Demonstrating the GUI controls**

This hour finally tackles a subject that we've been dancing around for many hours already but haven't taken seriously yet—graphical user interface programming! A graphical user interface (or GUI) is a system of controls that are displayed on the screen and interactive, allowing the user to interact with the program. We have already been using a `Button` class quite a bit in past hours, and it has been extremely helpful, despite its simplistic functionality. In this hour, we take that simple example of a GUI control to the next level by creating truly customizable GUI components—a `Button` control, a `Label` control, and a `Slider` control. These are the building blocks for more complex GUI controls such as a list box or a drop-down combo box, which can be developed with a little bit of time and effort using the building blocks we'll develop. This hour does not get into GUI design theory, just the development of several commonly used GUI controls that are essential in a touch-screen environment.

Creating the GUI Controls

A graphical user interface (GUI) is absolutely essential for a game to be successful, even if that means using nothing more than labels and buttons on the screen that the user can click on.

Sprite Class Improvements

▼ **Try It Yourself**

Modifying the Sprite Class

To make the GUI controls more effective, the Sprite class must be tweaked just a little.

1. We need to change the definition of p_content and p_spriteBatch from private to protected so that they will be accessible to classes that inherit from Sprite. This way, we can load assets and draw without creating new reference variables in every subclass. Open the Sprite class and make the change:

   ```
   protected ContentManager p_content;
   protected SpriteBatch p_spriteBatch;
   ```

2. Just to be sure we are on the same page despite the changes made to this class in the past, here is the Load() method. Ignore past changes and just note this current version, which shows that the size and origin properties have been moved out of the try block:

   ```
   public virtual bool Load(string assetName)
   {
       try
       {
           image = p_content.Load<Texture2D>(assetName);
       }
       catch (Exception) { return false; }
       size = new Vector2(image.Width, image.Height);
       origin = new Vector2(image.Width / 2, image.Height / 2);
       return true;
   }
   ```

3. Add an error-handling line to the Draw() method so that it won't crash the program if the image is null. This is a common verification. Since our GUI controls will be using a few images in interesting ways, we just want to ensure that any image that is not loaded correctly won't crash the program—instead, it will just not show up.

```
public virtual void Draw()
{
    if (!visible) return;
    if (image == null) return;
    . . .
}
```

GUI Base Class: `Control`

All the GUI classes will be found in the GUI.cs source code file for the sake of convenience. Within that file, the classes will be wrapped inside the GameLibrary
namespace (the same namespace used by Sprite and Animation).

```
namespace GameLibrary
{
    . . .
}
```

The base GUI class is called Control, and it is primarily used to create a reference to
the ContentManager, SpriteBatch, and SpriteFont objects used in a game—all of
which are needed by the GUI. Control inherits from Sprite, so it supplies GUI controls (declared as subclasses of Control) with all the features of Sprite, including
loading and drawing. Methods are declared as virtual or override so they can be
used *and* overridden in each subclass. There are certainly more services the base
class could provide, such as touch input, but it turns out (during development) that
most of that code must reside in each individual class. Listing 20.1 contains the
source code for the Control class.

LISTING 20.1   Source Code for the Control Class

```
public abstract class Control : Sprite
{
    protected SpriteFont p_font;

    public Control(ContentManager content, SpriteBatch spriteBatch,
        SpriteFont font)
        : base(content, spriteBatch)
    {
        p_font = font;
    }

    public override bool Load(string filename)
    {
        return base.Load(filename);
    }

    public virtual void Update(TouchLocation touch)
    {
    }

    public override void Draw()
```

```
    {
        base.Draw();
    }
}
```

Label Control

A Label is the most fundamental type of GUI control, with the simple task of displaying a text message on the screen. This is more important than it might at first seem, because a Label control can be *moved* anywhere on the screen without affecting the call to Label.Draw() from the main program. This Label class is rather basic, providing a shadow feature with customizable Color properties for the text and shadow. Two Labels will be used in the sample project later in this hour. Listing 20.2 contains the source code for the Label class.

LISTING 20.2 Source Code for the Label Class

```
public class Label : Control
{
    public string text;
    public Color shadowColor;
    public Color textColor;
    public bool UseShadow;

    public Label(ContentManager content, SpriteBatch spriteBatch,
        SpriteFont font)
        : base(content, spriteBatch, font)
    {
        text = "";
        color = Color.White;
        textColor = Color.White;
        shadowColor = Color.Black;
        UseShadow = true;
    }

    public override void Update(TouchLocation touch)
    {
        base.Update(touch);
    }

    public override void Draw()
    {
        if (UseShadow)
        {
            p_spriteBatch.DrawString(p_font, text,
                new Vector2(position.X - 2, position.Y - 2), shadowColor);
        }
        p_spriteBatch.DrawString(p_font, text, position, textColor);
    }

    public Vector2 TextSize()
    {
        return p_font.MeasureString(text);
    }
}
```

Button **Control**

A Button is the second most common type of control needed for a rudimentary GUI system. Our Button class will load a 64×64 bitmap file called button.png (which must be in the content project). The great thing about this is that you can replace the image with one of your own. Due to the way the class works, I recommend using an image with the same dimensions but with your own "skin" theme. The button used in the example this hour is a gray box with a white outline. An important feature for a Button control is to display text and respond to user tap events. Our Button goes further by allowing its background and text colors to be changed independently for a customized look. Listing 20.3 contains the source code for the Button class.

LISTING 20.3   Source Code for the Button Class

```
public class Button : Control
{
    public string text;
    public Color shadowColor;
    public Color textColor;
    public bool UseShadow;
    public bool Tapped;

    public Button(ContentManager content, SpriteBatch spriteBatch,
        SpriteFont font)
        : base(content, spriteBatch, font)
    {
        text = "";
        color = Color.White;
        textColor = Color.White;
        shadowColor = Color.Black;
        UseShadow = true;
        Load("button");
    }

    public override void Update(TouchLocation touch)
    {
        base.Update(touch);
        Tapped = false;
        if (touch.State == TouchLocationState.Pressed)
        {
            Rectangle rect = Boundary();
            Vector2 pos = touch.Position;
            Point point = new Point((int)pos.X, (int)pos.Y);
            if (rect.Contains(point))
            {
                Tapped = true;
            }
        }
    }

    public override void Draw()
    {
        base.Draw();
```

```
        Vector2 size = TextSize();
        Vector2 pos2 = new Vector2(position.X + 2, position.Y + 2);
        Vector2 pivot = new Vector2(size.X / 2, size.Y / 2);
        p_spriteBatch.DrawString(p_font, text, position, shadowColor,
            0.0f, pivot, 1.0f, SpriteEffects.None, zindex);
        p_spriteBatch.DrawString(p_font, text, pos2, textColor, 0.0f, pivot,
            1.0f, SpriteEffects.None, zindex);
    }

    public Vector2 TextSize()
    {
        return p_font.MeasureString(text);
    }
}
```

Horizontal Slider Control

A slider control makes it possible to adjust a setting or to control some aspect of a game directly by the user, and resembles a movable sliding lever on the screen. There are two types of slider: horizontal and vertical. Although one common class *could* be used for both slider orientations, it would be more coding work, so it is more effective to just separate them into HSlider and VSlider controls. This is definitely a complex type of control compared to Label and Button. HSlider loads *three* images, so these bitmap files must all be found in the content project for the GUI code to run properly:

▶ hslider_bar.png

▶ hslider_end.png

▶ button.png

Remember, when you are creating your own game using these GUI controls, that you can skin the controls to your own liking. The slider button needn't be a circle at all! It can be *any* shape, including a custom image or a picture of a dragon—it does- n't matter, and it's up to you!

The left and right end images are shared, so if you create a custom skin for the con- trol, be sure that the end images are interchangeable. The middle piece is a line one (1) pixel wide, scaled to the width of the control (set with the HSlider.Limit prop- erty). If the limit is 100, the one-pixel-wide image is scaled by 100 times to reach the edge! The scale as well as other properties are borrowed from the base Sprite class embedded in Control, inherited by HSlider. There isn't much error handling, so if you try to set Limit to a negative number, it just will not work right or will crash. Listing 20.4 contains the source code for the HSlider class.

LISTING 20.4 Source Code for the HSlider Class

```
public class HSlider : Control
{
    public bool Moving;
    public Vector2 start;
    private int p_value;
    private int p_limit;
    Sprite sprLeftEnd, sprRightEnd, sprBar;

    public HSlider(ContentManager content, SpriteBatch spriteBatch,
        SpriteFont font)
        : base(content, spriteBatch, font)
    {
        scale = 1.0f;
        start = Vector2.Zero;

        Load("slider_tab");

        sprLeftEnd = new Sprite(content, spriteBatch);
        sprLeftEnd.Load("hslider_end");
        sprLeftEnd.origin = new Vector2(3, 16);

        sprRightEnd = new Sprite(content, spriteBatch);
        sprRightEnd.Load("hslider_end");
        sprRightEnd.origin = new Vector2(0, 16);

        sprBar = new Sprite(content, spriteBatch);
        sprBar.Load("hslider_bar");
        sprBar.origin = new Vector2(0, 16);
        Limit = 100;
    }

    public int Value
    {
        get { return p_value; }
        set
        {
            p_value = value;
            if (p_value < 0) p_value = 0;
            if (p_value > p_limit) p_value = p_limit;
            position.X = start.X + p_value;
        }
    }

    public int Limit
    {
        get { return p_limit; }
        set
        {
            p_limit = value;
            sprBar.scaleV = new Vector2((float)
                (p_limit + this.image.Width+1), 1.0f);
        }
    }
}
```

```csharp
public override void Update(TouchLocation touch)
{
    base.Update(touch);

    Moving = false;

    if (touch.State == TouchLocationState.Moved)
    {
        Rectangle rect = Boundary();
        Point point = new Point((int)touch.Position.X,
            (int)touch.Position.Y);
        if (rect.Contains(point))
        {
            Vector2 relative = Vector2.Zero;
            relative.X = touch.Position.X - position.X;
            position.X += relative.X;
            Value = (int)(position.X - start.X);
            if (position.X < start.X)
                position.X = start.X;
            else if (p_value > p_limit)
                position.X -= relative.X;

            Moving = true;
        }
    }
}

public override void Draw()
{
    //draw ends
    sprLeftEnd.position = new Vector2(start.X - 16, start.Y);
    sprLeftEnd.color = this.color;
    sprLeftEnd.Draw();
    sprRightEnd.position = new Vector2(start.X + 16 + p_limit, start.Y);
    sprRightEnd.color = this.color;
    sprRightEnd.Draw();

    //draw middle bar
    sprBar.position = new Vector2(start.X - 16, start.Y);
    sprBar.color = this.color;
    sprBar.Draw();

    //draw sliding circle
    base.Draw();

    //draw value text
    Vector2 size = p_font.MeasureString(p_value.ToString());
    p_spriteBatch.DrawString(p_font, p_value.ToString(), position,
        Color.Black, 0.0f, new Vector2(size.X/2, size.Y/2), 0.6f,
        SpriteEffects.None, 1.0f);
}

public void SetStartPosition(Vector2 pos)
{
    position = pos;
    start = pos;
}
}
```

Vertical Slider Control

The Vertical Slider control, or VSlider, shares all the same functionality as HSlider, but calculations are shifted 90 degrees in a vertical orientation. So, all the "X" properties used in the HSlider's functionality become "Y" properties in VSlider in order for it to work properly. Here are the bitmaps required by the control (and note that button.png is shared):

- vslider_bar.png

- vslider_end.png

- button.png

Listing 20.5 contains the source code for the VSlider class.

LISTING 20.5 Source Code for the VSlider Class

```
public class VSlider : Control
{
    public bool Moving;
    public Vector2 start;
    private int p_value;
    private int p_limit;
    Sprite sprTopEnd, sprBottomEnd, sprBar;

    public VSlider(ContentManager content, SpriteBatch spriteBatch,
        SpriteFont font)
        : base(content, spriteBatch, font)
    {
        scale = 1.0f;
        start = Vector2.Zero;

        Load("slider_tab");

        sprTopEnd = new Sprite(content, spriteBatch);
        sprTopEnd.Load("vslider_end");
        sprTopEnd.origin = new Vector2(16, 3);

        sprBottomEnd = new Sprite(content, spriteBatch);
        sprBottomEnd.Load("vslider_end");
        sprBottomEnd.origin = new Vector2(16, 0);

        sprBar = new Sprite(content, spriteBatch);
        sprBar.Load("vslider_bar");
        sprBar.origin = new Vector2(16, 0);
        Limit = 100;
    }

    public int Value
    {
        get { return p_value; }
        set
        {
            p_value = value;
```

```
            if (p_value < 0) p_value = 0;
            if (p_value > p_limit) p_value = p_limit;
            position.Y = start.Y + p_value;
        }
    }

    public int Limit
    {
        get { return p_limit; }
        set
        {
            p_limit = value;
            sprBar.scaleV = new Vector2(1.0f, (float)
                (p_limit + this.image.Height + 1));
        }
    }

    public override void Update(TouchLocation touch)
    {
        base.Update(touch);

        Moving = false;

        if (touch.State == TouchLocationState.Moved)
        {
            Rectangle rect = Boundary();
            Point point = new Point((int)touch.Position.X,
                (int)touch.Position.Y);
            if (rect.Contains(point))
            {
                Vector2 relative = Vector2.Zero;
                relative.Y = touch.Position.Y - position.Y;
                position.Y += relative.Y;
                Value = (int)(position.Y - start.Y);

                if (position.Y < start.Y)
                    position.Y = start.Y;
                else if (p_value > p_limit)
                    position.Y -= relative.Y;

                Moving = true;
            }
        }
    }

    public override void Draw()
    {
        //draw ends
        sprTopEnd.position = new Vector2(start.X, start.Y - 16);
        sprTopEnd.color = this.color;
        sprTopEnd.Draw();
        sprBottomEnd.position = new Vector2(start.X, start.Y + 16 + p_limit);
        sprBottomEnd.color = this.color;
        sprBottomEnd.Draw();

        //draw middle bar
        sprBar.position = new Vector2(start.X, start.Y - 16);
```

```
        sprBar.color = this.color;
        sprBar.Draw();

        //draw sliding circle
        base.Draw();

        //draw value text
        Vector2 size = p_font.MeasureString(p_value.ToString());
        p_spriteBatch.DrawString(p_font, p_value.ToString(), position,
            Color.Black, 0.0f, new Vector2(size.X / 2, size.Y / 2), 0.6f,
            SpriteEffects.None, zindex);
    }

    public void SetStartPosition(Vector2 pos)
    {
        position = pos;
        start = pos;
    }
}
```

Demonstrating the GUI Controls

The initialization code for a GUI demo or a game using GUI controls will always be much more involved and code-intensive than the processing code where the controls are updated and drawn, because there are so many properties involved in creating and customizing a nice-looking, interactive GUI. Our example this hour demonstrates a GUI with Labels, Buttons, HSliders, and VSliders, and is quite functional, as you can see in Figure 20.1. The source code for the GUI Demo program is found in Listing 20.6.

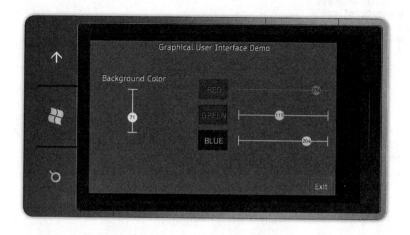

FIGURE 20.1
The example demonstrates labels, buttons, and sliders.

On the left is a vertical slider used to adjust the background color. Why? Just to show that the slider works and does something interesting. Maybe in a game a VSlider would be used to adjust the power level of a catapult or an artillery gun. Really, the use for these controls is up to the game's designer and is just implemented by the programmer (or team). On the right side are three buttons labeled RED, GREEN, and BLUE. Beside each button is a slider.

Clicking a button changes the color component to a random value from 0 to 255, and automatically moves the slider to that location. The slider can also be moved manually, and this in turn will change the button's color to reflect the change to that color component. The end result of all this color manipulation is seen in the small, unassuming Exit button at the lower-right corner of the screen. Note that the Limit property of both HSlider and VSlider changes its overall size and defines the limits of the sliding button. The three color sliders have a range of 0 to 255, whereas the smaller vertical slider has a range of 0 to 100.

LISTING 20.6   Source Code for the GUI Demo Program

```
public class Game1 : Microsoft.Xna.Framework.Game
{
    GraphicsDeviceManager graphics;
    SpriteBatch spriteBatch;
    SpriteFont font;
    Random rand;
    TouchLocation oldTouch;

    Label lblTitle, lblColor;
    Button[] buttons;
    HSlider[] hsliders;
    VSlider vslider;
    Color bgcolor;

    public Game1()
    {
        graphics = new GraphicsDeviceManager(this);
        Content.RootDirectory = "Content";
        TargetElapsedTime = TimeSpan.FromTicks(333333);
        oldTouch = new TouchLocation();
        rand = new Random();
        bgcolor = Color.CornflowerBlue;
    }

    protected override void Initialize()
    {
        base.Initialize();
    }

    protected override void LoadContent()
    {
        spriteBatch = new SpriteBatch(GraphicsDevice);
        font = Content.Load<SpriteFont>("WascoSans");
```

```
lblTitle = new Label(Content, spriteBatch, font);
lblTitle.text = "Graphical User Interface Demo";
lblTitle.position = new Vector2(400 - lblTitle.TextSize().X / 2, 0);

//create buttons
buttons = new Button[4];
buttons[0] = new Button(Content, spriteBatch, font);
buttons[0].text = "RED";
buttons[0].position = new Vector2(400, 150);
buttons[0].textColor = Color.Red;
buttons[0].color = Color.DarkRed;
buttons[0].scaleV = new Vector2(1.5f, 1.0f);

buttons[1] = new Button(Content, spriteBatch, font);
buttons[1].text = "GREEN";
buttons[1].position = new Vector2(400, 230);
buttons[1].textColor = Color.Green;
buttons[1].color = Color.DarkGreen;
buttons[1].scaleV = new Vector2(1.5f, 1.0f);

buttons[2] = new Button(Content, spriteBatch, font);
buttons[2].text = "BLUE";
buttons[2].position = new Vector2(400, 310);
buttons[2].textColor = Color.Cyan;
buttons[2].color = Color.DarkCyan;
buttons[2].scaleV = new Vector2(1.5f, 1.0f);

buttons[3] = new Button(Content, spriteBatch, font);
buttons[3].text = "Exit";
buttons[3].position = new Vector2(750, 450);
buttons[3].scaleV = new Vector2(1.2f, 0.8f);

//create horizontal sliders for color editing
hsliders = new HSlider[3];
hsliders[0] = new HSlider(Content, spriteBatch, font);
hsliders[0].SetStartPosition(new Vector2(500, 150));
hsliders[0].color = Color.Red;
hsliders[0].Limit = 255;

hsliders[1] = new HSlider(Content, spriteBatch, font);
hsliders[1].SetStartPosition(new Vector2(500, 230));
hsliders[1].color = Color.LightGreen;
hsliders[1].Limit = 255;

hsliders[2] = new HSlider(Content, spriteBatch, font);
hsliders[2].SetStartPosition(new Vector2(500, 310));
hsliders[2].color = Color.Cyan;
hsliders[2].Limit = 255;

//create vertical slider for bg color editing
vslider = new VSlider(Content, spriteBatch, font);
vslider.SetStartPosition(new Vector2(140, 170));
vslider.color = Color.Yellow;
vslider.Limit = 100;

//create label for slider
lblColor = new Label(Content, spriteBatch, font);
lblColor.text = "Background Color";
```

```
        lblColor.position = new Vector2( 140 - lblColor.TextSize().X/2,
            100);
    }

    protected override void Update(GameTime gameTime)
    {
        if (GamePad.GetState(PlayerIndex.One).Buttons.Back ==
            ButtonState.Pressed)
            this.Exit();

        TouchCollection touchInput = TouchPanel.GetState();
        if (touchInput.Count > 0)
        {
            TouchLocation touch = touchInput[0];
            oldTouch = touch;

            lblTitle.Update(touch);
            UpdateButtons(touch);
            UpdateSliders(touch);
            vslider.Update(touch);
            lblColor.Update(touch);
        }

        base.Update(gameTime);
    }

    void UpdateButtons(TouchLocation touch)
    {
        //update buttons
        int tapped = -1;
        for (int n = 0; n < buttons.Length; n++)
        {
            buttons[n].Update(touch);
            if (buttons[n].Tapped) tapped = n;
        }

        //was a button tapped?
        int c = rand.Next(256);
        switch (tapped)
        {
            case 0:
                buttons[0].color = new Color(c, 0, 0);
                hsliders[0].Value = c;
                break;
            case 1:
                buttons[1].color = new Color(0, c, 0);
                hsliders[1].Value = c;
                break;
            case 2:
                buttons[2].color = new Color(0, 0, c);
                hsliders[2].Value = c;
                break;
            case 3:
                this.Exit();
                break;
        }
    }
```

```
void UpdateSliders(TouchLocation touch)
{
    //update horizontal sliders
    int moving = -1;
    for (int n = 0; n < hsliders.Length; n++)
    {
        hsliders[n].Update(touch);
        if (hsliders[n].Moving) moving = n;
    }

    switch(moving)
    {
        case 0:
            buttons[0].color = new Color(hsliders[0].Value, 0, 0);
            break;
        case 1:
            buttons[1].color = new Color(0, hsliders[1].Value, 0);
            break;
        case 2:
            buttons[2].color = new Color(0, 0, hsliders[2].Value);
            break;
    }

    //colorize Exit button based on colors
    buttons[3].color = new Color(hsliders[0].Value,
        hsliders[1].Value, hsliders[2].Value);

    //update vertical slider
    if (vslider.Moving)
    {
        bgcolor = Color.CornflowerBlue;
        bgcolor.R -= (byte)vslider.Value;
        bgcolor.G -= (byte)vslider.Value;
        bgcolor.B -= (byte)vslider.Value;
    }
}

protected override void Draw(GameTime gameTime)
{
    GraphicsDevice.Clear(bgcolor);
    spriteBatch.Begin(SpriteSortMode.Deferred,
        BlendState.AlphaBlend);

    lblTitle.Draw();

    foreach (Button b in buttons)
        b.Draw();

    foreach (HSlider hs in hsliders)
        hs.Draw();

    vslider.Draw();
    lblColor.Draw();

    spriteBatch.End();
    base.Draw(gameTime);
}
```

```
void print(int x, int y, string text, Color color)
{
    var pos = new Vector2((float)x, (float)y);
    spriteBatch.DrawString(font, text, pos, color);
}
}
```

Summary

This hour added some extremely important new concepts to our WP7 programming capabilities, which now include graphical user interface control programming. That subject alone often requires one or more full-time specialists in a triple-A game studio, and GUI programmers are usually in high demand because it is a learned skill not easily shared, and the requirements tend to change with every game, requiring a GUI programmer to come up with creative GUI solutions for the designer. The four GUI controls presented this hour should meet our needs for the time being, but there are many more possibilities!

Q&A

Q. *It seems as though a lot of initialization code is needed just to get a GUI to work right. Is there a better way to do it?*

A. It is possible to store GUI control settings in a configuration or script file that can be read and used to create the GUI controls in a game. To make this work, all controls would have to be added to a List (as a sort of Sprite group).

Q. *What would you recommend doing if there are too many settings to fit on one screen full of GUI controls?*

A. Use a "tabbed" system with a pair of Prev and Next buttons that cycle through various screens of GUI controls.

Workshop

Quiz

1. What is the name of the base GUI class?

2. What is the name of the GUI class that handles drawing text?

3. What are the names of the GUI classes that slide?

Answers

1. Control

2. Label

3. HSlider and VSlider

Exercises

The Button control can be used to create an option list in which one option is selected out of several and highlighted differently to reflect that it is the current option. This would be extremely helpful in a settings screen for a game, if used only to select one of two options in a True/False manner. See whether you can create an experimental optional list, which need not be a unique GUI control, just an example of how the functionality *might* be put into a reusable class. Demonstrate how selecting one button of the option group deselects the others. By scaling the buttons and orienting them in a stack, a rudimentary list box/combo box–style control can be created.

HOUR 21

Finite State Gameplay

What You'll Learn in This Hour:

▶ Finite state gameplay
▶ Finite state theory
▶ State-driven game entity behavior
▶ Adaptive states: rudimentary A.I.
▶ Testing game state

This hour begins work on the first stage of a sample game that will demonstrate all the concepts covered up to this point in the book. The first stage of the game will see the game screens developed and displayed based on the current state, as well as early state-based behaviors for gameplay objects. The game is an interesting take on the space theme we've been using all along. There will be a black hole and gameplay will revolve around it—literally!

Finite State Gameplay in Theory

Finite state refers to a condition that will have a limited number of possible values. The age of a person is a finite state value range from 0 to around 80, with no exceptions. To ensure that an age does not exceed the bounds, the actual limits must be used, not just the most common limits. So, age really should be 0 to 120, because even today there are a few people still alive who were born in the nineteenth century. Let's study finite state theory and then write some sample code to see how well it works in a game.

Finite State Theory

The speed of a car is a finite state range from 0 to around 100. But what if we're dealing with a sports car? In that case, the speed might go up to 200 or more (the

Bugatti Veyron has a top speed of 260, but it costs a million dollars). Then, what about top fuel dragsters that can reach speeds in excess of 300 miles per hour? As you can see, the range is not easily determined because there are always exceptions to the rule, challenges for our assumptions. There are even land-speed-record cars that can go faster than these numbers. What we have to do, then, is reduce the scope of the object we're describing with finite state variables. For instance, we might limit the scope to consumer passenger vehicles that cost less than $40,000, to come up with a safe range of 0 to 120 (as a reasonable upper limit).

Finite states need not be numeric or even purely composed of whole numbers, either. We can have a finite state variable dealing with very small numbers indeed, such as the trace widths of computer chips, measured in billionths of a meter (nanometer), or even non-numeric states. Consider a light switch. It is either on or off. There is no in-between value because to hold the switch in between still causes the light to be either on or off. There is no "somewhat on" or "somewhat off" in a two-state switch.

Enumerations can also be used to describe the possible states of an object. For instance, the condition of a food item at a grocery store might have these possible values: Fresh, Good, Aged, or Spoiled. It is the job of the store employees to keep track of the state of their food items. Usually, when the state of, say, a banana goes from Fresh to Good, the price will be discounted. When the state degrades from Good to Aged, the price will be reduced further for perhaps one final day, and then if it hasn't sold, it is discarded.

We humans categorize items all day long. That's a very significant way that our brains work. We are *surprised* upon encountering a new thing, which can bring on emotional excitement or intrigue! Have you ever noticed that when you find something new, you often feel like a child again? For children, everything in the world is a new experience almost every day, which is what made childhood so much fun for most people (all things being equal). When something *new* or *weird* is discovered, the first thing we do is try to categorize it. "Hey, look, it's a bird! No, it's a plane! No, it's Superman!" Hunting in the deep forest is an exciting sport for many people because they never know what they'll run into in the woods. Biologists are often attracted to the field because of the excitement of finding new species and trying to categorize them. The same might be said of anthropology, the study of ancient human remains, and the related field, archaeology, the study of their civilizations. I was attracted to computer science for the same reason: Often, code would produce completely unexpected results, which I found exciting. Indeed, all the sciences involve discovery at the root of the field, so naturally curious people are those who enjoy the unexpected challenge of categorizing new things.

State-Driven Game Entity Behavior

Teaching computers to recognize new things and categorizing them is one area of work at the height of artificial intelligence research today. We will be looking at just large-scale game state this hour, but the potential is here for giving behaviors to game entities (represented with `Sprite` objects in the sample game). The behaviors have been explored somewhat already in the `Animation` class, but that was intended primarily to accommodate drawing with special effects, like rotation and alpha fading. The `OrbitalMovement` class was actually a behavior packaged as an `Animation` subclass, so we might use that class again for our game. The states of a game entity might be classified in terms of simple navigation—choosing a direction and velocity and moving, or heading toward a target location at a certain velocity. Some decision-making logic might be added so that an entity will *follow* or *run away from* another entity. These are all behaviors that can be programmed into a reusable class that will give a game much more of a scripted quality rather than a "hard-programmed" quality, which tends to be less flexible.

"State" can be set and used in logic using something as simple as a number variable, where the state is a discrete value from 0 to 100, with each number representing a different behavior for the entity. The state value might be used as a lookup index into an enumeration of behaviors that are available to all entities in a game. Consider these, for example:

▶ IDLE = 0

▶ RANDOM = 1

▶ CHASING = 2

▶ FLEEING = 3

▶ SHADOWING = 4

▶ HIDING = 5

These are all properties that can be encoded into an enumeration so that an entity's behavior is determined with a simple integer variable used as the index.

Adaptive States: Rudimentary A.I.

The use of a state variable and enumerated state values may be considered a simple form of intelligence, but complex systems are made of simple items and rules that determine how they interact. Consider how an ant colony with only reactionary behavior can accomplish the stripping of food from nearby shrubs without a guiding intelligence directing them? One might consider their simple behaviors collectively as a hive intellect. Agitate one of the ants so that it dies, and a pheromone is given off, causing all nearby ants to charge toward the threat and exude the pheromone themselves, so that soon half the colony is on the attack. A similar process directs bee behavior, and indeed all hive species.

A static state variable with an enumeration of behaviors works well for most games. But if more advanced behavior is needed, a change is needed to the way behaviors are chosen for the entity. The behaviors themselves don't change. In other words, the action items in the enumeration do not change. What changes is the way in which the *index* arrives at a value that is meaningful within the enumeration.

Consider sprite movement and animation for a minute. A sprite has a position based on `Vector2`, with floating-point X and Y properties. These floats do not have to equal a specific whole number representing a pixel in order for the sprite to continue to draw. If the sprite is drawn only when the X and Y position values equal a whole number, the sprite will most often be invisible! What's happening in the case of sprite rendering is a natural form of adaptive state-based behavior. In short, the value is rounded to arrive at the nearest whole number. How that value changes from 10.00378 to 10.00377 is the issue, not whether the whole-number part, 10, is affected. The decimal value might seem irrelevant since the sprite does not move from the 10 position unless the decimal crosses a rounding border (0.0 or 5.0), causing the whole number to change when evaluated. For instance, 9.9 is equivalent to 10.4 when the whole number is considered, even though these numbers could be a million miles apart in decimal terms. It's the *way* in which the values change that concerns adaptive state programming.

Although the indexed enumeration structure does not change, the values must change for the adaptive algorithms to make any sense. Using the list given previously, updating the index from 0.0 toward 1.0 will cause the entity to go from IDLE to RANDOM, which might not make any sense in the game. But bumping the entity several times while it is IDLE might push it into a FLEEING state. This is just an example, because the enumeration would need to be relevant to the game at hand. Instead of the items being just casually ordered, they are ordered in terms of "fear" or "aggression," and the RANDOM item has been removed because it does not make sense in this context (it is more of an ambivalent or apathetic behavior):

▶ FLEEING = -2

▶ HIDING = -1

▶ IDLE = 0

▶ SHADOWING = 1

▶ CHASING = 2

In this new ordering, note that the values reflect the fear factor of the game entity. As long as nothing happens to it, the state will remain at IDLE. If another sprite bumps into it, the state might go down a bit. The amount of change is dependent on the gameplay, but if a value of 0.2 represents a rock being thrown by an enemy, then it will take three rock hits before the entity goes from IDLE to HIDING:

1. state = 0 (IDLE)

2. state -= 0.2 (-0.2)

3. state -= 0.2 (-0.4)

4. state -= 0.2 (-0.6)

5. state = -0.6 (HIDING)

The HIDING state will persist until it reaches -1.5, which is rounded to the FLEEING state of -2. If our game entity starts throwing rocks back at the other guy, perhaps scoring a hit will increase the state by 0.3 or some other fine-tuned value. Also, a natural tendency to return to the IDLE or neutral state must be included in the game logic. This might be a small amount added to the state variable every frame, such as 0.001 (when negative) or -0.001 (when positive) so that inactivity will cause the entity to go back to IDLE. The natural balance factor should not be so strong that gameplay events are overridden. Getting hit or scoring a hit should always be far greater an impact (pun not intended) than the balancing value applied at every update.

Testing Game State

I have prepared an example for this hour that will demonstrate finite state programming in an effective way, while also launching the start of our sample game that will be built over the remainder of the book.

IGameModule

To get started, we will use an interface class to describe the format of all state classes so that they can be invoked from the main game with a generic call. In other words, we don't want to write a bunch of conditions to look for a specific state and launch that screen; we want all the screens to have the same functionality so that they can be called from an indexed array. The methods listed here *must* be implemented in all classes that share this interface. Another thing about an interface class is that it can't have any variables. There is an argument to be made in favor of just using an abstract class rather than an interface class. If you really need to have class variables and some private items, go with an abstract, because those cannot be defined in an interface.

```
interface IGameModule
{
    void LoadContent(ContentManager content);
    void Update(TouchLocation touch, GameTime gameTime);
    void Draw(GameTime gameTime);
}
```

By the Way

> Interface classes cannot contain variables (properties) or scope modifiers.

TitleScreenModule

The first module we'll cover is the `TitleScreenModule` class. This class inherits from `IGameModule`. Since that is an interface class, `TitleScreenModule` must incorporate all the methods defined in `IGameModule`. Each of these screens is like a miniprogram on its own, and that's the whole point—we don't want the main game to get too complicated with variables for each game state. Having a class for every state might seem like overkill, but it helps keep the game more organized, which leads to better results. Figure 21.1 shows the title screen module, and the source code is found in Listing 21.1. There are three buttons that trigger a different game state (Start Game, Options, Game Over), and an Exit button that ends the program.

FIGURE 21.1
The title screen module.

LISTING 21.1   Source Code for the `TitleScreenModule` Class

```
class TitleScreenModule : IGameModule
{
    Game1 game;
    SpriteFont font;
    SpriteFont guifont;
```

```
Label lblTitle;
Button[] btnMenu;

public TitleScreenModule(Game1 game)
{
    this.game = game;
}

public void LoadContent(ContentManager content)
{
    font = content.Load<SpriteFont>("WascoSans");
    guifont = content.Load<SpriteFont>("GUIFont");

    lblTitle = new Label(content, game.spriteBatch, font);
    lblTitle.text = "Title Screen";
    Vector2 size = font.MeasureString(lblTitle.text);
    lblTitle.position = new Vector2(400-size.X/2, 10);

    btnMenu = new Button[4];
    btnMenu[0] = new Button(content, game.spriteBatch, guifont);
    btnMenu[0].text = "Start Game";
    btnMenu[0].position = new Vector2(400, 160);
    btnMenu[0].scaleV = new Vector2(3.0f, 1.2f);

    btnMenu[1] = new Button(content, game.spriteBatch, guifont);
    btnMenu[1].text = "Options";
    btnMenu[1].position = new Vector2(400, 250);
    btnMenu[1].scaleV = new Vector2(3.0f, 1.2f);

    btnMenu[2] = new Button(content, game.spriteBatch, guifont);
    btnMenu[2].text = "Game Over";
    btnMenu[2].position = new Vector2(400, 340);
    btnMenu[2].scaleV = new Vector2(3.0f, 1.2f);

    btnMenu[3] = new Button(content, game.spriteBatch, guifont);
    btnMenu[3].text = "Exit";
    btnMenu[3].position = new Vector2(400, 430);
    btnMenu[3].scaleV = new Vector2(3.0f, 1.2f);
}

public void Update(TouchLocation touch, GameTime gameTime)
{
    int tapped = -1;
    int n = 0;
    foreach (Button btn in btnMenu)
    {
        btn.Update(touch);
        if (btn.Tapped)
            tapped = n;

        n++;
    }

    switch (tapped)
    {
        case 0:
            game.gameState = Game1.GameStates.PLAYING;
            break;
```

```
        case 1:
            game.gameState = Game1.GameStates.OPTIONS;
            break;
        case 2:
            game.gameState = Game1.GameStates.GAMEOVER;
            break;
        case 3:
            game.Exit();
            break;
    }
}

public void Draw(GameTime gameTime)
{
    lblTitle.Draw();

    foreach (Button btn in btnMenu)
    {
        btn.Draw();
    }
}
}
```

PlayingModule

The `PlayingModule` class represents the normal playing state of the game when the player is engaged in the main gameplay. If the player chooses to manually exit, or wins the game, or loses the game, then the state will return to either the title screen or the game over screen. The source code is found in Listing 21.2, and Figure 21.2 shows the output. There isn't much to see here, but it's important to simulate the flow of the game with a Return button that jumps back to the title screen.

FIGURE 21.2
The game playing module.

LISTING 21.2   Source Code for the `PlayingModule` Class

```
class PlayingModule : IGameModule
{
    Game1 game;
    SpriteFont font;
    SpriteFont guifont;
    Label lblTitle;
    Button btnReturn;

    public PlayingModule(Game1 game)
    {
        this.game = game;
    }

    public void LoadContent(ContentManager content)
    {
        font = content.Load<SpriteFont>("WascoSans");
        guifont = content.Load<SpriteFont>("GUIFont");

        lblTitle = new Label(content, game.spriteBatch, font);
        lblTitle.text = "Game Play Screen";
        Vector2 size = font.MeasureString(lblTitle.text);
        lblTitle.position = new Vector2(400 - size.X / 2, 10);

        btnReturn = new Button(content, game.spriteBatch, guifont);
        btnReturn.text = "Return";
        btnReturn.position = new Vector2(400, 430);
        btnReturn.scaleV = new Vector2(3.0f, 1.2f);
    }

    public void Update(TouchLocation touch, GameTime gameTime)
    {
        btnReturn.Update(touch);
        if (btnReturn.Tapped)
            game.gameState = Game1.GameStates.TITLE;
    }

    public void Draw(GameTime gameTime)
    {
        lblTitle.Draw();
        btnReturn.Draw();
    }
}
```

OptionsModule

The game options screen would allow the player to change the audio levels or toggle the mute option, among other settings. Figure 21.3 shows the output, which looks similar to the preceding screen—and for good reason, because these should behave in a similar way but contain unique content. Listing 21.3 contains the source code for the class.

FIGURE 21.3
The game
options module.

LISTING 21.3 Source Code for the `OptionsModule` Class

```
class OptionsModule : IGameModule
{
    Game1 game;
    SpriteFont font;
    SpriteFont guifont;
    Label lblTitle;
    Button btnReturn;

    public OptionsModule(Game1 game)
    {
        this.game = game;
    }

    public void LoadContent(ContentManager content)
    {
        font = content.Load<SpriteFont>("WascoSans");
        guifont = content.Load<SpriteFont>("GUIFont");

        lblTitle = new Label(content, game.spriteBatch, font);
        lblTitle.text = "Options Screen";
        Vector2 size = font.MeasureString(lblTitle.text);
        lblTitle.position = new Vector2(400 - size.X / 2, 10);

        btnReturn = new Button(content, game.spriteBatch, guifont);
        btnReturn.text = "Return";
        btnReturn.position = new Vector2(400, 430);
        btnReturn.scaleV = new Vector2(3.0f, 1.2f);
    }

    public void Update(TouchLocation touch, GameTime gameTime)
    {
        btnReturn.Update(touch);
        if (btnReturn.Tapped)
            game.gameState = Game1.GameStates.TITLE;
    }

    public void Draw(GameTime gameTime)
    {
```

```
        lblTitle.Draw();
        btnReturn.Draw();
    }
}
```

GameOverModule

The game over screen is shown in Figure 21.4. Like the previous two modules, this just displays the module name (using a Label control), and a Return button at the bottom. It would be filled in with actual content to reflect that the player either won or lost the round or the game. Does it seem as though there is a lot of duplicated code here, with the label and button and font and so forth? Don't be concerned with optimization if that occurs to you while you're looking at these source code listings. There is no real content here yet, but each module will have its own unique logic and functionality, and all we see so far is structure. Listing 21.4 contains the source code for the class.

FIGURE 21.4
The game over module.

LISTING 21.4   Source Code for the GameOverModule Class

```
class GameOverModule : IGameModule
{
    Game1 game;
    SpriteFont font;
    SpriteFont guifont;
    Label lblTitle;
    Button btnReturn;

    public GameOverModule(Game1 game)
    {
        this.game = game;
    }
```

```
    public void LoadContent(ContentManager content)
    {
        font = content.Load<SpriteFont>("WascoSans");
        guifont = content.Load<SpriteFont>("GUIFont");

        lblTitle = new Label(content, game.spriteBatch, font);
        lblTitle.text = "Game Over Screen";
        Vector2 size = font.MeasureString(lblTitle.text);
        lblTitle.position = new Vector2(400 - size.X / 2, 10);

        btnReturn = new Button(content, game.spriteBatch, guifont);
        btnReturn.text = "Return";
        btnReturn.position = new Vector2(400, 430);
        btnReturn.scaleV = new Vector2(3.0f, 1.2f);
    }

    public void Update(TouchLocation touch, GameTime gameTime)
    {
        btnReturn.Update(touch);
        if (btnReturn.Tapped)
            game.gameState = Game1.GameStates.TITLE;
    }

    public void Draw(GameTime gameTime)
    {
        lblTitle.Draw();
        btnReturn.Draw();
    }
}
```

Game1

Listing 21.5 contains the main source code for the example. This file contains the
GameStates enumeration and shows how to instantiate (remember, that's a fancy
word that means "to create an object from the blueprint of a class") each of the
modules, and call their mutual Update() and Draw() methods. Despite having four
different classes for the four modules, they are all defined as an array of
IGameModule! That is the key to using these behavioral/state classes—being able to
swap them at any time without rewriting much code. That array is then indexed
with the state variable.

LISTING 21.5   Main Source Code for the Example

```
public class Game1 : Microsoft.Xna.Framework.Game
{
    public enum GameStates
    {
        TITLE = 0,
        PLAYING = 1,
        OPTIONS = 2,
        GAMEOVER = 3
    }
```

```
public GraphicsDeviceManager graphics;
public SpriteBatch spriteBatch;
SpriteFont font;
Random rand;
TouchLocation oldTouch;
public GameStates gameState;
IGameModule[] modules;

public Game1()
{
    graphics = new GraphicsDeviceManager(this);
    Content.RootDirectory = "Content";
    TargetElapsedTime = TimeSpan.FromTicks(333333);
    oldTouch = new TouchLocation();
    rand = new Random();
}

protected override void Initialize()
{
    base.Initialize();
}

protected override void LoadContent()
{
    spriteBatch = new SpriteBatch(GraphicsDevice);
    font = Content.Load<SpriteFont>("WascoSans");

    modules = new IGameModule[4];
    modules[0] = new TitleScreenModule(this);
    modules[1] = new PlayingModule(this);
    modules[2] = new OptionsModule(this);
    modules[3] = new GameOverModule(this);
    foreach (IGameModule mod in modules)
    {
        mod.LoadContent(Content);
    }
    gameState = GameStates.TITLE;
}

protected override void Update(GameTime gameTime)
{
    if (GamePad.GetState(PlayerIndex.One).Buttons.Back ==
        ButtonState.Pressed)
        this.Exit();

    TouchCollection touchInput = TouchPanel.GetState();
    TouchLocation touch = new TouchLocation();
    if (touchInput.Count > 0)
    {
        touch = touchInput[0];
        oldTouch = touch;
    }

    //update current module
    modules[(int)gameState].Update(touch ,gameTime);

    base.Update(gameTime);
}
```

```
protected override void Draw(GameTime gameTime)
{
    GraphicsDevice.Clear(Color.CornflowerBlue);
    spriteBatch.Begin(SpriteSortMode.Deferred, BlendState.AlphaBlend);

    //draw current module
    modules[(int)gameState].Draw(gameTime);

    spriteBatch.End();
    base.Draw(gameTime);
}
}
```

Summary

This hour set the stage for our sample game that will continue to be built over the remaining three hours. Now that we have a state-based game, it will be simply a matter of filling in each game module with content. Admittedly, the options and game over modules were just used for the demonstration and probably are not needed in our small sample game, but the illustration was helpful.

Q&A

Q. *When we're using a "fuzzy" state variable with a "discrete" list of enumerated states, at what point does the behavior shift from one discrete state to another?*

A. The behavior is usually managed with a floating-point variable that shifts from one state to another by rounding up or down.

Q. *How could a behavioral system make changes to its own state variable?*

A. This is as complex a question as is the whole field of artificial intelligence, but by exploring these ideas, you can devise some fascinating A.I. behaviors for even fairly simple games.

Workshop

Quiz

1. What is a good way to represent state values in C# code?

2. What differentiates an interface from a normal class?

3. What data type should a behavioral state variable be defined as?

Answers

1. With an enumeration (enum)

2. An interface class must be implemented, and cannot have any variables, only methods.

3. Floating point (float or double)

Exercises

Add your own game module to the example in this hour and make room for it on the title screen with a new button. Next, give your new module some functionality so that it isn't boring like the others—perhaps a moving or animating sprite from an earlier demo? Yes, by using this state system, we could combine all the previous examples into one program and bring them up by tapping a button!

HOUR 22

The Physics of Gravity

What You'll Learn in This Hour:

- ▶ **Simulating gravity**
- ▶ **Escape velocity**
- ▶ **Calculating "gravity"**
- ▶ **The Gravity Demo**

This hour digs into some trigonometry again in order to explore the fascinating subject of game physics. Although the overall topic is broad, we will focus solely on the calculations for computing the effect of gravity on two massive objects. This hour, along with the preceding one, is developing code and concepts that will be used in sample game that will be completed by Hour 24. The gameplay will involve simulating the construction of a Hawking radiation reactor. The theory proposed by Stephen Hawking states that black holes emit a small amount of radiation from the poles of a black hole. The game will involve shooting energy satellites into orbit around the black hole with the goal of establishing a stable orbit. While satellites are orbiting, they are gathering energy and beaming it back to the player's ship, like a solar power satellite, but the energy is beamed away from the black hole toward the ship where it is gathered. It's a simple concept for a game, with simple rules, but the gameplay should be fun.

Simulating Gravity

Gravity is an interesting phenomenon of physics. Every moment of every day, you are literally falling inward toward the center of the earth. The surface of the earth keeps you from falling farther, but the same force that causes a person parachuting out of an airplane to fall downward, which is the same force that causes satellites in orbit to gradually lose position and require constant adjustments, causes you to fall downward at every moment. It actually takes quite a bit of energy to stand up against the force of the earth's gravity. Fortunately, a human body is relatively small, so the gravity exerted is not too great that we can't survive. But try to imagine, the same gravity pulling you toward the center of the earth also keeps the moon in orbit! The moon is gradually losing its orbit, by the way. Over time, it will draw closer and closer to the earth and eventually collide. The time frame is huge, but it is happening nonetheless.

Escape Velocity

To break out of the earth's gravity field requires a huge amount of thrust! The velocity required to do so is called *escape velocity*, which is the velocity required to escape the gravity of a planet or another large, massive object. Gravity, according to physics, is called gravitational potential energy. The term *escape velocity* is somewhat incorrect, but the term has stuck over the years. Velocity, as you have learned in this book, affects movement in a specific direction calculated with cosine (for X) and sine (for Y). Escape velocity is actually a *speed*, not a velocity, because an object moving at *escape speed* will break orbit no matter which direction it is moving in.

Earth's escape velocity is 6.96 miles per second (11.2 kilometers per second). In terms of aircraft speed, that is Mach 34, about 10 times faster than a bullet! But these terms are applicable only to *ballistic objects*, like a rocket launched from the surface. *Ballistic* is a term that means something is *fired* or *launched* and then the object coasts once it reaches a desired speed. The ballistic rocket that launched the Apollo astronauts toward the moon had to reach escape velocity with two or more rocket stages, plus an outer space thruster that sent the spaceship coasting toward the moon. But a spacecraft lifting off from the earth does not need to reach this ballistic escape velocity if it can just maintain a consistent thrust for a longer period. A U.S. Air Force F-22 Raptor jet, for instance, has enough thrust to go ballistic in terms of its own weight (meaning it can continue to speed up while going straight up, without ever slowing down), with fuel being the only limitation.

Calculating "Gravity"

This is not really "gravity" we're calculating, but rather the force two objects exert on each other. The result looks very much like the pull of gravity. Just note that the code we're about to write is simplified for a gameplay mechanic, not for spacecraft trajectories.

The formulas involved in "rocket science" are not overly complicated, but we're going to use a simpler technique to simulate gravity between any two massive objects. The end result will be similar as far as a game is concerned. What we need to be concerned with is the mass, position, and acceleration factor for each object.

Using these three basic pieces of information, we can cause two massive objects to affect each other gravitationally. During every update, the position, acceleration, and velocity are all updated. While the two objects are far apart, their interaction will be negligible. But as they draw closer, the acceleration factor will affect the velocity, which will cause the two objects to speed up toward each other. In the terms of rocket science, this is called "the whiplash effect." NASA and other space agencies often use whiplash gravity to propel their spacecraft toward a destination more quickly, costing less fuel as a result. After we have a simulation running, we can try this out!

To cause two massive objects to interact, first we have to calculate the distance between them. This will have a direct effect on the amount of force the objects exert upon each other. This code takes into account the situation in which the two objects have collided, in which case the distance factor is inverted:

```
double distX = this.position.X - other.position.X;
double distY = this.position.Y - other.position.Y;
double dist = distX*distX + distY*distY;
double distance = 0;
if (dist != 0) distance = 1 / dist;
```

Next, we use these distance values to calculate the acceleration of the object. Since this is directly affected by the distance to the other object, the acceleration will increase as the objects grow closer, which further increases acceleration. That is the nature of the whiplash effect, and it works well as long as the objects do not collide:

```
this.acceleration.X = (float)(-1 * other.mass * distX * distance);
this.acceleration.Y = (float)(-1 * other.mass * distY * distance);
```

Velocity is updated directly with the acceleration values:

```
this.velocityLinear.X += this.acceleration.X;
this.velocityLinear.Y += this.acceleration.Y;
```

The position, likewise, is updated directly with the velocity values:

```
this.position.X += this.velocityLinear.X;
this.position.Y += this.velocityLinear.Y;
```

It is very easy to lose track of game objects that interact with this gravitational code. If two objects collide, so that the distance between them is zero, then they will fling away from each other at high speed. I recommend adding boundary code to the velocity and acceleration values so that this doesn't happen in a playable game.

The Gravity Demo

The sample project can be found again under the name "Black Hole Game" in this hour's resource files. Because all the concepts and code learned during these last remaining chapters is directly applied to the sample game in the final hour, the project will just grow and evolve, and we'll continue to use the same name, as well as use code developed during previous hours. The example will be based on the game state example in the preceding hour, and we'll use the `PlayingModule.cs` file rather than `Game1.cs` as has been the norm previously. Figure 22.1 shows the example from this hour running.

FIGURE 22.1
The "plasma" sprite is rotating around the black hole in an elliptical orbit.

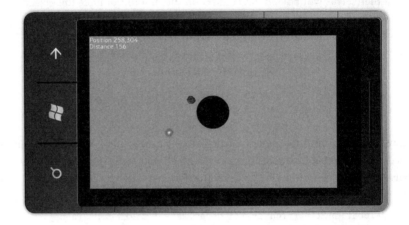

This program requires several bitmap files. You can copy them directly out of the project included in the book resource files, or create your own. For the "black hole" image, I have just created a filled black circle with transparency around the outside. The "plasma" image is an alpha blended particle that I've had for quite a while, and have used as a weapon projectile in some past games. The asteroid in this example is just window dressing, included to show how an object with an `OrbitalMovement` animation looks compared to the calculated trajectories of a `MassiveObject` object. To get a head start on the gameplay that will be needed for this game, I have added some code to cause the orbiting power satellites (currently represented just as a "plasma" ball) to get sucked into the black hole if they get too close. When this happens, the gravity code is replaced with the `OrbitalMovement` animation class. In Figure 22.2, we see that the projectile, or "plasma" sprite, has been captured by the black hole.

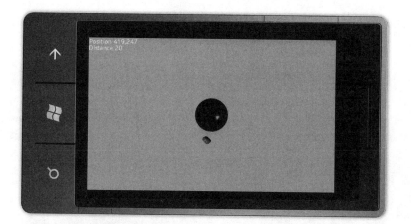

FIGURE 22.2
The "plasma" sprite has been captured by the black hole.

MassiveObject Class

A new class called MassiveObject, which inherits from Sprite, will handle our gravitational needs. Listing 22.1 provides the source code for this new class.

LISTING 22.1   Source Code for the MassiveObject Class

```
class MassiveObject : Sprite
{
    public double mass;
    public Vector2 acceleration;
    public float radius,angle;
    public bool captured;

    public MassiveObject(ContentManager content,
        SpriteBatch spriteBatch)
        : base(content, spriteBatch)
    {
        mass = 1.0f;
        acceleration = Vector2.Zero;
        radius = 50.0f;
        angle = 0.0f;
        this.captured = false;
    }

    public void Update(GameTime gameTime)
    {
    }

    public override void Draw()
    {
        base.Draw();
    }

    public void Attract(MassiveObject other)
    {
        //calculate DISTANCE
```

```
        double distX = this.position.X - other.position.X;
        double distY = this.position.Y - other.position.Y;
        double dist = distX*distX + distY*distY;
        double distance = 0;
        if (dist != 0.0) distance = 1 / dist;
        //update ACCELERATION (mass * distance)
        this.acceleration.X = (float)(-1 * other.mass * distX
            * distance);
        this.acceleration.Y = (float)(-1 * other.mass * distY
            * distance);
        //update VELOCITY
        this.velocityLinear.X += this.acceleration.X;
        this.velocityLinear.Y += this.acceleration.Y;
        //update POSITION
        this.position.X += this.velocityLinear.X;
        this.position.Y += this.velocityLinear.Y;
    }
}
```

PlayingModule.cs

This is the main source code file for the Gravity Demo, where the black hole and other MassiveObject (Sprite) objects are created, updated, and drawn. In other words, this is our main source code file. The original game state code is still present in the other files, but that has been removed from PlayingModule.cs. To return to the title screen, it's still possible to set game.gameMode as before! Listing 22.2 shares the source code for the class.

LISTING 22.2   Source Code for the PlayingModule Class

```
public class PlayingModule : IGameModule
{
    Game1 game;
    SpriteFont font;
    Random rand;
    MassiveObject blackHole;
    MassiveObject asteroid;
    MassiveObject plasma;

    public PlayingModule(Game1 game)
    {
        this.game = game;
        rand = new Random();
    }

    public void LoadContent(ContentManager content)
    {
        font = content.Load<SpriteFont>("WascoSans");

        blackHole = new MassiveObject(game.Content,
            game.spriteBatch);
        blackHole.Load("blackhole");
        blackHole.position = new Vector2(400, 240);
        blackHole.velocityAngular = -.05f;
```

```
        blackHole.scale = 1.0f;
        blackHole.mass = 100;

        asteroid = new MassiveObject(game.Content,
            game.spriteBatch);
        asteroid.Load("asteroid");
        asteroid.columns = 8;
        asteroid.totalFrames = 64;
        asteroid.size = new Vector2(60, 60);
        asteroid.radius = 80;
        asteroid.animations.Add(new OrbitalMovement(
            new Vector2(400,240), 80, 0, 0.08f));
        asteroid.scale = 0.5f;

        plasma = new MassiveObject(game.Content,
            game.spriteBatch);
        plasma.Load("plasma32");
        plasma.position = new Vector2(200, 240);
        plasma.mass = 1;
        plasma.velocityLinear = new Vector2(1.0f, 7.0f);
    }

public void Update(TouchLocation touch, GameTime gameTime)
{
        int time = gameTime.ElapsedGameTime.Milliseconds;

        blackHole.Update(gameTime);
        blackHole.Rotate();

        asteroid.angle += 0.001f;
        asteroid.Update(gameTime);
        asteroid.Rotate();
        asteroid.Animate(time);
        asteroid.Animate();

        plasma.Update(gameTime);
        plasma.Rotate();
        plasma.Animate();
        if (!plasma.captured)
        {
            plasma.Attract(blackHole);

            if (game.RadialCollision(plasma, blackHole))
            {
                plasma.captured = true;
                OrbitalMovement anim1 = new OrbitalMovement(
                    blackHole.position, 20 + rand.Next(20),
                    plasma.rotation, 0.8f);
                plasma.animations.Add(anim1);
                CycleColorBounce anim2 = new CycleColorBounce(
                    0, 10, 10, 0);
                plasma.animations.Add(anim2);
            }
        }
    }
}

public void Draw(GameTime gameTime)
{
```

```
        blackHole.Draw();
        asteroid.Draw();
        plasma.Draw();

        string text = "Position " +
            ((int)plasma.position.X).ToString() + "," +
            ((int)plasma.position.Y).ToString();
        game.spriteBatch.DrawString(font, text,
            new Vector2(0, 0), Color.White);

        float dist = game.Distance(plasma.position, blackHole.position);
        text = "Distance " + ((int)dist).ToString();
        game.spriteBatch.DrawString(font, text,
            new Vector2(0, 20), Color.White);
    }
}
```

Game1.cs

The source code to Game1.cs has not changed since the example in the preceding hour, but we need some reusable methods in this example added to the Game1.cs file, where they will be more useful. We have seen all of this code before, but just to be thorough, Listing 22.3 contains the complete code for the file with the additions.

LISTING 22.3   Main Source Code for the Example

```
public class Game1 : Microsoft.Xna.Framework.Game
{
    public enum GameState
    {
        TITLE = 0,
        PLAYING = 1,
        OPTIONS = 2,
        GAMEOVER = 3
    }

    public GraphicsDeviceManager graphics;
    public SpriteBatch spriteBatch;
    public GameState gameState;
    SpriteFont font;
    Random rand;
    TouchLocation oldTouch;
    IGameModule[] modules;

    public Game1()
    {
        graphics = new GraphicsDeviceManager(this);
        Content.RootDirectory = "Content";
        TargetElapsedTime = TimeSpan.FromTicks(333333);
        oldTouch = new TouchLocation();
        rand = new Random();
    }
```

```
protected override void Initialize()
{
    base.Initialize();
}

protected override void LoadContent()
{
    spriteBatch = new SpriteBatch(GraphicsDevice);
    font = Content.Load<SpriteFont>("WascoSans");

    modules = new IGameModule[4];
    modules[0] = new TitleScreenModule(this);
    modules[1] = new PlayingModule(this);
    modules[2] = new OptionsModule(this);
    modules[3] = new GameOverModule(this);

    foreach (IGameModule mod in modules)
    {
        mod.LoadContent(Content);
    }

    gameState = GameState.PLAYING;
}

protected override void Update(GameTime gameTime)
{
    if (GamePad.GetState(PlayerIndex.One).Buttons.Back ==
        ButtonState.Pressed)
        this.Exit();

    TouchCollection touchInput = TouchPanel.GetState();
    TouchLocation touch = new TouchLocation();
    if (touchInput.Count > 0)
    {
        touch = touchInput[0];
        oldTouch = touch;
    }

    //update current module
    modules[(int)gameState].Update(touch ,gameTime);

    base.Update(gameTime);
}

protected override void Draw(GameTime gameTime)
{
    GraphicsDevice.Clear(Color.CornflowerBlue);
    spriteBatch.Begin(SpriteSortMode.Deferred,
        BlendState.AlphaBlend);

    //draw current module
    modules[(int)gameState].Draw(gameTime);

    spriteBatch.End();
    base.Draw(gameTime);
}
```

```
public bool BoundaryCollision(Rectangle A, Rectangle B)
{
    return A.Intersects(B);
}

public bool RadialCollision(Sprite A, Sprite B)
{
    float radius1 = A.image.Width / 2;
    float radius2 = B.image.Width / 2;
    return RadialCollision(A.position, B.position,
        radius1, radius2);
}

public bool RadialCollision(Vector2 A, Vector2 B,
    float radius1, float radius2)
{
    float dist = Distance(A, B);
    return (dist < radius1 + radius2);
}

public float Distance(Vector2 A, Vector2 B)
{
    double diffX = A.X - B.X;
    double diffY = A.Y - B.Y;
    double dist = Math.Sqrt(Math.Pow(diffX, 2) +
        Math.Pow(diffY, 2));
    return (float)dist;
}

public float TargetAngle(Vector2 p1, Vector2 p2)
{
    return TargetAngle(p1.X, p1.Y, p2.X, p2.Y);
}

public float TargetAngle(double x1, double y1, double x2,
    double y2)
{
    double deltaX = (x2 - x1);
    double deltaY = (y2 - y1);
    return (float)Math.Atan2(deltaY, deltaX);
}
}
```

Summary

This hour developed some vital new code that will be needed for the Black Hole game that is currently in development and will be completed by Hour 24. The gravity code demonstrated here will be used to move the power satellites around the black hole to gather energy for the player, who must launch them at the right angle and velocity to maintain an orbit.

Q&A

Q. *When an object gets too close to the black hole, it is "sucked in" and goes into an orbit using the* `OrbitMovement` *class. Why?*

A. Due to the way the "gravity" code affects acceleration, any sprite that goes through the center of the black hole will be flung off the screen at a high velocity. To keep this from happening, we simulate the object being captured by the black hole in a low orbit.

Q. *What would happen if the other objects in the game influenced the black hole back, rather than just having the black hole exert gravity on everything?*

A. For the simulation, masses are exaggerated, with the black hole having a much smaller mass than a real black hole would have. So if we apply the gravity acceleration code to the black hole from all other objects, the black hole will move around a bit, perhaps even go off the screen. Go ahead and try it for yourself!

Workshop

Quiz

1. What trig functions do we use to rotate an object at a fixed radius?

2. What are the XNA versions of these trig functions?

3. Which custom class in our state system will be used for primary gameplay?

Answers

1. Sine and cosine

2. `Math.Sin()` and `Math.Cos()`

3. `PlayingModule`

Exercises

You might recall a similar example back in Hour 13, "Sprite Transform Animation." In that hour, we used the `OrbitalMovement` class to rotate many asteroid sprites around the center of the screen in a similar manner. But you know what would be even more realistic? An ellipse rather than a circle. See whether you can work out an algorithm to move a sprite in an elliptical orbit rather than circular. Hint: Try adjusting the velocity a bit when the angle is within a certain range.

HOUR 23

Rocket Science: Acceleration

What You'll Learn in This Hour:

- ▶ **Building the game**
- ▶ **Gravity well regions**
- ▶ **Enhancing** `MassiveObject`
- ▶ **Gameplay source code**

Now we can begin working on the gameplay involving user input and the logic for the game. This first part of the game developed this hour will focus on the player's spacecraft, the black hole, and objects moving in space. The player will need to orient and fire energy-gathering satellites into orbit around the black hole to gather energy, while the ship is also consuming energy to maintain its position. The goal of the game is to get enough energy to keep the ship from falling into the black hole. There will be little by way of polish in this hour, with just the primary gameplay being developed. Polish will be reserved for Hour 24, "The Black Hole Game."

Building the Game

The Black Hole game is based on most of the code we've developed in each of the previous hours of the book, and there really is no single previous hour that gets more credit than others since each hour has built upon the hours that came before. Let's dig into the game by going over the major sections and get something up and running fairly quickly. Then we'll continue our work on the game into the following hour, where it will get some polish and fine-tuning of the fun factor.

> This game is based on the theories of Stephen Hawking. If you're interested in black hole physics, be sure to read his popular books for more information! *The Universe in a Nutshell* is one of my favorites.

Gravity Well Regions

There are three regions around the black hole that affect game objects. The outer gravity well affects objects passing by, drawing them toward the black hole with relatively light force. This force is increased by an equal amount in the next two inner regions, with each region generating an equivalent gravity "tug" on objects. But the cumulative effect of all three gravity wells in the inner region of the black hole will cause objects to become hopelessly trapped.

The third and innermost region might be thought of as the *event horizon*, that region of a black hole where things disappear into the void, never to be seen again. It is this region that mathematics cannot penetrate, so while it appears that gravity increases toward infinity in the middle of a black hole, the truth of the matter is, there may be *nothing* at the very center of a black hole! The gravity might be so powerful that matter just rotates around the center of mass and no matter actually exists at that center point, which would be quite small at the center of a black hole. Then again, there might be a superdense material like a neutron star. It is at this point that physics just cannot explain it, because we don't actually have a black hole nearby to study. Even if we did, it's not like a spacecraft could be sent to investigate!

Figure 23.1 shows an illustration of the gravity well of the black hole in the game. The outer gravity well is quite large and draws most game objects inward at a steady "weight" or "pull," with some help from the inner core of the black hole, also exerting force. The inner gravity well is the region where energy can be mined by the "Hawking" satellites. At any rate, that's one of the enjoyable aspects of this game, pondering the infinite possibilities!

The code to simulate the gravitational pull of the black hole is coming up. Now let's just take a look again at some of our earlier helper methods used in this game. All the collision code in the Black Hole game is based around this RadialCollision() method and its overloaded friend:

```
public bool RadialCollision(Sprite A, Sprite B)
{
    float radius1 = A.image.Width / 2;
    float radius2 = B.image.Width / 2;
    return RadialCollision(A.position, B.position,
```

```
        radius1, radius2);
}

public bool RadialCollision(Vector2 A, Vector2 B, float radius1,
    float radius2)
{
    float dist = Distance(A, B);
    return (dist < radius1 + radius2);
}

public float Distance(Vector2 A, Vector2 B)
{
    double diffX = A.X - B.X;
    double diffY = A.Y - B.Y;
    double dist = Math.Sqrt(Math.Pow(diffX, 2) +
        Math.Pow(diffY, 2));
    return (float)dist;
}
```

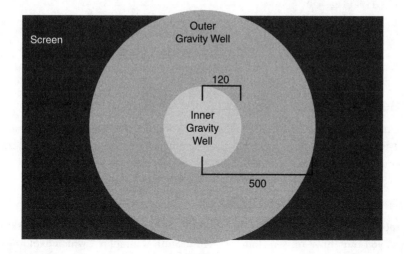

FIGURE 23.1
The gravity well of the black hole covers most of the Windows Phone screen.

Enhancing `MassiveObject`

Some minor changes need to be made to `MassiveObject` to support some new features needed in the game that were not in the example in the preceding hour. Following is what the class now looks like, with the new variables and updated constructor:

```
class MassiveObject : Sprite
{
    public string name;
    public bool captured;
    public double mass;
    public Vector2 acceleration;
    public float radius, angle;
    public int lifetime, startTime;

    public MassiveObject(ContentManager content,
        SpriteBatch spriteBatch)
        : base(content, spriteBatch)
    {
        name = "object";
        mass = 1.0f;
        acceleration = Vector2.Zero;
        radius = 50.0f;
        angle = 0.0f;
        captured = false;
        lifetime = 0;
        startTime = 0;
    }
// . . . note: some code omitted here
}
```

Game1.cs

There are no changes to be made to Game1.cs, because the main source code file is now PlayingModule.cs. In the final hour coming up, we will again use the game state modules for a more polished gameplay experience.

Gameplay Source Code

The most significant code of the game is found in PlayingModule.cs. If you skipped ahead, you may have missed Hour 21, "Finite State Gameplay," which explained how to use states to improve a game in many ways. The PlayingModule class is the primary gameplay class where the bulk of the game code will be found. The first lines of code in the class declare all the variables, including the key objects variable, defined as a List of MassiveObjects. We also see the black hole, the super core gravity well, and the player's ship here, among other things. Figure 23.2 shows the game as it is just getting started, and Listing 23.1 shows the source code for the class.

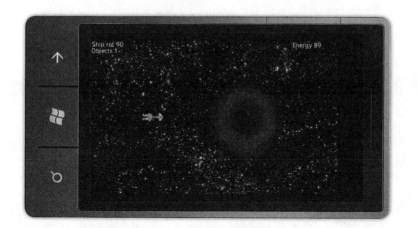

FIGURE 23.2
The Black Hole
game soon
after startup.

LISTING 23.1   Source Code for the **PlayingModule** Class

```
public class PlayingModule : IGameModule
{
    Game1 game;
    SpriteFont font;
    Random rand;
    Sprite background;
    MassiveObject blackHole;
    MassiveObject superCore;
    MassiveObject ship;
    float energy = 100.0f;
    int startTime, lifetime;
    List<MassiveObject> objects;

    public PlayingModule(Game1 game)
    {
        this.game = game;
        rand = new Random();
        startTime = 0;
        lifetime = 4000;
    }

    public void LoadContent(ContentManager content)
    {
        font = content.Load<SpriteFont>("WascoSans");

        background = new Sprite(game.Content, game.spriteBatch);
        background.Load("space");
        background.origin = Vector2.Zero;

        blackHole = new MassiveObject(game.Content, game.spriteBatch);
        blackHole.Load("blackhole");
        blackHole.position = new Vector2(500, 240);
        blackHole.scale = 2.0f;
        blackHole.mass = 40;
        blackHole.color = new Color(255, 100, 100, 200);
        blackHole.velocityAngular = 0.1f;
```

```
superCore = new MassiveObject(game.Content, game.spriteBatch);
superCore.image = blackHole.image;
superCore.position = new Vector2(blackHole.position.X,
    blackHole.position.Y);
superCore.scale = blackHole.scale * 0.4f;
superCore.mass = 60;
superCore.color = new Color(200, 100, 100, 180);
superCore.velocityAngular = 4.0f;
superCore.origin = new Vector2(64, 64);

//create objects list
objects = new List<MassiveObject>();

//create player ship
ship = new MassiveObject(game.Content, game.spriteBatch);
ship.Load("ship");
ship.position = new Vector2(200, 240);
ship.mass = 100f;
ship.scale = 0.2f;
ship.rotation = MathHelper.ToRadians(90);
}
```

The Update() method is a bit monolithic at this stage, but the code is easier to follow this way than if it had been divided into several smaller methods. I usually divide a method like this when it grows too large to be easily maintained, but since the gameplay code in PlayingModule is only 300 lines long, there isn't too much to consume here at once. There's a lot going on here in Update(), but we won't break up the code listing and break the flow of the code, which can be distracting.

First of all, the blackHole and superCore objects are updated. Then we go into a foreach loop that processes all the MassiveObject objects in the objects list (there's a tongue twister!). Each object is updated, rotated, and animated. Within the foreach is where the bulk of the code is found for the game.

When one of the satellites grows to a certain size (from collecting energy), that triggers a subset of code here in the foreach block where the player's ship actually attracts the satellite toward it, using the same code used to simulate the gravitational pull of the black hole on the same objects. The slight gravity "tug" causes the satellites to veer toward the ship and increase the chances of their being caught by it, without making it *too easy* for the player. After all, the ship doesn't move yet, it only rotates in place!

Next up is the code that tugs objects inward toward the black hole, if they are in range. Figure 23.3 shows another screenshot of the game, this time with a *lot* of satellites in orbit. Note the addition of animated asteroids in the scene. The asteroids serve no purpose, but just fill in some detail to make the scene look more interesting. A new asteroid is added every few seconds at a random direction and velocity, and over time they do tend to add up to quite a large mass of rotation around the black hole, which only increases the fun factor. Now, there is also potential use for these asteroid sprites beyond just "for looks."

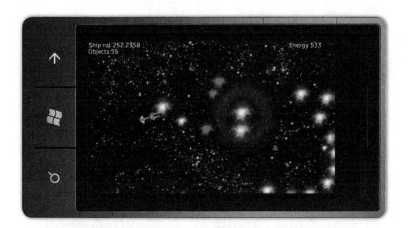

FIGURE 23.3
A large number of objects are orbiting the black hole, and they tend to fall in quite frequently.

Listing 23.2 contains the source code for the Update() method.

> It's quite a challenge to come up with *mass* values for the black hole, the super core, and each of the objects that not only result in a realistic simulation of gravity's effect on objects of mass but also make the game *fun*. Fun is more important than realism, but we want to have a little of both if possible. But when a trade-off is required, always go with that which helps the game to sell: the fun factor.

LISTING 23.2 Source Code for the Update() Method

```
public void Update(TouchLocation touch, GameTime gameTime)
{
    int time = gameTime.ElapsedGameTime.Milliseconds;

    blackHole.Update(gameTime);
    blackHole.Rotate();
    superCore.Update(gameTime);
    superCore.Rotate();


    foreach (MassiveObject obj in objects)
    {
        if (!obj.alive) continue;

        obj.Update(gameTime);
        obj.Rotate();
        obj.Animate(time); //frame animation
        obj.Animate(); //mod animation


        //allow ship to collect energy satellites for bonus energy
        if (obj.scale > 3.0f && obj.name == "satellite")
        {
```

```
        obj.Attract(ship);
        obj.color = Color.White;

        if (game.RadialCollision(obj.position, ship.position,
            obj.size.X, 40))
        {
            obj.alive = false;
            energy += obj.scale;
        }
    }

    if (!obj.captured)
    {
        //attract when object is near the black hole
        if (game.RadialCollision(obj.position,
            blackHole.position, 10, 500))
        {
            obj.Attract(blackHole);
            obj.Attract(superCore);

            //is object touching the outer edges of the black hole?
            if (game.RadialCollision(obj.position,
                blackHole.position, 10, 120))
            {
                obj.color = Color.Red;

                if (obj.name == "satellite")
                {
                    obj.scale += 0.1f;
                    energy += 0.5f;
                }

                obj.Attract(blackHole); //outer black hole
                obj.Attract(superCore); //inner black hole

                //oh no, object is caught by the black hole!
                if (game.RadialCollision(obj.position,
                    superCore.position, 16, 60))
                {
                    obj.captured = true;
                    obj.lifetime = 3000;
                    obj.startTime = (int)
                        gameTime.TotalGameTime.TotalMilliseconds;
                    OrbitalMovement anim1 = new OrbitalMovement(
                        blackHole.position, 10 + rand.Next(40),
                        obj.rotation, -0.8f);
                    obj.animations.Add(anim1);
                }
            }
            else
            {
                obj.color = Color.White;
            }
        }
    }

    //when captured, time runs out
    if (obj.lifetime > 0)
    {
```

```
            if (obj.startTime + obj.lifetime <
                gameTime.TotalGameTime.TotalMilliseconds)
                obj.alive = false;
        }

        //see if object has gone too far out of bounds
        if (obj.position.X < -200 || obj.position.X > 1000 ||
            obj.position.Y < -200 || obj.position.Y > 700)
            obj.alive = false;
}

//update ship
ship.Update(gameTime);
ship.Rotate();
ship.Animate(time);
if (energy <= 0)
{
    ship.Attract(blackHole);

    //object is caught by the black hole
    if (game.RadialCollision(ship.position, superCore.position,
        64, 40))
    {
        ship.captured = true;
        ship.lifetime = 3000;
        ship.startTime = (int)
            gameTime.TotalGameTime.TotalMilliseconds;
        OrbitalMovement anim1 = new OrbitalMovement(
            blackHole.position, 10 + rand.Next(40),
            ship.rotation, -0.8f);
        ship.animations.Add(anim1);
    }

    //done being squished?
    if (ship.lifetime > 0)
    {
        if (ship.startTime + ship.lifetime <
            gameTime.TotalGameTime.TotalMilliseconds)
            ship.alive = false;
    }
}
else
{
    energy -= 0.05f;
    ship.velocityLinear.X = 0.0f;
}

//check user input
if (touch.State == TouchLocationState.Released)
{
    if (touch.Position.X > ship.position.X)
    {
        CreateSatellite();
    }
    else
    {
        if (touch.Position.Y < 200)
            ship.velocityAngular = -0.01f;
        else if (touch.Position.Y > 280)
```

```
                ship.velocityAngular = 0.01f;
            else
                ship.velocityAngular = 0;
        }
    }

    //time to add another random asteroid?
    if (startTime + lifetime < gameTime.TotalGameTime.
        TotalMilliseconds)
    {
        startTime = (int)gameTime.TotalGameTime.TotalMilliseconds;
        CreateAsteroid();
    }

    //clean out the dead objects
    foreach (MassiveObject obj in objects)
    {
        if (obj.alive == false)
        {
            objects.Remove(obj);
            break;
        }
    }
}
```

The Draw() method is next, with its source code in Listing 23.3. This is a rather small
method because the gameplay objects are managed.

LISTING 23.3   Source Code for the Draw() Method

```
public void Draw(GameTime gameTime)
{
    background.Draw();
    superCore.Draw();
    blackHole.Draw();
    ship.Draw();

    foreach (MassiveObject obj in objects)
    {
        if (obj.alive)
        {
            obj.Draw();
        }
    }

    string text = "Ship rot " + MathHelper.ToDegrees(
        ship.rotation).ToString();
    game.spriteBatch.DrawString(font, text, new Vector2(0, 0),
        Color.White);
    text = "Objects " + objects.Count.ToString();
    game.spriteBatch.DrawString(font, text, new Vector2(0, 20),
        Color.White);
    text = "Energy " + energy.ToString("N0");
    game.spriteBatch.DrawString(font, text, new Vector2(650, 0),
        Color.White);
}
```

Finally, we have two helper methods, `CreateAsteroid()` and `CreateSatellite()`, that generate a random asteroid and random satellite, respectively. These two methods, shown in Listing 23.4, are quite important to the gameplay because they determine whether the objects will actually move reasonably on the screen. I say *reasonably* rather than *realistically* because, again, we don't want absolute realism; we want *some* realism with gobs of fun gameplay. The asteroids aren't important to the gameplay, because they are just for looks, but we do want them to start off in such a way that they end up rotating around the black hole. Likewise, the satellite must be launched in such a way that it moves reasonably well. At this stage, our satellites move at a constant speed, but in the next (and final) hour, we will add GUI controls that allow the player to adjust the power.

LISTING 23.4 Source Code for the `CreateAsteroid()` and `CreateSatellite()` Methods

```
public void CreateAsteroid()
{
    MassiveObject obj = new MassiveObject(game.Content, game.spriteBatch);
    obj.Load("asteroid");
    obj.columns = 8;
    obj.totalFrames = 64;
    obj.scale = 0.1f + (float)rand.NextDouble();
    obj.size = new Vector2(60, 60);
    obj.radius = 80;

    //randomly place at top or bottom of screen
    obj.position = new Vector2(rand.Next(100, 800), -100);
    obj.velocityLinear = new Vector2(4.0f, (float)(rand.NextDouble() *
        6.0));
    if (rand.Next(2) == 1)
    {
        obj.position.Y = -obj.position.Y;
        obj.velocityLinear.Y = -obj.velocityLinear.Y;
    }

    obj.scale = 0.4f;
    obj.mass = 1;
    obj.velocityAngular = 0.001f;
    obj.lifetime = 0;
    obj.name = "asteroid";
    objects.Add(obj);
}

public void CreateSatellite()
{
    MassiveObject obj;
    obj = new MassiveObject(game.Content, game.spriteBatch);
    obj.Load("plasma32");
    obj.position = ship.position;
    obj.mass = 1;
    obj.scale = 0.5f;
    obj.lifetime = 0;
    obj.name = "satellite";
```

```
    //calculate velocity based on ship's angle
    float accel = 4.0f;
    float angle = ship.rotation - MathHelper.ToRadians(90);
    float x = (float)Math.Cos(angle) * accel;
    float y = (float)Math.Sin(angle) * accel;
    obj.velocityLinear = new Vector2(x,y);

    //load energy to launch
    energy -= 1;

    objects.Add(obj);
  }
}
```

This all sounds like fun, but is there even a way to lose the game? Certainly! If the player runs out of energy, the ship will fall into the black hole! At this stage, the ship just loses its "traction" or station-keeping thrusters and is drawn into the black hole, only to be whipped around by the acceleration code. Some sort of fantastic animation will have to be added so that the ship gets sucked into the black hole like the other objects—a task for the next hour! Figure 23.4 shows what happens now if the player runs out of energy. Another improvement to be made in the next hour is an energy bar rather than just a text display. We have a lot of work yet to do on this game, but it's already showing promise.

FIGURE 23.4
Running out of energy spells doom for the poor ship and its crew!

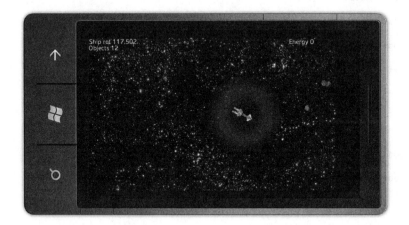

Summary

This hour got our Black Hole game off to a good start, with the fundamental game-play up and running, but the fun factor isn't quite there yet. In the next and final hour, we will address the shortcomings in the user interface and tweak the game-play so that this resembles less of a physics experiment and more of a game!

Q&A

Q. *How does the black hole sprite seem to "shimmer" over the background stars?*

A. The PNG file has an alpha channel, and the whole image is partially translucent.

Q. *When the ship gets pulled into the black hole, what should happen to it?*

A. That is the end of the game, but we haven't added such "polish" to the game yet.

Workshop

Quiz

1. What is the name of the method that causes two objects to affect each other's acceleration and velocity (that is, "gravity")? Note: This method was developed in the previous hour, and *used* in this hour.

2. What type of variable is `objects`?

3. What collision function is used to detect when an object falls into the black hole?

Answers

1. `MassiveObject.Attract()`

2. `List<MassiveObject>`

3. `RadialCollision()`

Exercises

Experiment with the mass values for the objects in the simulation to see what happens. Does more mass increase the acceleration of an object? What happens if you increase the mass of the black hole to a gigantic number like one million?

The Black Hole Game

What You'll Learn in This Hour:

▶ **Adding the finishing touches**
▶ **Modifying the** GameModule **interface class**
▶ MySoundEffect **class**
▶ GameOver **class**
▶ OptionsModule **class**
▶ TitleScreen **class**
▶ Game1 **class**
▶ MassiveObject **class**
▶ PlayingModule **class**

This hour puts the finishing touches on the Black Hole game that has really been in the works, more or less, for the past five hours. We first explored GUI programming back in Hour 20, "Creating a Graphical User Interface." Then we learned about finite states in Hour 21, "Finite State Gameplay," followed by calculating gravity in Hour 22, "The Physics of Gravity." These techniques are useful in any sort of game, and we're using them here for the final game with some pretty good results! The source code for the game is quite small, as these things go. Plus, since much of the "heavy lifting" code was developed in the preceding hour, we really can just focus on sprucing up the game a bit in this final hour!

Adding the Finishing Touches

Our Black Hole game is functional in terms of the mechanics of the game working and being fairly well balanced, so now we can spend time addressing the gameplay and "fun factor" of the game. The goal is to increase the replay value as much as possible. A neat idea for a game can fizzle pretty quickly unless there is a good reason for the player to come back. What is it about the game that would compel the player to keep playing for hours or days? The goal of an indie developer or a professional (obviously) is to sell a game. There are some games that will sell on the promise of short gameplay if the subject is compelling, but in this market replay sells. So, we'll see what we can do to improve gameplay and replay value.

Modifying the `GameModule` Interface Class

To make it possible to leave the `PlayingModule` and then return to it without shutting down and restarting the game, an enhancement is needed that will reset the gameplay to the starting values. So, a change will be made to the interface class, `GameModule`. Note the new `Reset()` method. This will meet our needs. Each of the game modules that use this interface will have to implement the new method:

```
interface IGameModule
{
    void Reset();
    void LoadContent(ContentManager content);
    void Update(TouchLocation touch, GameTime gameTime);
    void Draw(GameTime gameTime);
}
```

MySoundEffect Class

The `MySoundEffect` class, shown in Listing 24.1, was introduced back in Hour 18, "Playing Audio," and we'll need it here again. We'll need to make a minor tweak so that it's a little easier to use, by adding a `Play()` method directly to the class rather than requiring use of the instance object.

LISTING 24.1 Source Code for the MySoundEffect Class

```
public class MySoundEffect
{
    private Game1 game;
    private SoundEffect effect;
    private SoundEffectInstance instance;

    public MySoundEffect(Game1 game)
    {
        this.game = game;
        effect = null;
        instance = null;
    }

    public void Load(string assetName)
    {
        effect = game.Content.Load<SoundEffect>(assetName);
        instance = effect.CreateInstance();
    }

    public void Play()
    {
```

```
        if (game.globalAudio)
            instance.Play();
    }
}
```

> There is only one sound effect in the Black Hole game—when the ship launches a satellite. I know, the game is shamefully lacking in the audio department. Can you think of any events in the game that would benefit from a sound clip?

GameOverModule Class

The GameOverModule class does not need to use the Reset() method, but it has to be added to the class nonetheless because IGameModule mandates it. The GameOver class displays a message on the screen and waits for the user to press the Return button. This is kind of a no-brainer screen, but it is an important part of the gameplay and helps to separate this functionality from PlayingModule. Figure 24.1 shows the screen, and Listing 24.2 contains the source code.

FIGURE 24.1
Game over, man! Game over!

LISTING 24.2   Source Code for the GameOverModule Class

```
class GameOverModule : IGameModule
{
    Game1 game;
    Label lblTitle;
    Button btnReturn;

    public GameOverModule(Game1 game)
    {
        this.game = game;
    }

    public void Reset()
    {
    }
```

```
public void LoadContent(ContentManager content)
{
    lblTitle = new Label(content, game.spriteBatch,
        game.bigfont);
    lblTitle.text = "GAME OVER!";
    Vector2 size = game.font.MeasureString(lblTitle.text);
    lblTitle.position = new Vector2(400-size.X, 200);

    btnReturn = new Button(content, game.spriteBatch,
        game.guifont);
    btnReturn.text = "Return";
    btnReturn.position = new Vector2(400, 430);
    btnReturn.scaleV = new Vector2(2.0f, 1.0f);
}

public void Update(TouchLocation touch, GameTime gameTime)
{
    btnReturn.Update(touch);
    if (btnReturn.Tapped)
        game.gameState = Game1.GameState.TITLE;
}

public void Draw(GameTime gameTime)
{
    lblTitle.Draw();
    btnReturn.Draw();
}
}
```

OptionsModule Class

The `OptionsModule` class represents the Options screen in the game. This is often where game settings can be changed. In this small game, we'll need one global setting to make the screen useful—a global audio on/off switch. The screen is shown in Figure 24.2. Listing 24.3 shows the source code for the class.

FIGURE 24.2
The Options
screen.

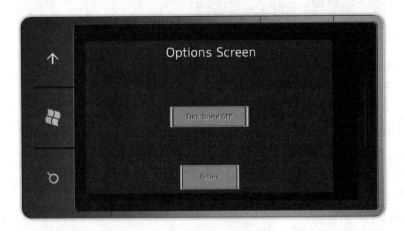

LISTING 24.3 Source Code for the OptionsModule Class

```
class OptionsModule : IGameModule
{
    Game1 game;
    Label lblTitle;
    Button btnReturn;
    Button btnAudio;

    public OptionsModule(Game1 game)
    {
        this.game = game;
    }

    public void Reset()
    {
    }

    public void LoadContent(ContentManager content)
    {
        lblTitle = new Label(content, game.spriteBatch,
            game.bigfont);
        lblTitle.text = "Options Screen";
        Vector2 size = game.font.MeasureString(lblTitle.text);
        lblTitle.position = new Vector2(400-size.X, 10);

        btnAudio = new Button(game.Content, game.spriteBatch,
            game.guifont);
        btnAudio.text = "";
        btnAudio.position = new Vector2(400, 240);
        btnAudio.scaleV = new Vector2(4.0f, 1.0f);

        btnReturn = new Button(content, game.spriteBatch,
            game.guifont);
        btnReturn.text = "Return";
        btnReturn.position = new Vector2(400, 430);
        btnReturn.scaleV = new Vector2(3.0f, 1.2f);
    }

    public void Update(TouchLocation touch, GameTime gameTime)
    {
        if (game.globalAudio)
            btnAudio.text = "Turn Sound OFF";
        else
            btnAudio.text = "Turn Sound ON";

        btnAudio.Update(touch);

        if (btnAudio.Tapped)
        {
            game.globalAudio = !game.globalAudio;
        }

        btnReturn.Update(touch);
        if (btnReturn.Tapped)
            game.gameState = Game1.GameState.TITLE;
    }
```

```
public void Draw(GameTime gameTime)
{
    lblTitle.Draw();
    btnAudio.Draw();
    btnReturn.Draw();
}
}
```

TitleScreenModule Class

The TitleScreenModule class has seen some major improvements since the early/crude version shown in an earlier hour. Now the buttons are colorful and rotate around a huge version of the animated black hole borrowed right out of the actual gameplay. See Figure 24.3 for the picture, and Listing 24.4 for the code.

FIGURE 24.3
The title screen features rotating buttons.

What happens to the buttons if you wait too long to make a selection? Actually, nothing! But it would be fun if they would fall into the black hole when the player waits too long!

LISTING 24.4 Source Code for the TitleScreenModule Class

```
class TitleScreenModule : IGameModule
{
    Game1 game;
    Label lblTitle;
    Button[] btnMenu;
    MassiveObject blackHole;
    MassiveObject superCore;
    Sprite background;

    public TitleScreenModule(Game1 game)
    {
        this.game = game;
```

```
        rand = new Random();
}

public void Reset()
{
}

public void LoadContent(ContentManager content)
{
        lblTitle = new Label(content, game.spriteBatch, game.bigfont);
        lblTitle.text = "The Black Hole Game";
        Vector2 size = game.font.MeasureString(lblTitle.text);
        lblTitle.position = new Vector2(400-size.X, 10);

        btnMenu = new Button[3];
        btnMenu[0] = new Button(content, game.spriteBatch, game.guifont);
        btnMenu[0].text = "PLAY!";
        btnMenu[0].scaleV = new Vector2(2.5f, 1.2f);
        btnMenu[0].color = Color.Orange;
        btnMenu[0].animations.Add(
            new OrbitalMovement( new Vector2(400, 240), 40, 0, 0.05f));

        btnMenu[1] = new Button(content, game.spriteBatch, game.guifont);
        btnMenu[1].text = "OPTIONS";
        btnMenu[1].color = Color.DarkRed;
        btnMenu[1].scaleV = new Vector2(2.1f, 1.0f);
        btnMenu[1].animations.Add(
            new OrbitalMovement(new Vector2(420, 220), 140, 0, 0.04f));

        btnMenu[2] = new Button(content, game.spriteBatch, game.guifont);
        btnMenu[2].text = "EXIT";
        btnMenu[2].color = Color.DarkSeaGreen;
        btnMenu[2].scaleV = new Vector2(1.6f, 0.8f);
        btnMenu[2].animations.Add(
            new OrbitalMovement(new Vector2(380, 260), 240, 0, 0.03f));

        background = new Sprite(game.Content, game.spriteBatch);
        background.Load("space");
        background.origin = Vector2.Zero;

        blackHole = new MassiveObject(game.Content, game.spriteBatch);
        blackHole.Load("blackhole");
        blackHole.position = new Vector2(400, 240);
        blackHole.scale = 4.0f;
        blackHole.mass = 40;
        blackHole.color = new Color(255, 100, 100, 200);
        blackHole.velocityAngular = 0.1f;

        superCore = new MassiveObject(game.Content, game.spriteBatch);
        superCore.image = blackHole.image;
        superCore.position = new Vector2(blackHole.position.X,
            blackHole.position.Y);
        superCore.scale = blackHole.scale * 0.4f;
        superCore.mass = 60;
        superCore.color = new Color(200, 100, 100, 180);
        superCore.velocityAngular = 4.0f;
        superCore.origin = new Vector2(64, 64);
}
```

```
public void Update(TouchLocation touch, GameTime gameTime)
{
    blackHole.Update(gameTime);
    blackHole.Rotate();
    superCore.Update(gameTime);
    superCore.Rotate();

    int tapped = -1;
    int n = 0;
    foreach (Button btn in btnMenu)
    {
        btn.Update(touch);
        btn.Animate();
        if (btn.Tapped)
            tapped = n;
        n++;
    }

    switch (tapped)
    {
        case 0:
            game.gameState = Game1.GameState.PLAYING;
            break;
        case 1:
            game.gameState = Game1.GameState.OPTIONS;
            break;
        case 2:
            game.Exit();
            break;
    }
}

public void Draw(GameTime gameTime)
{
    background.Draw();
    superCore.Draw();
    blackHole.Draw();
    lblTitle.Draw();
    foreach (Button btn in btnMenu)
    {
        btn.Draw();
    }
}
}
```

Game1 Class

The primary source code for the game is found in Listing 24.5, for the Game1 class.
Only a minor change is needed to support the new Reset() method. This makes
it easier to manage swapping between modules. For instance, exiting the
PlayingModule and returning to the TitleScreen, then back to PlayingModule, we
need to make sure the game is reset. That happens inside Game1. A new state backup
variable is also needed, oldState, to keep track of when the state changes, in order
to know when to call Reset().

LISTING 24.5   Source Code for the Game1 Class

```
public class Game1 : Microsoft.Xna.Framework.Game
{
    public enum GameState
    {
        TITLE = 0,
        PLAYING = 1,
        OPTIONS = 2,
        GAMEOVER = 3
    }

    public GraphicsDeviceManager graphics;
    public SpriteBatch spriteBatch;
    public GameState gameState, oldState;
    public Color backColor;
    Random rand;
    TouchLocation oldTouch;
    IGameModule[] modules;
    public bool globalAudio;
    public SpriteFont font, guifont, bigfont;

    public Game1()
    {
        graphics = new GraphicsDeviceManager(this);
        Content.RootDirectory = "Content";
        TargetElapsedTime = TimeSpan.FromTicks(333333);
        oldTouch = new TouchLocation();
        rand = new Random();
        backColor = new Color(32, 32, 32);
        globalAudio = true;
        gameState = GameState.TITLE;
        oldState = gameState;
    }

    protected override void Initialize()
    {
        base.Initialize();
    }

    protected override void LoadContent()
    {
        spriteBatch = new SpriteBatch(GraphicsDevice);
        font = Content.Load<SpriteFont>("WascoSans");
        guifont = Content.Load<SpriteFont>("GUIFont");
        bigfont = Content.Load<SpriteFont>("BigFont");

        modules = new IGameModule[4];
        modules[0] = new TitleScreenModule(this);
        modules[1] = new PlayingModule(this);
        modules[2] = new OptionsModule(this);
        modules[3] = new GameOverModule(this);

        foreach (IGameModule mod in modules)
        {
            mod.LoadContent(Content);
        }
    }
```

```
protected override void Update(GameTime gameTime)
{
    if (GamePad.GetState(PlayerIndex.One).Buttons.Back ==
        ButtonState.Pressed)
        this.Exit();

    TouchCollection touchInput = TouchPanel.GetState();
    TouchLocation touch = new TouchLocation();
    if (touchInput.Count > 0)
    {
        touch = touchInput[0];
        oldTouch = touch;
    }

    if (gameState != oldState)
    {
        oldState = gameState;
        modules[(int)gameState].Reset();
    }

    //update current module
    modules[(int)gameState].Update(touch ,gameTime);


    base.Update(gameTime);
}

protected override void Draw(GameTime gameTime)
{
    GraphicsDevice.Clear(backColor);
    spriteBatch.Begin(SpriteSortMode.Deferred,
        BlendState.AlphaBlend);

    //draw current module
    modules[(int)gameState].Draw(gameTime);

    spriteBatch.End();
    base.Draw(gameTime);
}

public bool BoundaryCollision(Rectangle A, Rectangle B)
{
    return A.Intersects(B);
}

public bool RadialCollision(Sprite A, Sprite B)
{
    float radius1 = A.image.Width / 2;
    float radius2 = B.image.Width / 2;
    return RadialCollision(A.position, B.position, radius1,
        radius2);
}

public bool RadialCollision(Vector2 A, Vector2 B, float radius1,
    float radius2)
{
    float dist = Distance(A, B);
    return (dist < radius1 + radius2);
```

```
    }

    public float Distance(Vector2 A, Vector2 B)
    {
        double diffX = A.X - B.X;
        double diffY = A.Y - B.Y;
        double dist = Math.Sqrt(Math.Pow(diffX, 2) +
            Math.Pow(diffY, 2));
        return (float)dist;
    }

    public float TargetAngle(Vector2 p1, Vector2 p2)
    {
        return TargetAngle(p1.X, p1.Y, p2.X, p2.Y);
    }

    public float TargetAngle(double x1, double y1, double x2,
        double y2)
    {
        double deltaX = (x2 - x1);
        double deltaY = (y2 - y1);
        return (float)Math.Atan2(deltaY, deltaX);
    }
}
```

MassiveObject Class

In an earlier hour, we introduced the new MassiveObject class to make working
with "gravity" calculations a bit easier than using global variables (or worse, having
to modify Sprite). So, this class just inherits from Sprite and adds a few new tidbits
of its own. Well, the class is now a full-blown entity that draws and updates, so we
need to take a look at the changes. Listing 24.6 shows the source code for the class.

LISTING 24.6 Source Code for the MassiveObject Class

```
class MassiveObject : Sprite
{
    public string name;
    public double mass;
    public Vector2 acceleration;
    public float radius,angle;
    public bool captured;
    public int lifetime, startTime;

    public MassiveObject(ContentManager content,
        SpriteBatch spriteBatch)
        : base(content, spriteBatch)
    {
        name = "object";
        mass = 1.0f;
        acceleration = Vector2.Zero;
        radius = 50.0f;
        angle = 0.0f;
        this.captured = false;
```

```
        lifetime = 0;
        startTime = 0;
    }

    public void Update(GameTime gameTime)
    {
        position.X += velocityLinear.X;
        position.Y += velocityLinear.Y;
    }

    public override void Draw()
    {
        base.Draw();
    }

    public void Attract(MassiveObject other)
    {
        //calculate DISTANCE
        double distX = this.position.X - other.position.X;
        double distY = this.position.Y - other.position.Y;
        double dist = distX*distX + distY*distY;
        double distance = 0;
        if (dist != 0.0) distance = 1 / dist;

        //update ACCELERATION (mass * distance)
        this.acceleration.X = (float)(-1 * other.mass * distX
            * distance);
        this.acceleration.Y = (float)(-1 * other.mass * distY
            * distance);

        //update VELOCITY
        this.velocityLinear.X += this.acceleration.X;
        this.velocityLinear.Y += this.acceleration.Y;

        //update POSITION
        this.position.X += this.velocityLinear.X;
        this.position.Y += this.velocityLinear.Y;
    }
}
```

PlayingModule Class

Now we come to the primary gameplay class of the game, PlayingModule. There's quite a bit of code here, so I won't break it up; it will just be listed without interruption. The gameplay could use some fine-tuning and tweaking, but the gist of it is that the player is the captain of a spaceship (insert filler story here). The ship has been caught in the strong gravity field of a black hole and you must help it to escape. Or the ship is mining the black hole for energy and gets caught. Whatever the story, it's a compelling little game that's worth your time to study.

As for the logic, when the energy level goes below 50, the ship begins to rotate around the black hole. When the energy reaches 0, the ship begins to also lose its orbit and slowly move inward, closer and closer to the event horizon. The player helps the ship stay out of the black hole by launching satellites/probes to collect energy. When the satellites are caught by the ship again, they will have gathered energy from the radiation field surrounding the black hole. If the ship has at least 1 or more energy, it will begin moving outward away from the black hole. When at least 50 energy is accumulated again, the ship will stop rotating. Remaining fixed in one position is definitely the preferred way to play, since you can launch satellites into a "known good" angle where the return will maintain your energy. That's it! Short and sweet.

Figure 24.5 shows the game running. The source code to the class is found in Listing 24.7.

FIGURE 24.5
The finished Black Hole game.

Did you Know?

The black hole simulated in this game uses a mass factor of only 100 total (between the blackHole and superCore objects), which is only 100 times more massive than the asteroids and satellites. It's this way for gameplay, but in the real universe, a typical black hole will be much more massive than a typical star. Plus, there is a supermassive black hole at the center of the Milky Way galaxy with a mass 4 million times greater than that of the Sun!

LISTING 24.7   Source Code for the PlayingModule Class

```
public class PlayingModule : IGameModule
{
    Game1 game;
    Button btnFire, btnQuit;
    Label lblAngle, lblPower;
    HSlider hsAngle, hsPower;
    Random rand;
```

```
    Sprite background;
    MassiveObject blackHole;
    MassiveObject superCore;
    MassiveObject ship;
    float energy;
    int startTime, lifetime;
    MySoundEffect launchSound;
    int lastLaunch, launchTime;

    List<MassiveObject> objects;

    public PlayingModule(Game1 game)
    {
        this.game = game;
        rand = new Random();
        objects = new List<MassiveObject>();
        ship = new MassiveObject(game.Content,game.spriteBatch);
        blackHole = new MassiveObject(game.Content,game.spriteBatch);
        superCore = new MassiveObject(game.Content,game.spriteBatch);
        hsAngle = new HSlider(game.Content, game.spriteBatch,game.guifont);
        lblAngle = new Label(game.Content,game.spriteBatch,game.guifont);
        hsPower = new HSlider(game.Content,game.spriteBatch,game.guifont);
        lblPower = new Label(game.Content,game.spriteBatch,game.guifont);
        btnFire = new Button(game.Content,game.spriteBatch,game.guifont);
        btnQuit = new Button(game.Content,game.spriteBatch,game.guifont);
        Reset();
    }

    public void Reset()
    {
        startTime = 0;
        lifetime = 4000;
        lastLaunch = 0;
        launchTime = 2000;
        energy = 100.0f;
        ship.position = new Vector2(200, 240);
        hsAngle.Value = 30;
        hsPower.Value = 50;
        ship.lifetime = 0;
        ship.radius = 250;
        ship.angle = MathHelper.ToRadians(180);
        ship.rotation = MathHelper.ToRadians(90);
        objects.Clear();
    }

    public void LoadContent(ContentManager content)
    {
        launchSound = new MySoundEffect(game);
        launchSound.Load("launch");

        background = new Sprite(game.Content, game.spriteBatch);
        background.Load("space");
        background.origin = Vector2.Zero;

        blackHole.Load("blackhole");
        blackHole.position = new Vector2(400, 240);
        blackHole.scale = 2.0f;
        blackHole.mass = 40;
```

```
    blackHole.color = new Color(255, 100, 100, 210);
    blackHole.velocityAngular = 0.1f;

    superCore.image = blackHole.image;
    superCore.position = new Vector2(blackHole.position.X,
        blackHole.position.Y);
    superCore.scale = blackHole.scale * 0.4f;
    superCore.mass = 60;
    superCore.color = new Color(200, 100, 100, 190);
    superCore.velocityAngular = 4.0f;
    superCore.origin = new Vector2(64, 64);

    //player ship
    ship.Load("ship");
    ship.mass = 20f;
    ship.scale = 0.2f;

    //angle slider
    hsAngle.SetStartPosition(new Vector2(170, 445));
    hsAngle.color = Color.Orange;
    hsAngle.Limit = 108;

    //angle label
    lblAngle.position = new Vector2(hsAngle.X, hsAngle.Y-40);
    lblAngle.text = "ANGLE";

    //power slider
    hsPower.SetStartPosition(new Vector2(530, 445));
    hsPower.color = Color.Orange;
    hsPower.Limit = 100;

    //power label
    lblPower.position = new Vector2(hsPower.X, hsPower.Y-40);
    lblPower.text = "POWER";

    //fire button
    btnFire.position = new Vector2(400, 440);
    btnFire.color = Color.Orange;
    btnFire.UseShadow = false;
    btnFire.text = "LAUNCH";
    btnFire.scaleV = new Vector2(1.5f, 0.7f);

    //quit button
    btnQuit.text = "X";
    btnQuit.position = new Vector2(800 - 20, 480 - 20);
    btnQuit.scaleV = new Vector2(0.3f, 0.5f);
}

public void Update(TouchLocation touch, GameTime gameTime)
{
    //update user controls
    btnFire.Update(touch);
    hsAngle.Update(touch);
    hsPower.Update(touch);
    lblAngle.Update(touch);
    lblPower.Update(touch);
    btnQuit.Update(touch);
```

```
//update gameplay objects
blackHole.Update(gameTime);
blackHole.Rotate();
superCore.Update(gameTime);
superCore.Rotate();
UpdateObjects(gameTime);
UpdateShip(gameTime);

//check user input
if (btnFire.Tapped)
{
    if (lastLaunch + launchTime < gameTime.TotalGameTime.
        TotalMilliseconds)
    {
        lastLaunch = (int)gameTime.TotalGameTime.
            TotalMilliseconds;
        launchSound.Play();
        CreateSatellite();
    }
}

//rotate ship with slider
float angle = hsAngle.Value * 3.3f;
ship.rotation = MathHelper.ToRadians(angle);
lblAngle.text = "ANGLE:" + angle.ToString("N0");

//set power label
lblPower.text = "POWER:" + hsPower.Value.ToString();

//time to add another random asteroid?
if (startTime + lifetime < gameTime.TotalGameTime.
    TotalMilliseconds)
{
    startTime = (int)gameTime.TotalGameTime.TotalMilliseconds;
    CreateAsteroid();
}

//user quit?
if (btnQuit.Tapped)
{
    game.gameState = Game1.GameState.TITLE;
}
}

public void UpdateObjects(GameTime gameTime)
{
    int time = gameTime.ElapsedGameTime.Milliseconds;

    foreach (MassiveObject obj in objects)
    {
        if (!obj.alive) continue;

        obj.Update(gameTime);
        obj.Rotate();
        obj.Animate(time);
        obj.Animate();
```

```
//allow ship to collect energy satellite
if (obj.scale >= 1.0f && obj.name == "satellite")
{
    //when large, cause satellites to seek the ship
    obj.Attract(ship);

    //reset satellite to white when seeking ship
    obj.color = Color.White;

    //look for collision with ship
    if (game.RadialCollision(obj.position, ship.position,
        obj.size.X, 40))
    {
        obj.alive = false;
        energy += obj.scale * 4;
        if (energy > 200) energy = 200;
    }
}

if (!obj.captured)
{
    //only attract when object is near the black hole
    if (game.RadialCollision(obj.position,
        blackHole.position, obj.size.X, 500))
    {
        obj.Attract(blackHole);

        //touching the outer edges of the black hole?
        if (game.RadialCollision(obj.position,
            blackHole.position, obj.size.X, 120))
        {
            //turn red when going through inner gravity well
            obj.color = Color.Red;

            if (obj.name == "satellite")
            {
                obj.scale += 0.1f;
                if (obj.scale > 5.0f) obj.scale = 5.0f;
                energy += 0.1f;
                if (energy > 200) energy = 200;
            }

            obj.Attract(superCore);

            //object is caught by the black hole
            if (game.RadialCollision(obj.position,
                superCore.position, 16, 60))
            {
                obj.captured = true;
                //set a lifetime delay once captured
                obj.lifetime = 3000;
                obj.startTime = (int)gameTime.TotalGameTime.
                    TotalMilliseconds;
                //cause object to spin around the black hole
                OrbitalMovement anim1 = new OrbitalMovement(
                    blackHole.position, 10 + rand.Next(40),
                    obj.rotation, -0.8f);
```

```
                                obj.animations.Add(anim1);
                    }
            }
            else
            {
                obj.color = Color.White;
            }
        }
    }

    //when captured, time runs out
    if (obj.lifetime > 0)
    {
        if (obj.startTime + obj.lifetime < gameTime.
            TotalGameTime.TotalMilliseconds)
            obj.alive = false;
    }

    //see if object has gone too far out of bounds
    if (obj.position.X < -200 || obj.position.X > 1000 ||
        obj.position.Y < -200 || obj.position.Y > 700)
        obj.alive = false;
    }
}

public void UpdateShip(GameTime gameTime)
{
    int time = gameTime.ElapsedGameTime.Milliseconds;

    ship.Update(gameTime);
    ship.Rotate();
    ship.Animate();

    //cause ship to fall into black hole
    if (!ship.captured)
    {
        //update ship position
        ship.X = 400 + (float)(Math.Cos(ship.angle) * ship.radius);
        ship.Y = 240 + (float)(Math.Sin(ship.angle) * ship.radius);

        //consume energy
        energy -= 0.05f;
        if (energy > 0)
        {
            //while we have energy, try to get away
            ship.radius += 0.2f;
            if (ship.radius > 250)
                ship.radius = 250;
        }

        if (energy < 50)
        {
            //rotate ship around black hole (custom)
            ship.angle += 0.01f;
            if (energy <= 0)
            {
                energy = 0;
                ship.radius -= 0.1f;
```

```
                //ship is caught by the black hole
                if (game.RadialCollision(ship.position,
                    superCore.position, 64, 40))
                {
                    ship.captured = true;
                    ship.velocityAngular = 1.0f;
                    ship.lifetime = 5000;
                    ship.startTime = (int)gameTime.TotalGameTime.
                        TotalMilliseconds;
                    OrbitalMovement anim1 = new OrbitalMovement(
                        blackHole.position, 10 + rand.Next(40),
                        0, 0.4f);
                    ship.animations.Add(anim1);
                }
            }
        }
    }

    //ship fell into black hole?
    if (ship.lifetime > 0)
    {
        if (ship.startTime + ship.lifetime <
            gameTime.TotalGameTime.TotalMilliseconds)
        {
            game.gameState = Game1.GameState.GAMEOVER;
            return;
        }
    }
}

public void Draw(GameTime gameTime)
{
    background.Draw();
    superCore.Draw();
    blackHole.Draw();
    ship.Draw();
    foreach (MassiveObject obj in objects)
    {
        if (obj.alive)
        {
            obj.Draw();
        }
    }
    btnFire.Draw();
    hsAngle.Draw();
    hsPower.Draw();
    lblAngle.Draw();
    lblPower.Draw();
    btnQuit.Draw();

    string text;
    text = "Energy " + energy.ToString("N0");
    game.spriteBatch.DrawString(game.font, text,
        new Vector2(650, 0), Color.White);
}
```

```
public void CreateAsteroid()
{
    MassiveObject obj = new MassiveObject(game.Content,
        game.spriteBatch);
    obj.Load("asteroid");
    obj.columns = 8;
    obj.totalFrames = 64;
    obj.scale = 0.1f + (float)rand.NextDouble();
    obj.size = new Vector2(60, 60);
    obj.radius = 80;

    //randomly place at top or bottom of screen
    obj.position = new Vector2(rand.Next(100, 800), -100);
    obj.velocityLinear = new Vector2(4.0f, (float)
        (rand.NextDouble() * 6.0));
    if (rand.Next(2) == 1)
    {
        obj.position.Y = -obj.position.Y;
        obj.velocityLinear.Y = -obj.velocityLinear.Y;
    }

    obj.scale = (0.5f + (float)rand.NextDouble()) * 0.5f;
    obj.mass = 1;
    obj.velocityAngular = 0.001f;
    obj.lifetime = 0;
    obj.name = "asteroid";
    objects.Add(obj);
}

public void CreateSatellite()
{
    MassiveObject obj;
    obj = new MassiveObject(game.Content, game.spriteBatch);
    obj.Load("plasma32");
    obj.position = ship.position;
    obj.mass = 1;
    obj.scale = 0.5f;
    obj.lifetime = 0;
    obj.name = "satellite";

    //calculate velocity based on ship's angle
    float accel = 1 + (float)(hsPower.Value / 10);
    float angle = ship.rotation - MathHelper.ToRadians(90);
    float x = (float)Math.Cos(angle) * accel;
    float y = (float)Math.Sin(angle) * accel;
    obj.velocityLinear = new Vector2(x,y);

    //use energy to launch satellite
    energy -= 1;

    objects.Add(obj);
}
}
```

Summary

This concludes the Black Hole game, and, well, the *whole book*! I hope you have enjoyed working with the WP7 platform, the emulator, and XNA Game Studio. These tools really are very rewarding, and you can't beat the price! If you have any questions or just want to chat, come visit my website at http://www.jharbour.com/forum. See you there!

Q&A

Q. *Is there any way to make this a two-player game?*

A. Multiplayer is a challenge on a single WP7 device, but it is possible to use networking to allow two or more players to compete. This would require some changes and additions to the code to support multiple players. It would be interesting to watch the power satellites compete for energy.

Q. *It seemed that the game was easier to play before the GUI controls were added. Can the gameplay include touchscreen and the GUI?*

A. Yes. In fact, it's a good idea to support more than one form of user input to cater to the variety of playing styles among players of your games.

Workshop

Quiz

1. What is the name of the method that adds a new satellite to the game?

2. What is the name of the method that adds a new asteroid to the game?

3. What is the name of the method that moves and attracts all the objects?

Answers

1. `CreateSatellite()`

2. `CreateAsteroid()`

3. `UpdateObjects()`

Exercises

There are still quite a few improvements that could be made to the game, not only to fine-tune the gameplay, but to make better use of the various game screens (like options). Experiment with the gameplay to see whether you can come up with any new settings that would make the gameplay more interesting.

Index